★ RUSTICA

FRANK CAMORRA AND
RICHARD CORNISH

A RETURN TO
SPANISH HOME COOKING

PHOTOGRAPHS BY ALAN BENSON

CHRONICLE BOOKS
SAN FRANCISCO

EMPIEZA EL CAMIÑO

THE JOURNEY BEGINS

I WAS HEADING DOWN THE AUTOPISTA ON THE WAY TO CÁCERES. IT WAS LATE SPRING IN 2008 BUT THE EXTREMEÑAN SUN WAS ALREADY HOT. THE COUNTRY WAS GREEN BUT TURNING TO BROWN ON THE HILLS AND RIDGES. THE NEW ROAD BYPASSED ALMOST EVERY TOWN. MY ONLY COMPANY WAS THE PIGS POKING THEIR SNOUTS OUT OF THE TRUCKS AS I OVERTOOK THEM ON THEIR WAY TO THE *JAMÓN* FACTORY. I TURNED ON THE RADIO. THE PROGRAM OF MOURNFUL FLAMENCO MUSIC GAVE WAY TO NEWS, THEN A DISCUSSION ON THE LATEST CONTROVERSY. IT WAS A NATIONAL SCANDAL: A SPANISH CHEF, THE TRADITIONALIST SANTI SANTAMARÍA, HAD VERBALLY ATTACKED ANOTHER CHEF, FERRAN ADRIÀ, A CUTTING-EDGE POSTMODERNIST. SANTAMARÍA HAD CRITICIZED ADRIÀ FOR HIS USE OF ARTIFICIAL ADDITIVES, GELS, THICKENERS, AND PRESERVATIVES AT THE EXPENSE OF LOCALLY PRODUCED ORGANIC INGREDIENTS. IT SEEMED EVERYBODY IN SPAIN HAD AN OPINION AND IT HIGHLIGHTED THE DEEP CONFUSION THAT THE SPANISH HAD TOWARD THEIR OWN FOOD. AN EXPERT WITH A DEEP VOICE TEXTURED BY TOBACCO ASKED A SERIES OF QUESTIONS THAT SPOKE VOLUMES. "BUT WHAT IS TRADITIONAL SPANISH FOOD? WHAT DO PEOPLE EAT IN THEIR HOMES TODAY? THEY ARE JUST AS LIKELY TO EAT A PRE-PREPARED MEAL FROM THE SUPERMARKET," HE SAID. "I TRULY FEAR THAT THE FOUNDATIONS OF OUR FOOD ARE BEING UNDERMINED."

It was in the year of that polemic that I traveled around Spain researching recipes from the Spanish people, from the chefs of Madrid to the widows of Galicia. With a heightened sense that their culinary culture was under attack, people spoke freely and openly about the food they made and ate. They took me into their kitchens and gardens and showed me the food they were preparing and growing. In most cases, it was an act of pure Spanish hospitality. But for many, it was part of their belief that recipes should be passed down and handed over for safekeeping.

For they knew the recipes were never "theirs," but simply a way of re-creating a cultural phenomenon that always had a life of its own. It was once explained to me that we cooks are simply the vehicles for these dishes to take shape. Without us they would simply remain ideas or words on a page — so whenever we cook these recipes, we invoke the idea of the food itself.

The Spaniards I spoke to responded so well when I explained I was searching for the foundations of Spanish food, the bedrock of traditions on which their cooking was based.

I told them I wanted to highlight some of the pillars of Spanish cooking and the culture in which their food is grown, prepared, and eaten. They gave me their recipes as gifts to share, not to covet and make my own.

I cannot tell you what attracted me to some dishes and not others. Perhaps I was looking for the food of my childhood. My family came to Australia from Spain in 1975, the year Franco died. I arrived at the age of five speaking only Spanish with a strong Andalusian accent. "If you're going to learn to speak English, then you're going to have to go to school," my Dad said. I remember my first day there feeling very, very small amid a cacophony of tongues. (To those who know me today, this seems quite laughable.) But every afternoon I went back home and there was always my Mum, who had spent the day in the house cleaning and preparing food. And it was food from Spain. It was the dishes she and her sister had grown up with. It may have been a plate of *cocido* (a meat and chickpea stew), or tripe with chorizo, or meatballs in beef broth.

This is probably why the food in this book is perhaps the simplest form of Spanish food — food that was particularly popular at a time when Spain was poor and had to be prepared in a manner determined by poverty. But poverty meant resourcefulness in feeding the family. Spanish people, particularly in the country, still grow a lot of their own food — so Spanish food is also about the type of soil the food grows in, the water that is available for the food to grow, the time of the year in which it is harvested and the long traditions of preparing food that stem from way back in time. I think the French call it *terroir*.

Over the course of 18 months, I visited Spain half a dozen times to research dishes. During that time, I think I ate my entire body weight several times over in food from almost every region, with a few notable exceptions. I didn't want to spread myself too thin, so there are parts of the country I deliberately left out. It was hard work but, as they say, someone had to do it.

The recipes in this book have been garnered from the people who live in the cities, towns and countryside of Spain. Every Spaniard can reel off recipes . . . the doctor, the post mistress, the mechanic, the IT professional, the farmer and the seamstress. They all have their recipes, and even if those dishes share the same name, they will inevitably vary in one way or another.

Without exception, people shared their time with me and told me and showed me how they made their food. I have been extremely privileged.

There was some food I ate that I felt couldn't translate to the personal kitchen. I remember enjoying a soup once popular in the poorest times in the Catalan countryside. It was made with just bread, water, garlic, thyme, salt and a little olive oil. It was a really lovely and restorative soup, but it just didn't seem to suit the modern context. Instead, I chose dishes I think people would enjoy making and eating today.

I also wanted to make a note of the "old school" techniques used across the nation. There is a new breed of young Spanish chefs who forget that good food comes from good basic technique. As much as I admire chefs like Ferran Adrià, he didn't emerge from a steaming foam. He learned his trade brilliantly. Unfortunately, there seems to be the equivalent of Ferran Adrià "cover bands," chefs who skip straight through their apprenticeship with their eyes closed and then try to re-create the style of food found at El Bulli. A famous Basque chef, Hilario Arbelaitz, described the situation by comparing Ferran Adrià to Pablo Picasso. "These young chefs are all trying to be Picasso. But there can only be one Picasso, and he too spent his early years learning to paint in the traditional manner. He was an exquisite figurative painter long before he was a Cubist."

The portion sizes in this book relate to the way Spanish people eat. Spaniards don't necessarily adhere to the "appetizer, main and dessert" triumvirate that dominates Anglo dining. Instead, they tend to share dishes at a table. When cooking from this book, note that one tapas portion size roughly equates to one canapé — so six tapas will be six portions of finger food. A *media ración* roughly relates to an appetizer-size portion, whereas a *ración* is a serving for one from a shared plate. To make a meal, a *ración* should be served with other dishes — so six *raciones* will serve six people as a main when accompanied by other dishes.

As much as possible, I have tried to give authentic representations of the recipes, but where ingredients are unobtainable or cooking times a little too long for the modern inclination, I have made slight and respectful adjustments. You may find cooking times vary depending on the oven you are using. As a general rule, if you are not using a fan-forced oven, set the oven temperature to 35°F higher than indicated in the recipe. These are everyday dishes to be cooked in your home and shared with family or friends. Please take as much time as you want to work through this book, for some of the techniques may require a suspension of disbelief. I hope you find as much pleasure in making these dishes as I did in collecting them and sharing them with you.

Finally, I'd like to dedicate this book to Vanessa, Pepe and Hugo.

Un abrazo!

LAS TAPAS MADRILEÑAS

MADRID'S TAPAS

★★★

SPAIN IS A NOCTURNAL NATION. SPANIARDS DON'T EAT DINNER UNTIL 10 O'CLOCK AT NIGHT. LUNCH IS NEVER TAKEN BEFORE 2 PM. BREAKFAST IS A QUICK COFFEE AND A PASTRY EATEN SOMETIME IN THE MORNING. SPAIN SHARES ITS TIME ZONE WITH THE REST OF EUROPE, WHICH MEANS IT GETS DARK LATE IN SPAIN— A SORT OF PERMANENT DAYLIGHT SAVING. A WHOLE STYLE OF EATING HAS EVOLVED TO SUIT THIS ELONGATED TWILIGHT AND IT'S CALLED TAPAS. I'M SURE EVERYONE IS FAMILIAR WITH TAPAS — SNACK FOOD THAT IS EATEN WITH A DRINK IN SPANISH BARS. SMALL PIECES OF VERY TASTY FOOD, PERHAPS A FEW BITES, NEVER MORE THAN A MOUTHFUL.

Madrid is the capital of Spain, yet apart from a few notable exceptions such as *callos* (tripe) and *cocido* (meat and chickpea stew), Madrid does not have a strong indigenous cuisine. Instead, it borrows heavily from the rest of the nation for its food. Over the centuries, people have come from all over the nation to work in the capital and they have brought with them their food. It is similar to immigrants arriving in our own country, setting up restaurants that reflect their national cuisine. Spaniards do exactly the same thing, setting up bars and making food from their home province. A family from Galicia will serve little bowls of steamed mussels, while a Basque will line up plates of *pintxos* — pieces of bread with anchovies, or a fish salad made with lots of mayonnaise. It is possible to spend a night walking around Madrid and eating food from each of the country's 17 regions (or the autonomous communities, to be correct).

There are parts of Madrid, particularly the center of the city, where the bars seem to line the streets. To the outsider, it would seem that all the *Madrileños* do is eat and drink. Even in the great tower-block communities in the suburbs, the ground floor will be taken up with bakeries, laundries and, of course, bars. It is important to realize that the purpose of visiting these bars is not just to take a seat and drink and eat: most of the socializing is done standing up. This is because there are never enough seats and, secondly, when you go to a bar, you're always on the way to somewhere else, whether it be a restaurant for dinner or, more likely, to another bar.

Because they are small and easily picked up with the fingers or a small fork, tapas dishes translate well to home entertaining. I have friends in Australia who now have tapas parties. Friends and family will all make a few little dishes and bring them along with a bottle of wine.

And that's what tapas is about — fun. Although the *Madrileños* take their tapas eating seriously, they never take the actual tapas dishes seriously. They are there on the plate in front of you one moment; next, they are in your mouth — salty, mouthwatering little treats to enjoy between sips of beer or wine and the effusive conversation that ever spills at a rapid speed and high volume from Madrid's tapas bars.

MADRID MAY BE ALMOST 200 MILES INLAND, BUT IT HAS ONE OF THE LARGEST FISH MARKETS IN THE WORLD. FISH ARE TRUCKED AND FLOWN IN FROM THE MEDITERRANEAN AND CANTABRIAN SEAS, THE ATLANTIC OCEAN AND WATERS FARTHER AWAY. THE SPANISH ARE FISH MAD. WALK PAST PEOPLE IN THE STREET AND YOU CAN HEAR THEM ON THEIR MOBILE PHONES HAVING A HEATED DISCUSSION ABOUT HAKE. *ESCABECHE* IS A PRESERVING TECHNIQUE THAT IS THOUSANDS OF YEARS OLD, YET I SAW THIS DISH BEING SERVED IN A FUNKY NEW SPOT IN MADRID WHERE YOUNG PEOPLE WERE TWO-DEEP AT THE BAR — AND HALF OF THEM WERE ORDERING THIS.

SARDINAS EN ESCABECHE Y PAN CRUJIENTE
MARINATED SARDINES ON CRISP BREAD WAFERS

24 TAPAS
12 MEDIAS RACIONES

I small baguette
24 fresh sardine fillets
seasoned all-purpose flour, to coat
1/3 cup olive oil
sea salt
some extra bread, to serve

ESCABECHE
7/8 cup extra virgin olive oil
2 red onions, finely sliced
a pinch of saffron threads
3 garlic cloves, finely sliced
5 bay leaves
2 thyme sprigs
I teaspoon black peppercorns
sea salt
3/4 cup good chardonnay vinegar
1 1/3 cups white wine
1 1/2 tablespoons chopped parsley

Using a very sharp bread knife, trim the ends, sides, top and bottom off the baguette to make a rectangle 4 1/2 inches long. Slice the bread across the top to make very thin, long wafers. Place the bread on a baking sheet, cover with another sheet the same size, then bake for 15 minutes, or until the bread browns slightly and becomes crunchy. Let cool on a wire rack, then store in an airtight container.

To make the *escabeche*: heat half of the olive oil in a heavy-bottomed saucepan over high heat and sauté the onion for 2 to 3 minutes, or until beginning to soften. Stir in the saffron, reduce the heat to medium, then add the garlic, bay leaves, thyme sprigs, peppercorns and a pinch of salt. Cook, stirring occasionally, for 15 to 20 minutes, or until the onion is soft but not colored. Stir in the vinegar, wine, remaining olive oil and 7/8 cup water, then cover and simmer for another 20 minutes. Stir in 1 tablespoon of the parsley, remove from the heat and let cool.

Meanwhile, preheat the oven to 300°F.

Dust the sardine fillets with the flour. Heat the olive oil in a large heavy-bottomed frying pan over medium-high heat. Add the sardines in batches, skin side down, and fry for 1 minute, then turn, season with sea salt and cook for another minute. Remove from the heat and drain on a paper towel.

Spoon some cooled *escabeche* into a glass or ceramic dish to cover the base. Add a layer of sardines, then cover with more *escabeche*. Repeat and pour the remaining liquid into the container. Cover and let stand for at least 15 minutes to allow the flavors to mingle.

To serve, select 24 of the best wafers, then remove the sardines from the marinade and place one on each wafer with a little *escabeche* mixture. Sprinkle with the remaining parsley and serve warm or at room temperature, with a little extra bread to soak up the marinade.

BANDERILLAS
SKEWERS OF ANCHOVIES, PEPPERS AND OLIVES

12 TAPAS

12 pickled baby onions

12 slices of pickled carrot

12 anchovies

12 *guindilla* pepper pieces, or any small, hot chile

24 pimiento-stuffed green olives

24 cornichons (baby gherkins)

SPAIN INVENTED NICHE MARKETS LONG BEFORE MARKETING PEOPLE APPEARED. THERE IS A BAR IN MADRID THAT ONLY SELLS SARDINES — AND ONLY ON SUNDAYS WHEN THE EL RASTRO MARKET IS IN FULL SWING. IT'S NEXT TO A SHOP THAT ONLY SELLS PICKLED OLIVES AND *BANDERILLAS*. THESE ARE SHORT WOODEN SKEWERS ONTO WHICH PICKLED VEGETABLES AND ANCHOVIES ARE PIERCED. IT COULD BE ANY SORT OF CRUNCHY PICKLED VEGETABLE, BUT GENERALLY OLIVES, ONIONS, GHERKINS AND *GUINDILLAS*, A TYPE OF BASQUE PEPPER THAT IS QUITE MILD BUT VERY TASTY, AND WHICH YOU CAN BUY FROM SPANISH GROCERY SHOPS. THE WORD *BANDERILLA* ALSO REFERS TO THE SKEWER THAT MATADORS STICK INTO BULLS. HERE WE'RE USING THEM TO STICK INTO THINGS THAT CAN'T FIGHT BACK.

Take 12 toothpicks and skewer an onion, carrot slice, anchovy, *guindilla* piece and two olives and two cornichons on each one. Serve with plenty of beer.

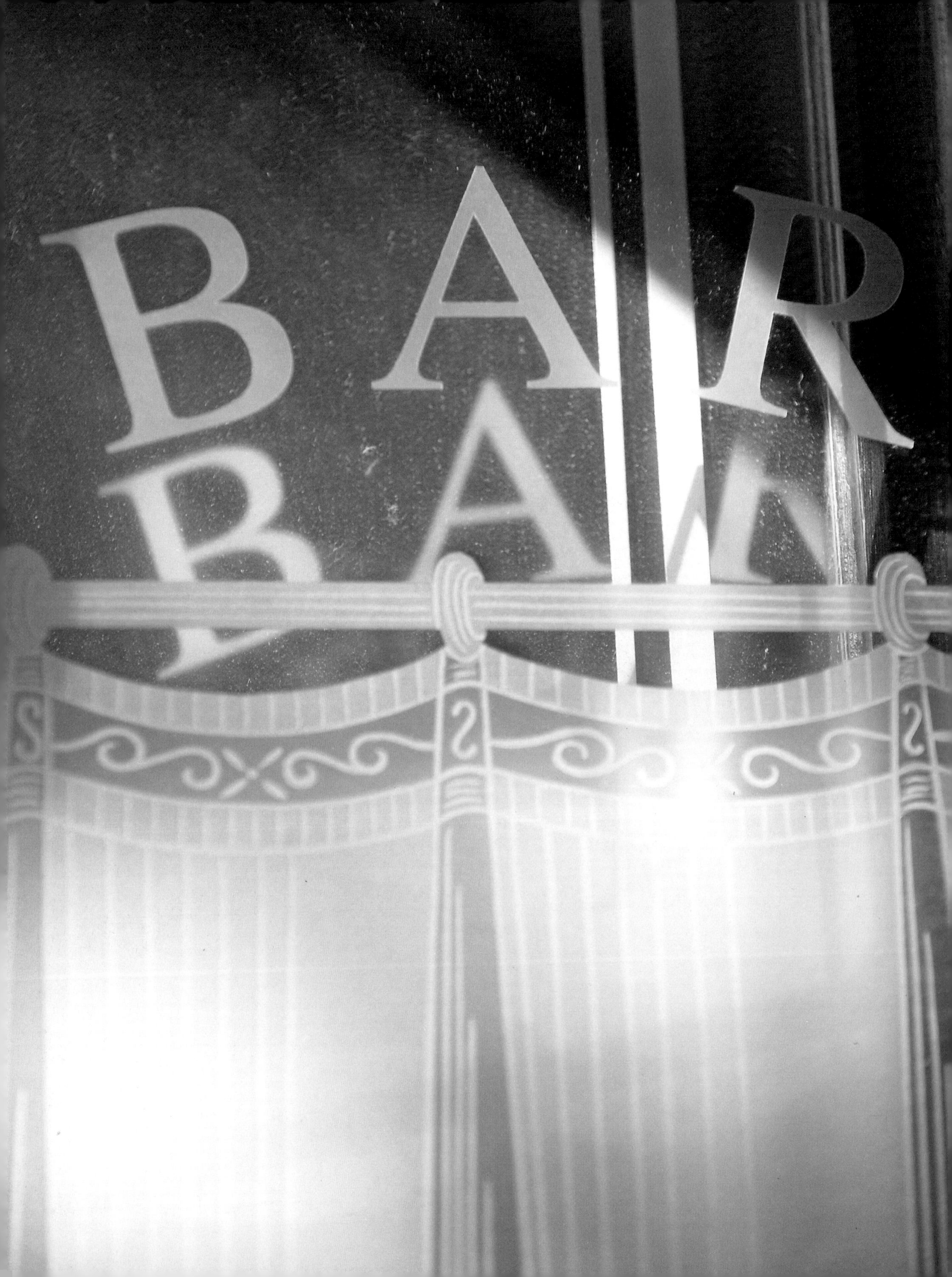
BAR

TO THE SOUTH OF MADRID, IN A TOWN CALLED ARANJUEZ, SITS THE OLD SUMMER PALACE OF THE KINGS. OPPOSITE THE PALACE IS CASA JOSÉ, A FAMILY RESTAURANT IN A CENTURIES-OLD HOUSE. THE CHEF, FERNANDO DEL CERRO, SHOWED ME AROUND THE MARKET GARDENS ON THE FLATS OF THE RÍO TAJO, WHERE HE BUYS THE FRUIT AND VEGETABLES FOR HIS KITCHEN. LIKE FERGUS HENDERSON IN LONDON OR DAN BARBER IN NEW YORK, HE CHAMPIONS PRODUCE AND TRADITIONAL TECHNIQUES. MANY OF THE DISHES HE COOKED THAT DAY COULD BE MADE ONLY IN ARANJUEZ, BECAUSE THE PRODUCE THEY USE — LIKE THE ARANJUEZ STRAWBERRIES, WHICH ARE TOO DELICATE TO TRANSPORT — ARE GROWN NOWHERE ELSE. THIS RECIPE IS INSPIRED BY ONE OF HIS DISHES — STICKY CROQUETTES MADE FROM PORK TROTTERS, MIXED WITH TINY CAPERS, ROLLED IN BREADCRUMBS AND DEEP-FRIED.

CROQUETAS DE MANOS DE CERDO
DEEP-FRIED STICKY PORK CROQUETTES

30 TAPAS

4 pig's trotters

1 yellow onion

1 bunch parsley, leaves finely chopped, stalks reserved

1 garlic head

1/3 cup wine vinegar

2 tablespoons tiny capers in salt, rinsed and drained

1/2 white onion, very finely chopped

1 teaspoon coarse sea salt

1 teaspoon freshly ground black pepper

safflower oil, for deep-frying

seasoned all-purpose flour, to coat

2 eggs, lightly beaten

4 1/2 cups panko breadcrumbs (see glossary)

fine sea salt, to sprinkle

Place the trotters in a very large stockpot with the yellow onion, parsley stalks, garlic and vinegar. Cover with 9 quarts water. Bring to a boil, then reduce the heat to low and simmer for about 3 1/2 hours. Drain the trotters, reserving the garlic. Set aside the trotters until cool enough to handle, then remove the skin, fat and meat, discarding the bone and cartilage. Slip the garlic cloves out of their skins.

Finely chop the trotter skin, fat and meat and place in a large bowl. Add the garlic cloves, chopped parsley, capers, white onion, sea salt flakes and black pepper and mix well.

Moisten a work surface with water, then place a large piece of plastic wrap on the work surface (the water will stop the plastic moving). Place half of the trotter mixture on the plastic wrap and form into a sausage shape, then roll up to form a log. Twist both ends of the plastic and roll the mixture back and forth over your work surface until you have a tight sausage approximately 1 1/4 inches in diameter. Repeat with another piece of plastic wrap and the remaining mixture, then place the rolls on a baking sheet and refrigerate overnight.

Unwrap the rolls, then cut them into slices 1/2 inch thick using a very sharp knife.

Fill a deep fryer or large heavy-bottomed saucepan one-third full of oil and heat to 350°F, or until a cube of bread dropped into the oil browns in 15 seconds.

Dust the slices in flour, then dip in the beaten eggs, allowing the excess to drain off. Roll in the breadcrumbs. Deep-fry for 2 minutes, or until golden brown. Drain on a paper towel, sprinkle with fine sea salt and serve hot.

MADRID IS ONE OF THE POWERHOUSES OF INNOVATION, WHERE A TRADITIONAL DISH MAY UNDERGO A MAKEOVER THAT RENDERS IT UNRECOGNIZABLE TO THE INHABITANTS OF ITS BIRTHPLACE. BUT WHEN DONE WITH RESPECT FOR THE INGREDIENTS, SOMETIMES CULINARY CHANGE CAN BRING ABOUT SOMETHING EXCELLENT. *PULPO A LA GALLEGA* IS A SIMPLE DISH OF OCTOPUS SLICES RESTING ON DISCS OF POTATO COOKED IN THE SAME WATER AS THE OCTOPUS. IT IS SERVED ON A PLATE AND DRESSED WITH OLIVE OIL AND PIMENTÓN. THIS VERSION IS BECOMING QUITE POPULAR IN MADRID AND ACKNOWLEDGES THE EVOLUTION OF CHEF SKILLS AND DINER EXPECTATIONS — WITHOUT CHANGING THE INGREDIENTS AT THE HEART OF THE DISH. THIS TERRINE IS SET WITH NOTHING MORE THAN THE GELATIN NATURALLY OCCURRING IN THE OCTOPUS.

TERRINA DE PULPO

OCTOPUS TERRINE

12 TAPAS

8 MEDIAS RACIONES

4½ lb frozen octopus tentacles, thawed

I teaspoon *agridulce* paprika, preferably from La Vera (see page 154)

4 tablespoons finely chopped parsley

2 lb boiling potatoes, washed but not peeled

fine sea salt

I red onion, finely diced

½ cup extra virgin olive oil

I tablespoon smoked paprika

Plunge the octopus tentacles into a large saucepan of boiling unsalted water for 15 seconds, then remove. Return the water to a boil, then repeat this plunging process another four times, allowing the water to reach boiling point between each immersion. On the last immersion, leave the octopus in the saucepan, reduce the heat to barely a simmer, then cook for 30 to 40 minutes, or until tender — the outside pink layer should be intact. Remove the octopus from the water and let cool.

Line a 4 x 10 inch terrine mold with plastic wrap.

Trim the tentacles to the same length as the terrine mold, measuring from the thick end of the tentacles down. Place them in a bowl, add the *agridulce* paprika and half of the parsley and mix together well. Arrange the legs, top to tail, to fill the terrine, using the smaller legs to fill the gaps. Cover with plastic wrap, then place a heavy weight on top of the octopus and refrigerate overnight.

Several hours before serving, place the potatoes in a large saucepan, cover with cold water, add a pinch of salt and bring to the boil. Reduce the heat and simmer for 45 minutes, or until tender. Drain the potatoes and let cool, then peel. Place in a large bowl and crush with a fork until roughly mashed. Add the onion, olive oil, paprika, I teaspoon sea salt and the remaining parsley and mix well.

Remove the octopus terrine from the mold. Using a very sharp knife, cut into slices ¼ inch thick, then place on a cold plate. Serve with the room-temperature potato salad.

TAPEO

THE TAPAS PROMENADE

Most Spanish people live in apartments. Apart from family and very close friends, entertaining in the family home is rare. Instead, the public spaces of the street and bars are where people meet and socialize. The Spanish are experts in walking. They have a great sense of style and understated flair as they move through the crowded streets. Indeed, the *tapeo* is a cultural phenomenon: there is a sense of exuberance, of something happening, of being part of an event, of just being. The secret is in existing completely in the moment. Walking is not just an activity to get somewhere, it is an art in itself. And in that public display can be very private and intimate moments: the caress of a young man's hand on the small of his girlfriend's back; a father cradling his newborn's head; two women elegantly kissing each other's cheek... and old married couples, walking sedately to the bar, holding each other's hand as they have done for years.

THE SPANIARDS LOVE THEIR MEATBALLS OR *ALBÓNDIGAS*. THEY ARE A REGULAR HOME MEAL, BUT ALSO APPEAR ON THE MENUS OF THE MOST RUSTIC OF BARS AND WELL-REGARDED RESTAURANTS ALIKE. A MERE MOUTHFUL, THEY ARE ALWAYS MOIST, JUICY AND FLAVORSOME. LUNCHING ONE DAY AT ONE OF MADRID'S WELL-KNOWN MODERN RESTAURANTS, ANDRÉS MADRIGAL'S ALBOROQUE, I WAS SERVED THE MOST STUNNING DISH. HE HAD BROUGHT TOGETHER THE CLASSIC COMBINATION OF SQUID AND FAVA BEANS, WHICH ARE TRADITIONALLY BRAISED, AND HE USED THEM TO MAKE *ALBÓNDIGAS* WITH SMALL PIECES OF CUTTLEFISH EMBEDDED IN A LIGHT FLAVORSOME MOUSSE THAT WAS SET BY POACHING.

ALBÓNDIGAS DE SEPIA

SQUID BALLS WITH FAVA BEANS

24 TAPAS

6 MEDIAS RACIONES

2 1/4 lb squid hoods, cleaned

4 garlic cloves

1 tablespoon finely chopped parsley

1 tablespoon finely chopped mint

sea salt

2 egg whites

a pinch of freshly grated nutmeg

zest of 1 lemon

1/4 cup whipping cream

a pinch of freshly ground white pepper

1/3 cup extra virgin olive oil

1 yellow onion, finely chopped

a pinch of saffron threads

3 bay leaves

1 1/8 cups white wine

1 1/3 cups shelled fava beans

crusty bread, to serve

Finely chop one-third of the squid hoods and half of the garlic, then place in a bowl with the parsley, mint and a pinch of salt. Mix well.

Cut the remaining squid into 1-inch squares, then place in a food processor and process until a coarse purée forms. Place in a bowl sitting over a larger bowl filled with ice. Add the egg whites, nutmeg, lemon zest, cream and white pepper and combine very well. Add the finely chopped squid mixture, combine well, then cover with plastic wrap and refrigerate while preparing the rest of the dish.

Thinly slice the remaining garlic, then heat the olive oil in a large heavy-bottomed saucepan over medium heat. Add the onion and a pinch of salt and sauté for 2 to 3 minutes, or until the onion is beginning to soften. Add the saffron and stir for 1 minute, then reduce the heat to low. Add the sliced garlic and bay leaves and cook for 10 minutes, then add the wine. Increase the heat to high and bring to a boil, then reduce the heat to low and simmer for 10 minutes. Add 2 1/2 cups water, increase the heat to high and bring to a boil, then reduce the heat again and simmer for 10 minutes.

Meanwhile, using damp hands, shape tablespoons of the squid mixture into balls, placing them on a baking sheet lined with parchment paper. Once you have finished rolling them, carefully place the balls in the sauce and simmer over very low heat for 45 minutes, turning occasionally.

Add the fava beans to the sauce and simmer for another 5 minutes. Check the seasoning and serve hot, with plenty of crusty bread to soak up the sauce.

NOT FAR FROM THE HEART OF MADRID IS CASA PACO. IT'S A BAR. A BAR FULL OF BLOKES DRINKING *CHATOS* — LITTLE GLASSES OF CHILLED RED WINE. IT'S NOT FANCY, BUT IT IS BEAUTIFUL. THERE'S A CARVED WOODEN BAR, TILED WALLS AND A SMALL SQUARE GLASS CABINET ON ONE CORNER OF THE BAR WHERE THERE IS ALWAYS A *TORTILLA*, A SMALL STACK OF *LOMO* (PORK LOIN) AND CHORIZO, A FEW ROUNDS OF *MANCHEGO* CHEESE AND A GREAT BIG PINK BLOCK OF PORK TERRINE THAT THE WAITER EMILIO CUTS INTO CUBES THAT TAKE A GOOD FEW BITES TO GET THROUGH. THIS IS A RICH AND SWEET TERRINE THAT IS PERFECT FOR A SPECIAL OCCASION.

TERRINA DE HÍGADO

SPICED PORK LIVER TERRINE

12 TAPAS

6 MEDIAS RACIONES

I lb pork liver, cleaned and cut into 1-inch dice

²/₃ lb pork shoulder, cut into 1-inch dice (see Note)

I teaspoon freshly ground nutmeg

I teaspoon freshly ground toasted juniper berries

3 tablespoons brandy

3 tablespoons amontillado sherry

3 teaspoons fine sea salt

I teaspoon freshly ground black pepper

I large yellow onion, roughly chopped

½-lb piece of pork back fat, cut into ½-inch dice, chilled

3 tablespoons whipping cream

⅓ lb finely sliced pork back fat or mild pancetta

fresh bread, to serve

DAY 1

Place the pork liver, pork shoulder, nutmeg, juniper, brandy, sherry, sea salt and black pepper in a bowl. Mix together well, then cover tightly and refrigerate overnight.

Meanwhile, drop the chopped onion into a large saucepan of boiling salted water and cook for 3 to 4 minutes. Remove with a slotted spoon, drain on a paper towel and allow to cool, then cover and refrigerate overnight.

DAY 2

Using a meat grinder fitted with the coarse grinding plate, grind the chilled back fat into a large bowl. (If you don't have a meat grinder, use a sharp knife to finely chop the fat.)

Drain the liver mixture. Change the grinding plate to fine, then grind the marinated liver mixture into the bowl with the back fat. (If you don't have a meat grinder, use a food processor to blend the marinated liver into a rough purée, then mix in your ground pork.)

Using scrupulously clean hands, combine well, then mix in the cream and blanched onion. Cover and refrigerate for at least 2 hours (or overnight if you prefer).

Preheat the oven to 300°F.

Line a 4 x 10 inch terrine mold with the sliced back fat or pancetta in slightly overlapping layers, leaving the sides overhanging; reserve several slices to cover the terrine. Pour the mixture into the lined mold, then tap it firmly on the bench several times to expel any air bubbles. Lay the remaining back fat or pancetta slices over the terrine mixture, then fold over the overhanging pieces of fat to cover.

Cover the terrine tightly with foil and place in a deep roasting pan. Pour in enough hot water to come halfway up the sides of the terrine. Bake for 90 minutes, then carefully remove from the hot water bath and let cool. Remove the foil and loosely cover the terrine with plastic wrap, then place a weight on top and refrigerate overnight.

DAY 3

Carefully remove the terrine from the mold. If this proves difficult, loosen the terrine by placing it in a bath of hot water for 30 to 60 seconds to melt the fat that may be holding it in place.

Cut the terrine into twelve slices I inch thick, then cut each slice into three "batons." Place three batons on each serving plate. Serve with plenty of fresh bread, and perhaps a few cornichons and some homemade spicy conserve.

NOTE If you don't have a meat grinder, buy the pork shoulder already ground instead, and don't marinate it in the liver mixture on Day I of the recipe. Use as instructed on Day 2.

LOS CAMAREROS

THE WAITERS

Lunch is always late in Spain. At the time the rest of the world normally eats — say 12 to 1 pm — Spanish waiters (*camareros*) are just starting their day's work by sitting down to their staff meal before the onslaught of *comida* (lunch). The *camareros* are not journeymen service staff filling in time between university classes or acting jobs. They are career waiters. Looking after people is their life's work. Some strut through the room puffing out their chests like little roosters signalling their importance in the proceedings. Others put on an air of flair and pizzazz with flourishes of the hands and head that both silently communicate instructions to other staff members and deliberately entertain the guests. Some move serenely, creating as little wake as possible, placing dishes down unnoticed, filling a glass without being seen, then quietly moving on to the next table.

EVERY TIME I AM IN MADRID, I MAKE A BEELINE TO SEE JAIME. HE'S A GALICIAN GUY WHOSE KITCHEN IS A SMALL HOTBOX OF A GRILL ROOM WITH ONLY A PANE OF GLASS SEPARATING HIM FROM THE STREET. IN THAT FLUORESCENT-LIT CHAMBER, HE PERFORMS HIS NIGHTLY THEATER OF COOKING *OREJAS* (PIG'S EARS) AND *MOLLEJAS* (SWEETBREADS) ON THE HOT PLATE. HE SERVES GOOD BEER AND ROUGH GALICIAN WINE POURED INTO WHITE CERAMIC BOWLS. HIS BAR IS QUITE AUSTERE, EXCEPT FOR THE SOUND OF FLAMENCO COMING FROM THE SPEAKERS — JAIME LOVES FLAMENCO! I LOVE HIS PIG'S EARS, MADE SOFT WITH HOURS OF COOKING AND VERY TASTY BY BEING MARINATED IN *ADOBO* — A MIX OF HERBS, GARLIC AND *PIMENTÓN* (SPANISH PAPRIKA). WHEN I SEE HIM, I ASK THE SAME QUESTION: "¿*TIENES OREJAS?*" (DO YOU HAVE EARS?). HE JUST FLAPS HIS EARS WITH HIS HANDS AND LAUGHS. HIS PIG'S EARS ARE HARD TO MAKE, SO INSTEAD I HAVE INCLUDED HIS RECIPE FOR SWEETBREADS — SMALL SAVORY *ADOBO*-FLAVORED BITES THAT ARE PERFECT WITH A GLASS OF BEER.

MOLLEJAS DE CORDERO
GRILLED LAMB SWEETBREADS

12 TAPAS
6 MEDIAS RACIONES

¾ lb lamb sweetbreads, soaked
   overnight in salted water
1 yellow onion, halved
5 garlic cloves
1 tablespoon white wine vinegar
fine sea salt
1 teaspoon smoked paprika
3 tablespoons extra virgin olive oil
1 tablespoon finely chopped parsley
1 teaspoon dried oregano
1 teaspoon fennel seeds, toasted

Drain the sweetbreads and trim off any scraggy bits. Place in a large saucepan with the onion halves, 2 garlic cloves, the vinegar and a pinch of salt. Cover with cold water and place over medium-high heat. Bring to just below a boil, then reduce the heat to medium-low and simmer for 1 minute. Remove from the heat and allow the sweetbreads to cool in the liquid.

Finely chop the remaining garlic cloves and place in a bowl with the paprika, olive oil, parsley, oregano, fennel seeds and 1 teaspoon sea salt. Mix well. Drain the cooled sweetbreads and gently stir them through the olive oil mixture. Cover with plastic wrap and refrigerate overnight.

Heat a grill pan or heavy-bottomed frying pan over high heat until very hot. Working in batches, cook the sweetbreads on one side for 1 minute. Season, then turn, season again and cook for another minute. Place on a warm serving plate and serve immediately.

MUM WOULD ALWAYS HAVE A POTATO SALAD IN THE FRIDGE OVER SUMMER: ROUGHLY CUT POTATOES, RIPE TOMATOES, ONIONS, OLIVES AND A LITTLE EGG. A LITTLE PLATE OF THIS MAKES A GREAT LUNCH ON A HOT DAY. I HAD A FLASH OF THIS CHILDHOOD MEMORY ONE SUMMER IN MADRID. IT WAS LATE AFTERNOON AND THE *ENSALADA CAMPERA* THE BARMAN WAS SERVING UP WAS ALMOST IDENTICAL TO MUM'S. I WATCHED AS A FEW MATES GATHERED TOGETHER FOR A QUIET BEER AFTER WORK AND ORDERED A LITTLE PLATE OF THIS. THEY ALL ATE FROM THE SAME PLATE, TAKING THE ODD NIBBLE NOW AND THEN, RESTING THEIR FORK, TINE SIDE DOWN, ON THE PLATE BETWEEN BITES. IT'S THIS SHARING AND COMMUNAL EATING THAT MAKES TAPAS SO SPECIAL.

ENSALADA CAMPERA
SUMMER POTATO SALAD

12 TAPAS
6 MEDIAS RACIONES

1¾ lb fingerling potatoes, washed but not peeled

fine sea salt

6 eggs

6 ripe tomatoes, peeled and seeded (see glossary), roughly chopped

3 green bell peppers, seeded and ribs removed, cut into ½-inch squares

1 red onion, chopped into large dice

1½ cups green olives

1 tablespoon chopped parsley

⅔ cup fruity extra virgin olive oil

⅓ cup aged sherry vinegar

7-oz can Spanish tuna, drained

Place the potatoes in a saucepan, cover with cold water and add a pinch of salt. Bring to a boil, then reduce the heat and simmer for 45 minutes, or until tender.

Meanwhile, place the whole eggs in a saucepan, cover with plenty of cold water and bring to a boil over medium heat. Reduce the heat to low and simmer for 4 minutes. Drain, refresh in cold water and peel.

Place the tomatoes, bell peppers, onion, olives, parsley, olive oil, vinegar and 2 teaspoons sea salt in a bowl. Mix well and set aside.

Drain the potatoes, and when cool enough to handle, peel and slice into ½-inch rounds. Add the potatoes and tuna to the salad and gently mix through with your fingers, then place on a serving plate. Cut the eggs into quarters, arrange them over the salad and serve immediately.

LAS HUERTAS

THE KITCHEN GARDENS

★ ★ ★

IT WAS LATE MORNING AND I WAS WATCHING A STOCKY OLD MAN WALKING ACROSS A MEDIEVAL STONE BRIDGE WITH A BIG BUCKET OF TOMATOES ON HIS SHOULDER. FOLLOWING HIM WAS HIS WIFE, CARRYING AN ARMLOAD OF ZUCCHINI AND A PLASTIC BAG FILLED WITH SMALL APPLES. SOON CAME OTHER COUPLES, SOME CARRYING SACKS, OTHERS PUSHING WHEELBARROWS. ONE MAN HAD TIED BLUE PLASTIC CRATES TO HIS HORSE'S BACK AND FILLED THEM WITH GRAPES. SLOWLY THEY ALL LUMBERED UP TO THEIR VILLAGE ON TOP OF THE HILL.

This was their daily ritual: work in their *huerta* — what we'd call a kitchen garden — during the day, and return to their home in the afternoon. Their little *huertas* were patchworked across the fertile flats of the Río Francia that meanders a few hundred yards below their millennia-old town of Mirandar del Castañar in the Sierra de Francia, an hour south of Salamanca in western Spain. Here, people grow what they eat and eat what they grow.

Across Spain there are thousands of small towns in which self-sufficiency is not a lifestyle choice but a matter of survival. In their *huertas* — small plots of land about a third of an acre in size — a family can grow almost all its food. A *huerta* can be a bit like the English allotment, a plot of land on the edge of the village, or just a piece of land next to a house or even in the middle of town. I have even seen a *huerta* on a finger of land running by the airport trainline in Barcelona. The Spanish hate to see fertile land go to waste, no matter who it belongs to.

Traditionally, the Sierra de Francia has been one of the most isolated areas in Spain. Before roads were built, the steep hills and mountains made movement between even relatively close villages a laborious affair. During the time of the Moors, some noble Christian families moved here for protection. Well into the early 20th century, there were villages accessible only by foot or on the back of a donkey. When a team of filmmakers arrived in this region in the 1930s, they documented a way of life almost unchanged since the Middle Ages. The Spanish classic *Tierra sin Pan* (*Land Without Bread*) shows villagers living hand-to-mouth from their kitchen gardens, keeping bees in hollow logs and hunting for game in the surrounding hills.

The area now has automatic teller machines and Wi-Fi Internet connection, but many of the old people still spend their lives tending to their *huertas*. They walk, sometimes several miles, twice a day, watering their gardens by hand from the natural springs that flow through their plots, weeding, sowing and harvesting.

Being a *campesino* (peasant) in the 21st century doesn't hold much allure for young people and many of the *huertas* now lie abandoned, choked with weeds. That said, I have met IT professionals and bankers who have turned their backs on the intangible commodities of modernity to return to the family kitchen garden to grow beautiful vegetables. Several work with some of Spain's most noted chefs, growing internationally renowned produce — some varieties of which are endemic to their village.

The dishes in this chapter reflect the food traditionally cooked by the people of this area. Based on garden vegetables, including home-grown and sun-dried legumes, they are all really quite hearty and filling meals, all tasting wonderfully rich — as befits the tradition of poverty from which they spring.

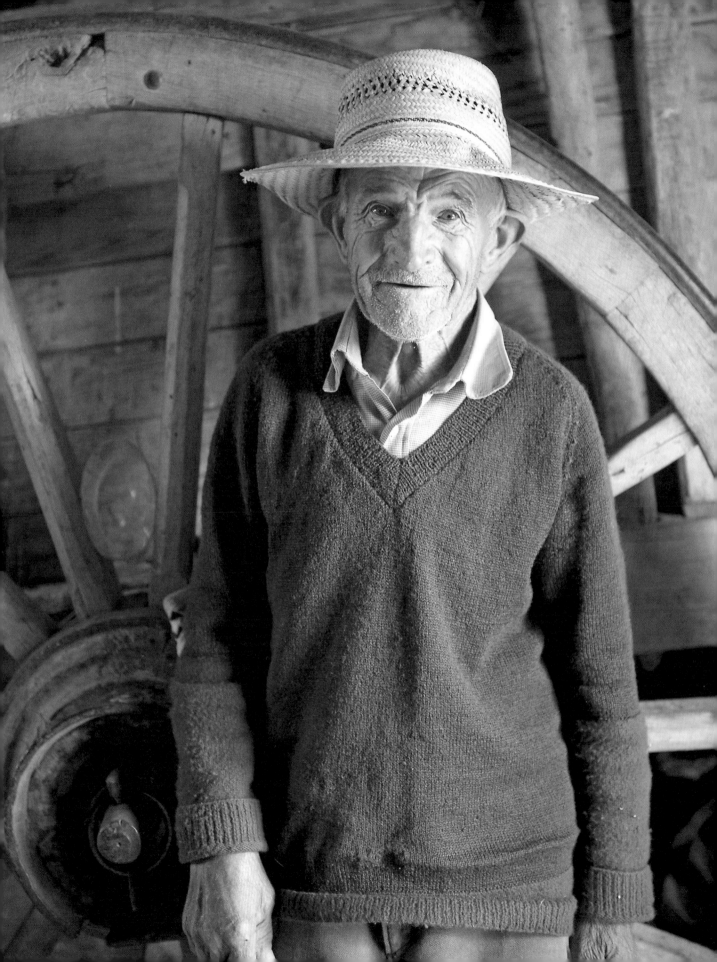

THE AROMA OF SLOW-COOKED LEEKS FILLED THE ENTIRE TOWN SQUARE. FOLLOWING THE RICH SMELL LED ME TO THE ALMOST HIDDEN KITCHEN OF TITO ROBLEDO, CHEF AND OWNER OF LAS PETRONILAS IN MIRANDA DEL CASTAÑAR. HIS PHILOSOPHY IS TO EMBRACE THE SIMPLE THINGS IN LIFE AND MAKE THE MOST OF THEM. EVERY DAY, A HANDFUL OF LOCALS WANDERS INTO HIS SMALL RESTAURANT, AND LAYS BUNCHES OF VEGETABLES FROM THEIR *HUERTAS*, WRAPPED IN NEWSPAPER, ON HIS BAR. THE DAY BEFORE WE ARRIVED, AN OLD COUPLE HAD SOLD HIM SOME OF THEIR EXCESS LEEKS: SMALL, PALE, TIGHT AND FIRM. THESE HE COOKED IN A SIMPLE STOCK AND SERVED LUKEWARM. THEIR AROMA WAS RICH AND ENTICING, THE OUTER LEAVES SOFT AND SILKY AND THE INNER CORE COOKED TO A BUTTER-LIKE CONSISTENCY. IT'S HARD TO GET SUCH PERFECT LEEKS, BUT YOU CAN MAKE THIS DISH TO A SIMILAR QUALITY BY CHOOSING THE SMALLEST, TIGHTEST LEEKS IN THE MARKET.

PUERROS COCIDOS
SLOW-COOKED BUTTERY LEEKS

4 MEDIAS RACIONES

6 small leeks, roots trimmed

⅓ cup olive oil

4 garlic cloves, thickly sliced

5 bay leaves

⅔ cup white wine

5 tablespoons butter

coarse sea salt

freshly ground black pepper

extra virgin olive oil, to drizzle

Cut the green tops off the leeks and discard or use for stock. Halve the leeks crossways and remove a few of the tough outer layers.

Heat the olive oil in a wide heavy-bottomed saucepan over medium heat. Add the garlic and sauté for 2 minutes, or until lightly browned, then add the bay leaves and the leeks in a single layer.

Add the wine, butter, a pinch of sea salt and enough warm water to almost cover the leeks. Increase the heat to high and bring to a boil. As soon as the liquid comes to a boil, reduce the heat to low, then cover and cook for 45 to 60 minutes, or until the leek centers are very soft when pierced with a skewer. Carefully remove the leeks from the liquid and set aside to cool.

Meanwhile, simmer the poaching liquid over high heat for 10 minutes, or until reduced by two-thirds.

Remove and discard the outer few layers of the leeks and arrange the stalks on a warm serving plate. Pour over most of the sauce, then sprinkle with sea salt and black pepper. Drizzle with a little extra virgin olive oil and serve warm.

GREEN BEANS ARE THE FIRST THING YOU SEE IN THE SPANISH KITCHEN GARDEN. THEIR SPRAWLING TENDRILS COVER HEAD-HIGH TRIPODS OF STICKS, MAKING THEM LOOK LIKE OVERGROWN TEEPEES. ON ANY SPARE PATCH OF LAND IN THE COUNTRY, VILLAGE OR TOWN, SOMEONE WILL TURN OVER THE SOIL AND PLANT SOME BEANS. *JUDÍAS* WERE ORIGINALLY FROM SOUTH AMERICA AND WERE FIRST GROWN IN SPAIN IN THE 1500S. UNLIKE SMALLER STRING BEANS OR FRENCH BEANS, THESE BEANS REQUIRE A BIT MORE COOKING FOR AN OPTIMUM LEVEL OF SOFTNESS.

JUDÍAS VERDES CON AJOS CONFITADOS

GREEN BEANS WITH GARLIC CONFIT

6 MEDIAS RACIONES

$1/2$ cup extra virgin olive oil

8 garlic cloves, very thinly sliced

$1^3/_4$ lb large green beans, ends trimmed and cut on the diagonal into 2-inch lengths

$1^1/_2$ teaspoons coarse sea salt

freshly ground black pepper

Heat the olive oil in a heavy-bottomed frying pan over very low heat. Add the garlic and sauté for 8 to 10 minutes, or until lightly colored and soft, then remove from the heat and pour into a small heatproof bowl. Do not allow the garlic to burn or it will taste bitter.

Meanwhile, drop the beans into a large saucepan of salted boiling water. When the water returns to a boil, cook for another 12 to 15 minutes, or until tender.

Drain the beans and place in a warm serving dish. Sprinkle with the sea salt and some black pepper and pour the oil and garlic mixture over. Toss gently and serve hot.

LAS TIERRAS DE LA FAMILIA

THE FAMILY LANDS

The Valez family *huerta* is surrounded by a drystone wall ringed by wild cherry and chestnut trees. One of half a dozen or so in that bend of the Río Francia, it is watered by hand from a spring welling up from deep under the hill. Many such *huertas* are terraced into the side of this hill, with the deep, fertile soil hand-carted from the river flats generations ago. The spring also feeds a *pozo* (well), where every time they wash their vegetables, they disturb a family of frogs basking on the mossy rocks. On this one small plot of land, no bigger than a suburban house block, I counted 45 different edible plants growing in the rich soil — fruit trees, leafy vegetables, tubers, legumes, garlic and onions, herbs, and half a dozen different types of pumpkin and zucchini.

On the summer day I visited the Valez family, there were four generations in that garden. Great-grandmother was sitting in the shade of a quince tree, minding her great-grandson. The baby's father, Manuel, was back home from Madrid for the weekend, where he works in a bank. Manuel's mother, Adelfa, joked that he only came back home when it was time to harvest the food. "Our real problems are the wild boars," says Celedo, the father. "They are always trying to break my fence and eat my vegetables. But if they do, I will find them and eat them!"

IT WAS THE END OF THE DAY AND I HAD BEEN TALKING TO AN OLD BLOKE IN HIS KITCHEN GARDEN. HE POINTED TO A ROW OF SQUAT BUSHES AND INSTRUCTED ME TO PULL OFF ONE OF THE LITTLE PODS. IN IT WERE TWO PERFECTLY FORMED CHICKPEAS. THEY WERE SMALL BUT NOT TINY, WITH THE FAINTEST FLUSH OF PINK THROUGH THE SKIN. HE TOOK ME ASIDE AND SAID TO ME IN A HUSHED VOICE THAT WAS CHEEKY YET RESPECTFUL:

"*¿DECÁLOGO DE UN BUEN GARBANZO? EL CULO DE UN GARBANZO ARRUGADO COMO EL CULO DE UNA VIEJA. EL PICO DEL GARBANZO DURO Y TERSO COMO EL PECHO DE UNA DONCELLA.*"

THIS IS TYPICAL OF THE NAUGHTY SPANISH IDIOM AND GOES SOMETHING LIKE: "WHAT ARE THE MAIN POINTS TO A GOOD CHICKPEA? THEY SHOULD BE ROUND LIKE AN OLD LADY'S BUM, BUT PERT AND FIRM LIKE A YOUNG LADY'S BREAST." LOOK AT A CHICKPEA AND YOU'LL KNOW WHAT HE WAS TALKING ABOUT.

WITH THEM, YOU MAKE THIS COOL BUT ENERGIZING SUMMER SOUP THAT CAN BE A LIGHT MEAL IN ITSELF.

PURÉ DE COCIDO DE VERANO
SUMMER CHICKPEA CREAM WITH RIPE TOMATOES

8 MEDIAS RACIONES

1 1/3 cups dried chickpeas,
    soaked overnight
1 large carrot, unpeeled
1 yellow onion, peeled and halved
1 garlic bulb, plus 1/4 clove,
    finely chopped
3 bay leaves
2 teaspoons fine sea salt, plus
    extra, to sprinkle
1/3 cup extra virgin olive oil,
    plus extra, to drizzle
3 ripe tomatoes, peeled, seeded
    (see glossary) and finely chopped

Drain the chickpeas and place in a large saucepan with the carrot, onion halves, garlic bulb and bay leaves. Cover with cold water and bring to a boil over high heat, then reduce the heat to medium and simmer for 1 to 1 1/2 hours, or until the chickpeas are soft but not losing their skins.

Remove the carrot, garlic bulb and bay leaves from the chickpeas. When cool enough to handle, peel and roughly chop the carrot and squeeze the garlic paste out of the cloves, then place both in the bowl of a large food processor. Using a slotted spoon, remove the chickpeas from the cooking liquid and add to the food processor with 1/3 cup of the cooking liquid. Process until smooth. Add the finely chopped garlic, the sea salt and olive oil and process for another minute. The purée should be smooth and liquid enough to fall easily from a spoon. If not, add a little more cooking liquid. Pour into a bowl, then cover and refrigerate until cold but not chilled.

To serve, ladle the soup into small bowls, then top with chopped tomato, a sprinkle of sea salt and a drizzle of extra virgin olive oil.

PEOPLE SAY TO ME THAT THERE ARE VERY FEW VEGETABLES EATEN IN SPAIN. I SAY TO THEM THAT THEY ARE EATING IN RESTAURANTS AND NOT SPANISH PEOPLE'S HOMES. TRADITIONALLY, SPANISH PEOPLE ATE THE VEGETABLES THEY COULD AFFORD OR THE ONES THEY COULD GROW. MEAT WAS FOR FEASTING, SO RESTAURANTS SERVED MORE MEAT DISHES: WHO WANTS TO PAY FOR VEGETABLES WHEN YOU'RE TAKING A NIGHT OFF FROM THE KITCHEN? WHEN WE WERE GROWING UP, MUM MADE THIS AMAZING DISH WITH SWISS CHARD AND IT IS TYPICAL OF HOW IT IS COOKED ACROSS SPAIN. THE STALKS ARE SLOWLY SAUTÉED WITH GARLIC AND ONION, THE TORN LEAVES ARE LATER ADDED WITH WATER, AND THE ENSUING STOCK IS THICKENED WITH FRIED BREAD. DON'T BE ALARMED BY THE COOKING TIME — TRUST ME WHEN I SAY THAT IT IS GOING TO BE OKAY TO COOK THE HECK OUT OF YOUR SWISS CHARD: IT'S ALL ABOUT FLAVOR. IF YOU'RE USING THE SLIGHTLY SMALLER AND MORE TENDER EUROPEAN CHARD, YOU CAN REDUCE THE COOKING TIME.

ACELGAS REHOGADAS

BRAISED SWISS CHARD

6 MEDIAS RACIONES

- 2 bunches of Swiss chard, about 4½ lb in total, stalks and leaves separated and rinsed
- ⅞ cup extra virgin olive oil
- 3 large yellow onions, finely chopped
- 6 garlic cloves, thickly sliced, plus 5 whole cloves, unpeeled
- 1 teaspoon fine sea salt
- ½ teaspoon ground turmeric
- 4½ oz two-day-old bread rolls, thickly sliced
- 1 tablespoon sherry vinegar

Cut off and discard the bottom 1 inch of the chard stalks. Very thinly slice the intact stalks and roughly shred the leaves, keeping them separate.

Heat ⅓ cup of the olive oil in a large heavy-bottomed frying pan over medium-high heat. Add the onions and sauté for 5 minutes, or until slightly brown. Add the sliced garlic, the sliced chard stalks and a good pinch of the sea salt. Reduce the heat to medium-low and cook, stirring occasionally, for 30 minutes, or until the stalks are very tender.

Add the shredded chard leaves and remaining salt and cook for another 5 minutes, or until the leaves are just wilted. Stir in the turmeric and 3 cups water and simmer over low heat for another 30 minutes, or until tender.

Meanwhile, heat the remaining olive oil in a heavy-bottomed frying pan over medium-high heat. Add the bread slices and the unpeeled garlic cloves and cook, shaking the pan frequently, until the bread is golden and crisp. Remove the bread, drain on a paper towel, then return the pan to the heat and cook the garlic cloves for another 2 to 3 minutes, or until slightly golden. Drain on a paper towel.

When cool enough to handle, break up the toasted bread slices with your hands. Peel the toasted garlic, then flatten with the flat side of a large knife and roughly chop.

Add the vinegar and toasted bread and garlic to the chard in the last few minutes of cooking. Season to taste and serve immediately.

ARTICHOKES ARE GOOD, YES? AND DEEP-FRYING MAKES FOOD TASTE BETTER, YES? SO WHEN YOU DEEP-FRY ARTICHOKES YOU DOUBLE THE GOODNESS? WELL, YES, TO TELL YOU THE TRUTH. THIS DISH OF SMALL ARTICHOKES, BOILED UNTIL SOFT, THEN SEASONED AND DEEP-FRIED IN A LITTLE SEMOLINA AND FINISHED WITH SOME GOLDEN ALMONDS AND A HIT OF LEMON ZEST MAKES A GREAT STARTER TO A MEAL. PASS AROUND A PLATE OF THESE AT YOUR NEXT GATHERING AND A RIPPLE OF PRAISE WILL FOLLOW YOU AROUND THE ROOM. THIS IS A GREAT BITE TO GO WITH A GLASS OF FINO OR EVEN AMONTILLADO SHERRY.

ALCACHOFAS FRITAS
DEEP-FRIED ARTICHOKES

12 TAPAS
6 MEDIAS RACIONES

1 lemon

12 artichokes

1⅓ cups olive oil

⅔ cup blanched almonds

2 cups fine semolina

1 tablespoon sea salt, plus extra,
  to sprinkle

2 tablespoons finely chopped parsley

Finely grate the zest of the lemon and set aside. Squeeze the juice into a large bowl of water to stop the artichokes browning as you peel them. Working one at a time, and using a small sharp knife, slice off most of the stem and the top one-third to half of the artichoke tops. Pull off the tough outer leaves to reveal the soft, pale yellow inner leaves, then peel the stem and slice the artichoke in quarters lengthways. Using a teaspoon, scoop out and discard the hairy choke. Place in the acidulated water and repeat with the remaining artichokes.

Bring a large saucepan of salted water to a boil over high heat. Add the drained artichokes and boil for 15 minutes, then drain again.

Meanwhile, heat half of the olive oil in a large frying pan over medium heat and fry the almonds for 6 to 8 minutes, or until golden, turning now and then. Remove the almonds with a slotted spoon, reserving the oil in the pan, and drain on a paper towel.

Preheat the oven to 300°F.

Combine the semolina and sea salt on a baking sheet. Working in two batches, toss the drained artichokes in the semolina until lightly coated.

Reheat the reserved olive oil in the frying pan over medium heat and cook half of the artichokes for 8 to 10 minutes, or until golden and crisp. Drain on a paper towel and keep warm in the oven. Discard any remaining oil in the pan and wipe the pan clean with a paper towel. Heat the remaining olive oil over medium heat and cook the remaining artichokes as before.

Pile the artichokes and fried almonds on a warm serving plate. Sprinkle with the lemon zest, parsley and some sea salt and serve warm.

BEFORE YOU EAT YOUR FIRST SPOONFUL OF THIS RICH SOUP, STOP. LEAN OVER THE BOWL AND GENTLY INHALE THE INTENSE AROMA OF THE SPICES AND SALT COD. IT IS BEAUTIFUL, TRULY BEAUTIFUL. THIS DISH IS FOUND THROUGHOUT SPAIN, BUT THIS VERSION COMES FROM SIERRA DE FRANCIA. SALT COD IS UBIQUITOUS ACROSS THE NATION. DRY, HARD AND, ONCE UPON A TIME, CHEAP, IT WAS TRANSPORTED FROM THE COAST ON THE BACK OF MULES AND WAS THE PROTEIN OF CHOICE IN CATHOLIC SPAIN — A COUNTRY THAT HELD FAST TO THE CHURCH'S RULES ON FASTING. THIS SOUP IS THICK AND RUSTIC AND SHOULD BE CONSUMED WITH PLENTY OF BREAD AND *TEMPRANILLO*. IT IS ALSO GOOD WITH *RUFETE*, THE WINE INDIGENOUS TO THE REGION — IT IS LIKE *TEMPRANILLO*, BUT WITH A HINT OF FENNEL.

POTAJE DE GARBANZOS CON ESPINACAS Y BACALAO
AROMATIC CHICKPEA POTAGE WITH SPINACH AND SALT COD

6 RACIONES

1 1/3 cups dried chickpeas, soaked overnight

1/2 head of garlic, plus 4 cloves, unpeeled

2 bay leaves

1/3 cup extra virgin olive oil

2 tomatoes

7 oz dried salt cod, soaked in cold water for 48 hours, changing the water four times

1 teaspoon saffron threads

2 tablespoons cumin seeds

4 egg yolks

1 teaspoon fine sea salt

1/2 teaspoon freshly ground black pepper

1 large bunch of spinach, about 1 lb in total, leaves only, washed and thickly shredded

1 slice of two-day-old *pasta dura* or other firm crusty bread

Drain the chickpeas and place in a large saucepan with the half head of garlic, bay leaves, half of the olive oil and the whole tomatoes. Cover with warm water and bring to a boil over high heat, then reduce the heat to medium and simmer for 1 to 1 1/2 hours, or until the chickpeas are soft but not losing their skins. Remove and reserve the garlic and tomatoes, but discard the tomato skins.

Meanwhile, drain the salt cod. Using your fingers, remove and discard the bones, tough skin and any fins or dark flesh, then break the flesh into small pieces.

Toast the saffron in a small dry frying pan over medium heat for 90 seconds, or until the threads begin to darken. Remove the saffron from the pan, then add the cumin seeds and toast for another 90 seconds, or until fragrant. Let cool, then grind the spices using a large mortar and pestle. Squeeze the reserved cooked garlic cloves out of their skins and add to the mortar with the reserved tomatoes and the egg yolks and pound until a smooth paste forms. (If you don't have a large mortar and pestle, grind the spices using a small one or a coffee grinder, then mix with the garlic, tomatoes and egg yolks in a food processor.)

Add the spice mixture, salt cod, sea salt and black pepper to the chickpeas. Mix well, stir in the shredded spinach and bring to a simmer.

Heat the remaining olive oil in a frying pan over medium heat. Add the bread slice and unpeeled garlic cloves and cook the bread until golden on each side. Drain the bread and garlic cloves on a paper towel. When cool enough to handle, peel the garlic and break the bread into small pieces. Place them both in a mortar with 2 tablespoons of liquid from the chickpea mixture and pound until a rough paste forms. Stir the mixture into the chickpeas and simmer for 3 to 4 minutes. Check the seasoning and serve in warm bowls.

THE FORESTS OF SPAIN HAVE ALWAYS BEEN DARK AND MYSTERIOUS PLACES, FULL OF WOLVES AND BANDITS. THERE ARE REMNANTS OF ANCIENT FORESTS IN MANY PARTS OF THE COUNTRY — GREAT OAK FORESTS COVERED IN ENOUGH MOSS TO MAKE THEM LOOK LIKE TOLKIEN FANTASIES, AND GLOOMY ARBUTUS FORESTS WHERE WILD BOARS LURK IN THE SHADOWS. EVERY AUTUMN AFTER THE FIRST STEADY RAINS, DROVES OF SPANIARDS ARMED WITH KNIVES AND BASKETS HEAD TO THE FORESTS IN SEARCH OF TREASURED *SETAS* (WILD MUSHROOMS). WILD MUSHROOMS ARE SO DIFFERENT TO THEIR SHED-RAISED COUSINS: THEY ARE RICH, SLIPPERY AND GIVE SO MUCH MORE TO A DISH — ALMOST LIKE NATURE'S STOCK CUBE. I HAVE BEEN TO THIS PART OF SPAIN SEVERAL TIMES DURING MUSHROOM SEASON AND THE NEXT FEW RECIPES REFLECT BOTH THE LOVE THE LOCALS HAVE FOR MUSHROOMS AND THE RESPECT I HAVE FOR THEIR RECIPES.

ALUBIAS BLANCAS CON CHANTERELLES

WHITE BEANS WITH WILD MUSHROOMS

6 MEDIAS RACIONES

$2/3$ cup extra virgin olive oil

1 white onion, sliced

$1/2$ red bell pepper, seeded and ribs removed, thinly sliced lengthways

3 bay leaves

1 garlic bulb, plus 2 thinly sliced cloves

$1 1/2$ cups dried cannellini beans, rinsed and soaked for 2 hours in cold water, then drained

$3 1/2$ oz chanterelle or oyster mushrooms, sliced $1/8$ inch thick

$3 1/2$ oz shiitake mushrooms, sliced $1/8$ inch thick

1 teaspoon coarse sea salt

$1/2$ teaspoon freshly ground black pepper

3 teaspoons sherry vinegar

a handful of chopped parsley

Heat $1/3$ cup of the olive oil in a large heavy-bottomed saucepan over high heat. Add the onion, reduce the heat to medium and cook, stirring occasionally, for 10 minutes, or until soft. Add the bell pepper, bay leaves and all the garlic and cook for another 10 minutes. Add the beans and enough water to cover, then bring to a gentle simmer. Reduce the heat to low and cook for 1 hour, or until the beans are soft and almost all of the cooking liquid has evaporated. Remove and reserve the cooked head of garlic.

Meanwhile, heat the remaining olive oil in a frying pan over high heat. Add the mushrooms, sea salt and black pepper and toss for 6 to 8 minutes, or until softened. Stir in the vinegar and cook for another 2 minutes, or until the mushrooms are slightly colored. Remove from the heat and stir in the parsley.

Squeeze the reserved cooked garlic cloves out of their skins, and add them to the beans with the mushrooms. Season to taste, then combine well and serve hot.

WHEN YOU HAVE SOMETHING GOOD AND YOU WANT TO SHARE IT AROUND, BUT THERE'S NOT ENOUGH FOR A BIG PIECE FOR EVERYONE, THE SPANISH ANSWER IS TO PUT IT IN A SOUP OR A RICE DISH. TIME AND TIME AGAIN, RIGHT ACROSS SPAIN, THERE ARE RICE DISHES THAT SOMEHOW CHAMPION THE GUEST INGREDIENT WITHOUT DETRACTING FROM THE INTEGRITY OF THE RICE. THE CHAMPION IN THIS CASE IS A WILD MUSHROOM CALLED *TROMPETAS DE LA MUERTE* (TRUMPETS OF DEATH). THESE MUSHROOMS ARE SO NAMED NOT BECAUSE THEY HERALD THE DEMISE OF THE INGESTOR BUT BECAUSE THEY ARE BLACK AND LOOK LIKE LITTLE TRUMPETS!

ARROZ CON TROMPETAS DE LA MUERTE

RICE WITH WILD MUSHROOMS

6 RACIONES

Heat half of the olive oil in a *perol* (see glossary) or frying pan over medium-high heat. Add the saffron and stir for 30 seconds, then add the onion and 1/2 teaspoon of the sea salt and cook for 5 minutes, stirring occasionally. Add half of the sliced garlic cloves, all of the thyme and bay leaves and cook, stirring occasionally, for another 5 minutes, or until the garlic is soft.

Increase the heat to high, then add the wine and boil for 2 minutes. Reduce the heat to medium, add the tomatoes and cook for 10 minutes, or until the tomatoes have reduced and thickened. Add the stock and bring to a boil, then stir in the rice and remaining 1 1/2 teaspoons sea salt. Reduce the heat to medium-low and simmer very gently, stirring occasionally, for 20 minutes.

Meanwhile, heat the butter and the remaining olive oil in a frying pan over medium heat. Add the remaining sliced garlic and the parsley and sauté for 2 to 3 minutes, or until the garlic is lightly browned. Add the mushrooms, season to taste and sauté for 5 minutes, or until tender.

When the rice has been cooking for 20 minutes and is tender, stir in the mushrooms. Remove from the heat and allow to stand for 10 minutes before serving.

1/2 cup extra virgin olive oil

a pinch of saffron threads

1 large white onion, finely sliced

2 teaspoons coarse sea salt

4 garlic cloves, thinly sliced

1 teaspoon thyme leaves

3 bay leaves

1 1/8 cups white wine such as verdelho

4 ripe tomatoes, peeled (see glossary) and puréed

6 1/2 cups chicken stock

1 1/4 cups Calasparra rice (see glossary)

2 tablespoons butter

a handful of roughly chopped parsley

9 oz fresh *trompetas de la muerte* (if unavailable, use sliced chanterelle, shiitake, or oyster or other wild mushrooms)

HOMENAJE A UN FILOSOFO

HOMAGE TO A PHILOSOPHER

When I first went to Miranda del Castañar, a man in a restaurant came up to me and asked, "Are you the Swedish journalist?" I said, "No, I am the Australian chef." The man said, "You'll do," and proceeded to escort me around the area for several days. The fact that he was a food and wine philosopher was not just serendipitous, not even synchronicity, but perhaps divine intervention. This is part of life in Spain: odd things just happen. One just has to go with the flow.

For two days, Fausto (yes, that was his name!) filled me with so much information about the food of Sierra de Francia that I thought my head would explode. What really impressed me was his love of the countryside and his knowledge of edible wild plants. In the country, foraging for nuts, berries and leaves is still an important part of the food culture. Fausto showed me sloe berries and wild fennel and one day took me to a dark forest of fruit-bearing trees — an ancient *madroño* (arbutus) forest. The fruit looked like thick-skinned strawberries. "This is all part of your heritage," he said to me. "These are the plants that the people survived on in hard times. These are the foods that kept people alive during the Civil War."

Fausto fears that Spaniards are slowly losing their culinary language skills, their ability to read their countryside — and as time moves on, there will be fewer people to pass the knowledge on. The population will eventually be unable to interpret their own land and recognize, for example, which berries are safe and which are lethal. Thankfully, there are people like Fausto all across Spain — people dedicated to collecting and passing on the knowledge about Spanish food, in all its forms.

IN TRUE SPANISH FASHION, NOTHING IN THE KITCHEN IS WASTED — NOT EVEN THE HEAT FROM THE BREAD KILN! IN DAYS GONE BY, AFTER BREAD WAS BAKED, A *CAZUELA* (CERAMIC POT) OF POTATOES, SITTING IN A POOL OF SEASONED STOCK, WAS PUSHED INTO THE KILN TO SLOWLY COOK FROM THE RESIDUAL HEAT TRAPPED IN THE BRICKS. MOST *PANADEROS* (BAKERS) NOW USE ELECTRIC OVENS, BUT THE NAME OF THIS DISH IS STILL THE SAME. I ENJOYED THIS DISH WHILE SPENDING TIME WITH TITO ROBLEDO FROM LAS PETRONILAS. HIS FRIEND, THE LOCAL DOCTOR, DROPPED BY WITH A BASKET OF WILD MUSHROOMS, WHICH TITO COOKED WITH THE POTATOES AND SERVED TO THE DOCTOR AND HIS WIFE. THE LOVELY SOFT DISH WAS THICKENED WITH A LITTLE EGG. TITO COMMENTED THAT HE FELT SAFE EATING WILD MUSHROOMS WITH A DOCTOR. "IF WE GET SICK, HE'LL BE ABLE TO CURE US," HE LAUGHED.

PATATAS PAÑADERA CON SETAS

SOFT POTATOES AND ONIONS WITH MUSHROOMS THICKENED WITH EGG

10 MEDIAS RACIONES
6 RACIONES

$2/3$ cup extra virgin olive oil

3 white onions, cut into fine wedges

4 bay leaves

3 green bell peppers, seeded and ribs removed, cut into slices $1/2$ inch thick

6 garlic cloves, thinly sliced

fine sea salt

2 lb roasting potatoes, cut into slices $1/2$ inch thick

2 cups chicken stock

$3 1/2$ oz shiitake mushrooms, cut into slices $1/4$ inch thick

$5 1/4$ oz oyster or other wild mushrooms, cut into slices $1/4$ inch thick

4 eggs, lightly beaten

4 tablespoons finely chopped parsley

Heat $1/3$ cup of the olive oil in a large heavy-bottomed saucepan over high heat. Add the onions, bay leaves, bell peppers, half of the sliced garlic and a good pinch of sea salt and sauté for 4 to 5 minutes, or until the onions begin to soften. Reduce the heat to medium-low, then cover and cook for 25 minutes, or until the peppers are tender, stirring regularly. Remove from the heat and stir the potato slices through.

Preheat the oven to 350°F.

Spread the potato mixture in a large roasting pan, season well and pour the stock over. Cover tightly with foil and bake for 60 to 70 minutes, or until the potatoes are tender.

Meanwhile, heat the remaining olive oil in a frying pan over high heat. Add the mushrooms, the remaining garlic and a pinch of sea salt. Toss to combine well, then reduce the heat to medium and cook for 10 minutes, or until slightly brown and soft. Remove from the heat, place in a bowl and let cool for a few minutes, then stir in the beaten eggs and parsley.

When the potatoes are cooked, remove the roasting pan from the oven and remove the foil. Pour the mushroom and egg mixture over, then stir it through gently, without breaking up the potatoes. Bake, uncovered, for another 6 to 8 minutes, or until the egg is nearly set, but still a little runny. Remove from the oven and serve warm.

HONEY IS HIGHLY REGARDED IN SPAIN. IT IS CONSIDERED TO BE A NATURAL PRODUCT THAT REFLECTS THE FLORA OF THE REGION, WITH SOME REGIONS PRODUCING HONEY THAT IS MORE HIGHLY PRIZED THAN OTHERS. THE HONEY FROM SIERRA DE FRANCIA USED TO BE MADE FROM HONEYCOMB COLLECTED FROM HIVES MADE IN HOLLOW LOGS. HONEY WAS ONE OF THE AREA'S FEW PRODUCTS AND WAS TRADED FOR GOODS AT THE NEARBY CITY OF SALAMANCA. SPANISH HONEY IS MUCH MORE HEADY AND FLORAL THAN AMERICAN HONEY. THESE LITTLE PASTRIES, FILLED WITH GOLDEN QUINCE AND RICOTTA CHEESE FLAVORED WITH CINNAMON AND HONEY, ARE LOVELY AND SWEET AND BEST SERVED WARM.

EMPANADILLAS DE MEMBRILLO
QUINCE PIES WITH RICOTTA AND HONEY

12 PIES

2 quinces
1/4 cup Calvados (apple brandy)
1/3 cup superfine sugar
1 cinnamon stick
finely grated zest of 1 lemon
7/8 cup ricotta cheese
2 tablespoons flavored honey
1/2 teaspoon ground cinnamon
1 egg, lightly beaten
confectioners' sugar, to dust

EMPANADILLA DOUGH

2 cups all-purpose flour,
   plus extra, to dust
1/4 cup superfine sugar
sea salt
1/4 oz fresh yeast
2 tablespoons warm milk
5 tablespoons unsalted butter,
   softened

Preheat the oven to 300°F.

Peel and core the quinces and cut each into eight wedges. Place in a baking dish with the Calvados, sugar, cinnamon stick, half of the lemon zest and 1/4 cup water. Cover with foil and bake for 1 hour. Remove the foil, pour in another 1/4 cup water and turn the quinces. Bake, uncovered, for another 30 minutes, or until the quinces are tender, then remove from the oven and let cool.

Meanwhile, for the empanadilla dough: sift the flour into a bowl, add the sugar and a pinch of salt and combine well. Dissolve the yeast in the warm milk and add to the flour with the butter and 3/4 cup warm water. Stir with a wooden spoon until a sticky dough forms, then mix the dough for another 2 to 3 minutes. Shape the dough into a ball, sprinkle with a little extra flour, cover with a cloth and let stand in a warm place for 1 hour.

Remove the cooled quinces from the poaching liquid and cut into slices 1/4 inch thick. Place in a bowl with the ricotta, honey, ground cinnamon and the remaining lemon zest and gently combine.

Reheat the oven to 350°F.

Cut the empanadilla dough into 12 equal portions. Roll out each ball on a lightly floured surface into a 4 1/2-inch round. Place a tablespoon of the ricotta mixture on one half of each round and brush the other edge with a little beaten egg. Fold over to form a half-moon shape, press to seal well, then crimp the edges using a fork and place on two lightly floured baking sheets. Brush the tops with beaten egg and bake for 15 to 20 minutes, or until golden.

Dust with confectioners' sugar while still hot and serve warm.

THERE ARE STILL ROUGH-AND-READY TYPES IN THE HILLS OF SIERRA DE FRANCIA. ONE OF THEM IS JOAQUÍN. HE LIVES JUST OUTSIDE MIRANDA DEL CASTAÑAR ON HIS PLOT OF LAND. HE HAS NEVER MARRIED AND COMES TO TOWN ONCE A WEEK FOR SUPPLIES, AND TO DELIVER SOME OF HIS CHERRIES WHEN THEY ARE IN SEASON. HE USED TO WALK INTO TOWN, BUT AFTER HE SHOT HIMSELF IN THE FOOT, HE FOUND IT EASIER TO RIDE ON HIS DONKEY THAT, FOR THE RECORD, IS BLIND IN ONE EYE, ACCOMPANIED BY AN ENTOURAGE OF THREE LOPING HUNTING DOGS AND TWO PRANCING GOATS. THE CHERRIES GROW WILD IN THE RIVER VALLEYS. MEDIUM-SIZED AND NOT OVERBLOWN WITH WATER, THEY'RE DARK, SLIGHTLY TART AND WONDERFULLY FLAVORED. I'VE NAMED THIS DESSERT IN HIS HONOR, USING BEST-QUALITY CHERRIES, GOAT'S CURD ICE CREAM (JOAQUÍN CAN'T USE AN ICE-CREAM MAKER AS HE DOESN'T HAVE ELECTRICITY) AND ANISE LIQUEUR (WHICH I'M SURE, JUDGING BY THE WAY HE RIDES HIS DONKEY, HE IS FAMILIAR WITH). USING FRESH GOAT'S CURD IN THIS DESSERT RETAINS ITS RUSTIC TEXTURE.

HELADO DE QUESO DE CABRA FRESCO CON CEREZAS 'JOAQUÍN'

RED AND WHITE CHERRIES WITH FRESH GOAT'S CURD ICE CREAM

SERVES 6

5 egg yolks
3/4 cup superfine sugar
2 3/4 cups heavy cream
9 oz goat's curd
l lb 9 oz red and white cherries
1/2 cup anise liqueur (see glossary)
2 tablespoons confectioners' sugar, sifted

In a large bowl, mix the egg yolks and superfine sugar until just combined.

Pour the cream into a saucepan and bring to a boil over medium heat. As soon as the cream reaches boiling, remove from the heat and stir 2 tablespoons of the hot cream into the egg mixture and mix well. Whisking continuously, gradually add the remaining hot cream until well combined.

Pour the mixture into a clean saucepan and stir over low heat for 5 minutes, or until the mixture thickens enough to coat the back of a wooden spoon. Remove from the heat, whisk in the goat's curd and let cool to body temperature. Place in an ice-cream maker and follow the manufacturer's instructions. (Alternatively, transfer to a shallow metal pan and freeze, whisking every couple of hours, until the ice cream is frozen and creamy in texture. Freeze for 5 hours or overnight.) Soften in the refrigerator for 30 minutes before serving.

Wash the cherries and pat dry. Place in a bowl, then add the anise and confectioners' sugar and toss well.

To serve, place the cherries in chilled serving bowls with a little of the liqueur. Add a scoop of the ice cream and serve immediately.

JEREZ, SAL Y PESCADO

SHERRY, SALT & FISH

★ ★ ★

PACO THE BARMAN POURED LITTLE GLASSES OF CHILLED MANZANILLA SHERRY. IN A WELL-WORN ROUTINE, HE SET DOWN A PLATE OF ANCHOVY-STUFFED OLIVES, WIPED DOWN THE COUNTER AND MADE A WRY COMMENT ABOUT THE HOT WEATHER. I TOOK A SIP OF MANZANILLA. IT WAS COOL, DRY, CRISP AND SLIGHTLY AROMATIC. THE CLATTERING OF PANS CAME FROM THE KITCHEN AND IN A FEW MOMENTS, A PLATE OF SHRIMP AND A GRILLED SNAPPER DRESSED WITH RED BELL PEPPER WAS PLACED NEXT TO THE SHERRY. THE GLASS WAS NOW DRIPPING WITH CONDENSATION IN THE WARM SEA AIR.

I was in Sanlúcar de Barrameda, a sherry town on the banks of the Guadalquivir River estuary. I walked outside. The sun was playing on the elaborate mosaics of the sherry warehouses lining the waterfront. Looming on the horizon beyond the little fishing boats bobbing on the water were great white pyramids of salt, harvested from the salt pans to the north.

From this one location come the three elements that dominate this part of Spain's cooking: sherry, salt and fish.

Although I enjoy, quite regularly, all of the half-dozen or so fortified Spanish wines that are commonly known as sherry, it is the two light, dry sherries — fino and manzanilla — that really fascinate me.

My dad always says that "sherry is not a drink. It's a way of life." True. Sherry is all about the fun, the talk, the nonsense and all the food that goes with it. It's a brisk little fortifying punctuation mark to life that the Spanish seem to enjoy any time of day without the slightest notion of guilt. Although sherry is consumed all over Spain, to understand the drink you have to eat the food that has co-evolved with it in its homeland, a tiny patch of the nation where sherry and seafood have created an undeniable local cuisine.

For a wine to be called *sherry* it must have been produced in a small triangle of Spain on the southern Atlantic coast marked by three sherry-making towns: El Puerto de Santa María on the ocean, Sanlúcar de Barrameda on the Guadalquivir River estuary and, up in the hills 12 miles inland, the town of Jerez de la Frontera. In between these towns is rolling, chalky country in which the Palomino grapes grow. The grapes are generally crushed in the countryside and taken into the towns, where the sherry is made in great cathedral-like bodegas filled with blackened oak barrels.

I could go on about how the wine is made with a layer of yeast floating on top, how the old sherry is mixed with the new sherry and how the oak affects the flavor. I am, however, a chef, and what inspires me most about sherry is its relationship with food — a phenomenon that cannot be overstated.

Drink fino or manzanilla on its own and it seems quite out of balance. It's too big, too dry, too yeasty — even salty. But when you sit down with a plate of deep-fried baby sole or some big fat grilled langoustines, everything comes together with a subtle satisfaction similar to getting that last square in a Rubik's cube to fall into place. The saltiness of the sherry complements the saltiness of the fish. The yeastiness works with the roundness of the fresh flesh and the crispness leaves the palate cleansed, ready for another mouthful.

These recipes have come from those Andalusian kitchens that excel at this type of cooking — simple summery dishes based heavily on seafood and fresh vegetables, with a few culinary twists that make the most of the ingredients but still leave room for the sherry to work its magic.

THIS IS A STUNNINGLY SIMPLE BUT ELEGANT TOMATO SALAD SERVED
IN BARS IN ANDALUSIA. IT REQUIRES ONLY THE BEST TOMATOES
AND THE FINEST DRIED OREGANO YOU CAN FIND — HOME-GROWN
IS GOOD, BUT THE DRIED OREGANO AVAILABLE IN MEDITERRANEAN
DELIS ALSO HAS GREAT FLAVOR. THE OREGANO SHOULD BE GROUND
INTO A DUST SO THAT IT DOESN'T CHANGE THE TEXTURE OF THE
TOMATOES, JUST THE FLAVOR. TO DO THIS, I RECOMMEND USING A
SPICE GRINDER OR SMALL DOMESTIC COFFEE GRINDER. IN THE BARS
OF ANDALUSIA, THIS RECIPE IS MADE TO ORDER AND ITS SHARPNESS
MAKES A GREAT FOIL TO THE OIL IN THE DEEP-FRIED DISHES. I LET IT
REST FOR A WHILE, TO ALLOW THE FLAVORS TO MARRY.

ENSALADA DE TOMATE

TOMATO SALAD

6 MEDIAS RACIONES

8 full-flavored tomatoes, such as
  beefsteak or black Russian

1/2 teaspoon dried oregano
  (see above)

2 garlic cloves

I teaspoon coarse sea salt, plus extra,
  to sprinkle

I tablespoon extra virgin olive oil

1/2 red onion, very thinly sliced

freshly ground black pepper

2 teaspoons best-quality white
  wine vinegar

If you have thick-skinned tomatoes, such as those generally sold in
supermarkets, peel them by scoring the base with a sharp knife and
placing them in a saucepan of boiling water for 30 seconds. Remove with
a slotted spoon, refresh in iced water, and when cool enough to handle,
peel away the skins.

Cut the tomatoes into slices 1/4 inch thick. Arrange them on a large
serving plate and sprinkle with the oregano.

Place the garlic on a cutting board and crush the cloves by pressing
down with the flat side of a large knife. Sprinkle the sea salt over the garlic,
then pound together, using the flat side of the knife again, until a smooth
paste forms. Transfer to a small bowl and stir in the olive oil.

Cover the tomato slices with the onion slices, then sprinkle with some
more sea salt and black pepper. Drizzle with the vinegar, then the olive oil
and garlic mixture. Cover and let stand at room temperature for I hour to
allow the flavors to mingle.

LIGHT BUT RICH, FRESH BUT DECADENT, THIS IS A DISH THAT WELL DESCRIBES THE CONTRASTING NATURE OF ANDALUSIAN FOOD. ENTIRE FISH ROE SACS ARE DELICATELY POACHED IN A FRAGRANT BOUILLON, THEN COOLED AND SLICED INTO NATURALLY PATTERNED ROUNDS. THESE ARE FOLDED THROUGH A SALAD OF FRESH SUMMER VEGETABLES DRESSED WITH AGED SWEET PEDRO XIMÉNEZ SHERRY VINEGAR. THE SAUCE IS THEN SOAKED UP BY DISCS OF YOUNG POTATOES. A SALAD SERVED IN BARS ACROSS ANDALUSIA, *ENSALADA DE HUEVAS* IS A CASUAL, UNSOPHISTICATED SNACK. IT GOES JUST AS WELL WITH AN ICE-COLD CRUZCAMPO, THE LOCAL BEER, OR A CHILLED GLASS OF FINO SHERRY. I USE TREVALLY ROE, BUT THIS IS NOT ALWAYS AVAILABLE. DESCRIBE TO YOUR FISHMONGER THE DISH YOU ARE MAKING AND HE WILL HELP YOU WITH THE RIGHT SORT OF ROE.

ENSALADA DE HUEVAS
SUMMER SALAD WITH POACHED FISH ROE

10 MEDIAS RACIONES
6 RACIONES

Pour 8 3/4 cups water into a large saucepan. Add the bay leaves, sherry and the yellow onion half and bring to a boil over high heat, then reduce the heat to medium. When the water is simmering, gently lower in the fish roe sacs. Simmer for 20 minutes, then remove the pan from the heat and allow the roe to cool in the poaching liquid.

Meanwhile, place the potatoes in a large saucepan, cover with cold water and add a pinch of salt. Bring to a boil and cook for 45 minutes, or until tender. Remove from the heat, then drain and let cool. When the potatoes are cool enough to handle, carefully peel them and slice into 1/2-inch rounds and place in a large serving bowl. Add the tomatoes, bell pepper and red onion, then season to taste with sea salt and white pepper. Drizzle with the olive oil and vinegar and toss gently to combine.

Remove the cooled fish roe sacs from the poaching liquid and slice into 1/2-inch rounds. Add to the salad with the fresh oregano. Mix very gently and serve at room temperature.

3 bay leaves
1/3 cup dry sherry
1/2 yellow onion
1 1/4 lb fresh fish roe sacs, from a fish such as trevally
1 1/4 lb fingerling or other boiling potatoes, washed but not peeled
coarse sea salt
6 ripe tomatoes, peeled, seeded (see glossary) and cut into 1/2-inch chunks
1 green bell pepper, seeded and ribs removed, finely chopped
1/2 red onion, very finely chopped
ground white pepper
2/3 cup extra virgin olive oil
2/3 cup aged Pedro Ximénez sherry vinegar
1 tablespoon fresh oregano

THESE DELICATE, CRISP FRITTERS ARE SERVED FRESH FROM THE DEEP-FRYER IN BARS ACROSS SOUTHERN SPAIN, BUT NOWHERE ARE THEY AS GOOD AS IN THE SEASIDE RESTAURANTS OF EL PUERTO DE SANTA MARÍA. HERE, AS ELSEWHERE, THEY ARE MADE WITH FRESH, WHOLE TINY SHRIMP NO BIGGER THAN YOUR LITTLE FINGERNAIL. IT'S THE COMBINATION OF SALTY SEA AIR, THE SMELL OF FRYING FRESH FISH AND GLASSES OF CHILLED SHERRY THAT ELEVATES THIS SIMPLE LITTLE FRITTER TO AN EXOTIC ART FORM. MADE WITH CHICKPEA FLOUR (AVAILABLE FROM HEALTH FOOD STORES AND INDIAN SUPERMARKETS), THE BATTER IS SLIGHTLY RUNNY, ALLOWING IT TO SPREAD IN THE HOT OIL TO FORM A DELICATE PASTRY. USE BABY SHRIMP IF YOU HAVE ACCESS TO THEM, BUT AS THEY ARE NOT COMMON, I HAVE ADAPTED THE TRADITIONAL RECIPE TO USE READILY AVAILABLE FRESH RAW SHRIMP. THESE FRITTERS ARE SLIGHTLY TRICKY TO GET THE HANG OF — IT MAY TAKE A FEW TRIES TO PERFECT THE FRYING TECHNIQUE. THIS RECIPE WAS GIVEN TO ME BY LOCAL CHEF FERNANDO CÓRDOBA.

TORTILLITAS DE CAMARONES

FRITTERS OF BABY SHRIMP

8 TAPAS

12 raw shrimp, peeled and deveined, heads reserved

2 bay leaves

coarse sea salt

1/3 cup chickpea flour

1/3 cup all-purpose flour

1 tablespoon finely chopped cilantro

1 tablespoon finely chopped parsley

2 tablespoons finely snipped chives

1 3/4 cups olive oil, for deep-frying

Place the shrimp heads in a saucepan with the bay leaves, a pinch of salt and 1 1/3 cups cold water. Bring to a boil over high heat, then reduce the heat to low and simmer for 5 minutes. Remove from the heat, strain the stock and discard the solids. Pour the stock into a clean saucepan and bring to a boil.

Meanwhile, finely chop the shrimp. When the stock comes to a boil, stir in the chopped shrimp and cook for 30 seconds, then remove from the heat and allow to cool a little.

Sift the chickpea and all-purpose flours into a bowl. Whisking continuously, gradually add the hot stock mixture to the flour mixture until a thin batter forms. Stir in the chopped herbs and let the batter to stand at room temperature for 15 minutes.

Heat the oil in a large heavy-bottomed frying pan or wok to 375°F, or until a cube of bread dropped into the oil browns in 10 seconds.

Working in batches, gently ladle 1/4 cup of the batter into the hot oil, ensuring you get an equal portion of the shrimp meat. The batter will spread quickly, so use the bowl of the ladle to even out the fritters and bathe them in the hot oil as they cook. Fry for 1 minute or until golden, then turn and cook for another minute on the other side. Drain on a paper towel, sprinkle with sea salt and serve immediately.

A FINE, PALE GOLDEN CRUST COVERS THE SALTY, SWEET FLESH OF THESE LITTLE FRIED FISH. THE SECRET IS IN THE SEASONING: A LIBERAL SPRINKLING OF THE BEST SALT, INSIDE AND OUT, THEN A GOOD COATING OF SEMOLINA AND FLOUR. MORE BAPTIZED IN VERY HOT OIL THAN DEEP-FRIED, THE FISH ARE PERFECTLY COOKED AND SO DELICIOUS. TO EAT THE FISH, THE ADVENTUROUS HOLD THE HEAD IN ONE HAND AND THE TAIL IN THE OTHER, SINK THEIR TEETH TO THE SPINE AND REMOVE THE DELICATE FLESH WITH THEIR LIPS. THE MORE TIMID USE A KNIFE AND FORK, BUT THE RESULTING SATISFACTION IS THE SAME. DO NOT DRY THE FISH PRIOR TO PREPARATION AS THEIR NATURAL JUICES BIND WITH THE FLOUR TO MAKE THE LIGHTEST OF COATINGS. THE MOST IMPORTANT PART IS TO CAREFULLY REMOVE ALL THE FINS DURING PREPARATION AS THESE CAN BE LESS THAN PLEASANT TO EAT. WE'VE SUGGESTED A FEW SPECIES IN THE RECIPE BELOW, BUT FISHMONGERS WITH MEDITERRANEAN BACKGROUNDS ARE GENERALLY FAMILIAR WITH THIS SIMPLE STYLE OF COOKING SO THEY'LL POINT YOU IN THE RIGHT DIRECTION FOR THE TYPE OF FISH TO DEEP-FRY.

PESCAITO FRITO

MIXED WHOLE FRIED FISH

6 RACIONES

6 snapper, flounder or sole, cleaned and scaled

6 silver whiting, cleaned and scaled

6 jack mackerel, cleaned and scaled

olive oil, for deep-frying

2 cups fine semolina

2 cups all-purpose flour

coarse sea salt

Remember not to dry the fish — the natural juices are essential for a crisp finish. Using a pair of kitchen scissors, trim all the fins from each fish.

Fill a deep fryer or large heavy-bottomed saucepan one-third full of oil and heat to 375ºF, or until a cube of bread dropped into the oil browns in 10 seconds.

Meanwhile, combine the semolina and flour on a large flat dish. Thoroughly season each fish inside and out with sea salt, then dust each with the flour mixture. Cook the fish in small batches, allowing 1½ to 2 minutes for the smaller fish and about 3 minutes for the larger fish.

Remove with a slotted spoon, drain on a paper towel, then season with sea salt and serve immediately.

THE FISH MARKET

In Spain, fishmongers have a cult-like status in the hearts of housewives. In smaller towns, some exceptional fishmongers may own a small boat and come to the town market with a basket of their own catch. I once witnessed one fishmonger trailed by a small swarm of women from his boat to his market stall. There they forced their way to be the first to buy his small catch of sea bream and still-writhing squid. The fish market in Jerez may not be Spain's biggest, but it is one of the best. For a while it was housed in a modern building with a stretched-fabric roof, giving the antics of the fishmongers working under it a bizarre circus-like feel.

The Jerez fishmongers share not just a professional obsession with freshness and quality but also a culture of competitive decoration. I arrived early one day to watch one gnarled fishmonger finish his centerpiece just as the first customers came through the doors. He was adjusting the giant sword of a marlin that was thrusting out of the fish's head. Around it he had garlanded tuna fillets. At the next stall, hake were displayed with their fire-red gills wide open to show their freshness, while the filleted skeletons were arranged as if they were consuming their own tails.

What I find truly admirable about the relationship between the fishmonger and the customer is that he will never ask, "What do you want?" He starts off the business by saying "Hello, what are you cooking today?" The customer will tell him and he will offer the best cut of the most suitable fish for that dish.

THE LAST TIME I ATE *SALPICÓN* WAS IN A BAR IN CÁDIZ, A CITY ON THE PERIPHERY OF THE SHERRY TRIANGLE. I HAD BEEN WATCHING A BRASS BAND PRACTICING FOR THE NEXT DAY'S BULLFIGHT IN THE COURTYARD OF A BLOCK OF FLATS. WHEN THE LAST TRUMPET FINISHED ECHOING OFF THE CONCRETE WALLS, THE BAND'S MUSIC WAS REPLACED BY THE SHRILL CALL OF A FLOCK OF GULLS CHASING A SCHOOL OF FISH IN THE BAY. THE SUN HOVERED OVER THE BAY OF CÁDIZ, ITS RAYS FLARING IN THE CLOUDS IN THE UPPER ATMOSPHERE, FLOODING THE WHOLE WESTERN SKY WITH RICH YELLOW LIGHT. THE BAND MEMBERS CAME INTO THE BAR SHORTLY AFTER ME. SOME DRANK BEER. MOST HAD SHERRY. THEY ALL ORDERED *SALPICÓN* — A COLD SALAD OF POACHED SEAFOOD AND SUMMER VEGETABLES. ALTHOUGH IT SOUNDS LIGHT, *SALPICÓN* HAS A DEPTH OF FLAVOR THAT MARRIES PERFECTLY WITH CHILLED MANZANILLA SHERRY.

SALPICÓN DE MARISCO
CHILLED SEAFOOD SALAD

6 MEDIAS RACIONES
4 RACIONES

4 bay leaves
2 cups dry sherry
4 garlic cloves
9-oz piece of skinless halibut, cut into
　1-inch chunks
7 oz cleaned squid hoods, cut into
　1-inch chunks
3¹/₂ oz scallops, trimmed
9 oz raw shrimp, peeled and deveined,
　leaving the tails intact
1 lb mussels, scrubbed and beards
　removed
4 ripe tomatoes, peeled, seeded
　(see glossary) and chopped
1 green bell pepper, seeded and ribs
　removed, cut into ¹/₄-inch dice
1 large cucumber, roughly peeled, halved
　lengthways, then seeded and cut into
　¹/₂-inch chunks
1 small red onion, finely chopped
3 tablespoons roughly chopped parsley
¹/₃ cup extra virgin olive oil
¹/₃ cup chardonnay vinegar
1 teaspoon ground white pepper
1 teaspoon coarse sea salt
crusty bread, to serve

Pour 4¹/₃ cups water into four separate saucepans. Add a bay leaf, ¹/₃ cup of the sherry and a garlic clove to each saucepan and bring to a boil.

Add the fish to one saucepan and cook for 6 minutes, then remove with a slotted spoon and place on a baking sheet. In the other three saucepans, cook the remaining seafood separately, cooking the squid for 2 to 3 minutes, and the scallops and shrimp for 1¹/₂ minutes each. Transfer all the cooked seafood to the baking sheet and allow to cool.

Place the mussels and the remaining sherry in a large frying pan and cook over high heat until the sherry comes to the boil. Cover the pan and cook, shaking the pan continuously, for 3 to 4 minutes, or until the mussels open. Pour the mussels into a colander set over a bowl, reserving ¹/₃ cup of the cooking liquid and discarding any mussels that haven't opened. When the mussels are cool enough to handle, remove them from their shells and place on the sheet with the other seafood.

Combine the tomatoes, bell pepper, cucumber, onion and parsley in a large bowl. Add the reserved mussel liquid, the olive oil, vinegar, white pepper and sea salt and mix well. Add the seafood and gently toss again. Refrigerate until chilled, then serve with crusty bread.

IN THE JEREZ FISH MARKET, I WAS ENTRANCED BY A BOX OF GREEN AND SAPPHIRE MACKEREL. IN THE EARLY MORNING SUN, THEIR SHINY SKINS WERE SHIMMERING WITH THE COLORS OF THE SEA. AS I MOVED AROUND THEM, THEIR PATTERNS CHANGED AND I COULD IMAGINE THEM SWIMMING IN A SCHOOL. MACKEREL HAVE A WONDERFULLY MOIST, DENSE FLESH, WHICH IS FULL FLAVORED AND QUITE MEATY. HERE WE'RE SERVING IT WITH *PIPIRRANA*, A CLASSIC LOCAL SALAD, WHERE THE SHARPNESS OF THE DRESSING BALANCES THE STURDINESS OF THE FISH.

CABALLA A LA PARRILLA CON PIPIRRAÑA

GRILLED MACKEREL SALAD

12 MEDIAS RACIONES
6 RACIONES

6 mackerel, about 5½ oz each, filleted
2 tablespoons parsley, finely chopped
1 tablespoon smoked paprika
6 garlic cloves, very finely chopped
⅞ cup extra virgin olive oil
2 green bell peppers
coarse sea salt
6 eggs
2 small cucumbers
6 ripe tomatoes, peeled, seeded (see glossary) and cut into thin wedges
½ red onion, finely sliced
1 cup green olives, pitted
⅓ cup good sherry vinegar
freshly ground black pepper
1 lemon, halved

Using a very sharp knife, score the skin of each mackerel fillet with four slashes. Combine the parsley, paprika, half of the chopped garlic and half of the olive oil in a large bowl. Add the fish fillets, massage the marinade into the fish, then cover with plastic wrap and refrigerate for 2 hours.

Preheat the oven to 400°F.

Place the bell peppers in a small roasting pan, sprinkle with sea salt and bake for 45 minutes, or until the skins are dark and the flesh is soft. Remove from the oven and reserve 2 tablespoons of the cooking juices. Peel the peppers and discard the stem and seeds. Cut the flesh into strips 1 inch thick.

Meanwhile, place the eggs in a saucepan, cover with plenty of cold water and bring to a boil over high heat. Cook for 5 minutes, then drain and refresh in cold water. Let cool, then peel.

Peel the cucumbers lengthways, leaving a hint of skin. Cut off the ends, then cut the cucumbers in half lengthways. Using a teaspoon, remove and discard the seeds. Cut the flesh into small pieces.

Place the tomato wedges, cucumbers, onion, olives and the remaining garlic in a bowl. Add the bell peppers and the reserved cooking juices. Pour the vinegar and remaining olive oil over, season to taste and combine well. Divide the salad among serving plates, then cut the eggs in half and arrange on the plates.

Heat a large frying pan or grill pan over high heat. Cook the fish fillets, skin side down, for 3 minutes, seasoning with sea salt, black pepper and a squeeze of lemon juice as they cook. Turn and cook for another 3 minutes and season again. Arrange the fish fillets over the salads and serve immediately.

CÁDIZ IS A VIBRANT TOWN OF STRAIGHT NARROW STREETS ON A HEADLAND PERCHED AT THE END OF A FINGER-LIKE PENINSULA. THE PEOPLE LIVING HERE — THE *GADITANOS*, CÁDIZ LOCALS — HAVE DEVELOPED THEIR OWN ACCENT AND SLANG AND ARE KNOWN ACROSS SPAIN FOR THEIR WICKED SENSE OF HUMOR. ONE OF MY FAVORITE DISHES FROM HERE IS SQUID AND CHICKPEAS. IT IS A CLASSIC PRESSURE-COOKER RECIPE, BUT IF YOU DON'T HAVE ONE, USE A LARGE HEAVY-BOTTOMED CASSEROLE DISH AND SIMMER IT FOR TWICE AS LONG, ADDING A LITTLE EXTRA WATER DURING COOKING TO KEEP THE INGREDIENTS COVERED.

CHOCOS CON GARBANZOS
BRAISED SQUID WITH CHICKPEAS

6 MEDIAS RACIONES

1½ lb squid, cleaned and cut into 1-inch pieces

2¾ cups dried chickpeas, soaked overnight

1 garlic bulb

1 teaspoon smoked paprika

⅞ cup fino sherry

3 tablespoons extra virgin olive oil

1 large yellow onion, quartered

6 ripe tomatoes, peeled, seeded (see glossary) and roughly chopped

3 bay leaves

7 oz fresh chorizo

1 teaspoon saffron threads

1 tablespoon mint, finely chopped

1 tablespoon parsley, roughly chopped

2 teaspoons whole black peppercorns

crusty bread, to serve

Place the squid in a 12-inch pressure cooker. Add the drained chickpeas, garlic, paprika, sherry, olive oil, onion, tomatoes and bay leaves. Cover with 3 cups cold water, seal and bring to a boil over high heat. Reduce the heat to medium-low and simmer for 45 minutes, then remove from the heat and let cool for at least 5 minutes before removing the lid, or as per the manufacturer's instructions. Remove and reserve the garlic bulb, then add the chorizo and simmer, uncovered, for another 15 minutes, or until the chickpeas are tender.

Meanwhile, toast the saffron threads in a small dry frying pan over medium heat just until the threads deepen in color, then place in a mortar and pestle. Add the mint, parsley and peppercorns and pound until a coarse paste forms. Squeeze the reserved garlic cloves from their skins into the mortar. Add 1 tablespoon of the chickpea cooking liquid and pound until a smooth paste forms.

Stir the mixture into the chickpeas and simmer for another 5 minutes. Serve hot, with plenty of crusty bread to soak up the juices.

THIS IS DRINKING FOOD. SIMPLE DRINKING FOOD. GET SOME DARK, FIRM-FLESHED FISH, SOAK IT OVERNIGHT IN A MARINADE, ROLL IT IN SOME FLOUR, THEN DEEP-FRY IT. IN SPAIN, THEY USE *CAZÓN*, OR SPOTTED DOGFISH. WHAT IS INTERESTING IS THE USE OF WATER IN THE MARINADE — AND THE LACK OF SALT. SALT DRAWS LIQUID OUT OF THE FISH; WATER PLUMPS IT UP. SO WHAT WE'RE DOING IS MAKING SUPER-SUCCULENT, SLIGHTLY SHARP, BITE-SIZE MORSELS OF FISH THAT ARE SO MOIST THEY FORM THEIR OWN BATTER WHEN ROLLED IN THE FLOUR. TRY THESE ON A HOT NIGHT WITH PLENTY OF BEER OR CHILLED FINO SHERRY.

CAZÓN FRITO EN ADOBO
DEEP-FRIED MARINATED SHARK

8 TAPAS

2¼ lb shark (or other dark, firm-fleshed fish) fillets, bones removed, cut into 1-inch chunks

2 tablespoons dried oregano

a handful of parsley, chopped

2 tablespoons sweet paprika

1½ tablespoons ground cumin

1 yellow onion, finely sliced

4 garlic cloves, roughly chopped

⅔ cup extra virgin olive oil

1 cup sherry vinegar

olive oil, for deep-frying

seasoned all-purpose flour, to coat

coarse sea salt, to sprinkle

Place the shark fillets in a large bowl with the herbs, spices, onion, garlic, olive oil, vinegar and ⅔ cup cold water. Mix together well, then cover and refrigerate overnight.

Fill a deep fryer or large heavy-bottomed saucepan one-third full of oil and heat to 350 to 375°F, or until a cube of bread dropped into the oil browns in 10 to 15 seconds.

Working in small batches, remove the shark from the marinade, gently shake off the excess liquid and dust well in the seasoned flour. Deep-fry for 1½ to 2 minutes, or until well browned and cooked through. Drain on a paper towel, sprinkle with sea salt and serve immediately.

TRADITIONAL *ENCEBOLLADO* IS A RICH, BRAISED ONION SAUCE THAT FORMS A GOLDEN-BROWN COLOR DURING ITS LONG, SLOW COOKING. IT IS OFTEN USED TO COOK SEAFOOD SUCH AS SAND CLAMS, AND CAN BE SLIGHTLY FIERY WHEN THE CHEF GIVES IT A GOOD HIT OF WHITE PEPPER. THE DOWNSIDE IS THAT WHEN TUNA IS COOKED IN *ENCEBOLLADO* THE FLESH CAN DRY OUT. ALTHOUGH I RESPECT THE CHEFS WHO COOK THIS DISH, IT DOES COME FROM ANOTHER ERA WHEN THE SPANISH ROUTINELY COOKED THE LIVING DAYLIGHTS OUT OF THEIR FISH. MANY OF THE YOUNGER SPANISH CHEFS NOW HAVE A LIGHTER TOUCH AND PREFER FISH "JUST COOKED." I USE ONIONS AND INSTEAD OF CARAMELIZING AND REDUCING THEM, I COOK THEM UNTIL QUITE SOFT BUT NOT DEFEATED. THE TUNA IS LIGHTLY SEASONED WITH OREGANO AND GIVEN A LITTLE "EL SCORCHO" IN A HOT FRYING PAN AND THEN DRESSED WITH THE COLORFUL, FLAVORFUL SHERRY AND SAFFRON SAUCE.

ATÚN ENCEBOLLADO
TUNA IN A RICH ONION AND MANZANILLA SAUCE

6 MEDIAS RACIONES

$7/8$ cup extra virgin olive oil

7 white onions, finely sliced

4 bay leaves

coarse sea salt

4 garlic cloves, finely sliced

$2/3$ cup manzanilla sherry

2 teaspoons dried oregano

I teaspoon whole black peppercorns

I teaspoon saffron threads

$2^1/4$ lb yellowfin tuna, cut into six equal portions

sea salt flakes

freshly ground black pepper

2 tablespoons olive oil

Heat $1/2$ cup of the extra virgin olive oil in a heavy-bottomed saucepan over medium-low heat. Add the onions, bay leaves and a pinch of salt and cook, stirring occasionally, for 8 to 10 minutes, or until the onions are soft but not colored. Add the garlic, then cover and cook for 10 minutes. Stir in the sherry, half of the oregano and all of the peppercorns. Reduce the heat to low and cook, uncovered, for 20 to 25 minutes, or until the onions are very soft.

Toast the saffron threads in a small dry frying pan over medium heat just until the threads begin to darken. Place in a mortar and pestle, add 2 tablespoons of the onion cooking liquid and pound until dissolved. Stir the saffron mixture into the onions and cook for another 3 minutes.

When the onion sauce is cooked, place the tuna in a bowl with the remaining oregano, sea salt flakes to taste, a pinch of black pepper and the remaining extra virgin olive oil. Mix well.

Heat the olive oil in a large frying pan over high heat and cook the tuna for 2 minutes on each side, seasoning both sides with sea salt as you go. Place in a large warm serving dish, pour the onion sauce over and serve hot.

LA BODEGA

THE CELLAR

In the city of Jerez de la Frontera, entire city blocks are taken up by white-walled bodegas. Inside those walls are practiced the archaic and arcane arts of sherry making. These great cathedral-like buildings were built not just to store wine, but were designed to "breathe": a simple system of shutters and doors allows air to circulate, keeping the wine at a constant temperature. These great dark halls are filled with the sweet, pleasant aroma of yeast. Yeasts form a layer on top of the sherry called *flor*, imparting to the wine its particular nuttiness.

Great stacks of blackened barrels — the *solera* — tower toward the ceiling. There's constant movement of men in boiler suits siphoning younger sherry from the top barrels into lower barrels. It's this blend of old and new wine that can give sherries their subtle layering of flavors. A few bodegas still have their own *tonelero*, the cooper who fashions the barrels, working in a vulcan's pit of coal fire, charred oak and red-hot bands of steel that hold the barrels in place.

From these Andalusian bodegas — part factory, part cloistered institutions — comes sherry. Sherry refers to a "rainbow" of wines, from light and dry to dark and sweet. Fino is a dry, pale, straw-colored wine with a crisp finish. Manzanilla is very similar to fino, but can only be made in Sanlúcar de Barrameda. Some say the coastal bodegas there are so influenced by their proximity to the sea that the wine has a faint salty tang.

Both fino and manzanilla are perfect with the seafood recipes in this chapter. My bar manager Andy describes amontillado and oloroso as the midfield players in the sherry world — darker, not quite as dry. Amontillado is a honey amber-colored wine that really works with cured meats, terrines, nuts, mushrooms and game. Oloroso is a little bit richer and more bronze and chocolate brown. It's slightly thicker and lends itself to cheese, meats and earthy vegetables.

Then there's Pedro Ximénez, also known as liquid dessert. Pedro Ximénez sherries are made with partially dried fruit and are very, very sweet. With its deep color and wonderful aromatic perfume, it is a great wine to use when cooking game and for making desserts. It is so powerful, however, that it can be too sweet to drink with dessert but instead is used as a sweet dressing.

Spaniards make fino, amontillado, oloroso and Pedro Ximénez all over Andalusia, but only the wines made in this little triangle on the Atlantic coast can be called *sherry*.

THESE HONEY-DRIZZLED PASTRY FLOWERS ARE ENJOYED WITH MORNING COFFEE, BUT ALSO MAKE A VERY IMPRESSIVE DESSERT WHEN SERVED SOUSED WITH A LITTLE PEDRO XIMÉNEZ SHERRY AND A SCOOP OF VANILLA ICE CREAM. THE DOUBLE FLOWER-LIKE MOLDS USED HERE CAN BE FOUND IN SOME SPECIALTY SHOPS, BUT DEEP 2-INCH COOKIE CUTTERS WILL DO THE JOB. THE MOLDS ARE TEMPERED IN SCORCHINGLY HOT OIL, THEN GENTLY SWIRLED IN THE FRAGRANT BATTER, ALLOWED TO DRIP FOR A FEW SECONDS, THEN DROPPED BACK INTO THE BUBBLING OIL. IT TAKES TIME TO MASTER THE ART SO IT MAY REQUIRE A FEW ATTEMPTS.

FLORES CON MIEL
DEEP-FRIED PASTRIES WITH HONEY

MAKES 8 FLOWER PASTRIES (30 IF USING A COOKIE CUTTER)

6 eggs

I cup milk

I¾ cups all-purpose flour

2 tablespoons anise liqueur (see glossary)

2 tablespoons olive oil

I teaspoon fennel seeds, toasted

extra virgin olive oil, for deep-frying

4 tablespoons full-flavored honey

confectioners' sugar, to dust

Preheat the oven to 300°F.

Using a balloon whisk or food processor, whisk the eggs for 5 to 10 minutes, or until they reach a ribbon-like consistency. Gently whisk in the milk. Sift in the flour, combine well, then stir in the anise, olive oil and fennel seeds.

Fill a deep fryer or large heavy-bottomed saucepan one-third full of olive oil and heat to 375°F, or until a cube of bread dropped into the oil browns in 10 seconds.

Drop the flower mold or cookie cutter into the oil for I minute.

Meanwhile, stir the batter once with a spoon to lift up the fennel seeds. Using tongs to hold the very top of the mold, remove the mold from the oil and dip immediately into the batter, turning to coat in the batter, and leaving just the very top of the mold bare. Allow the excess batter to drain off, then plunge the mold back into the hot oil. Deep-fry for I to I½ minutes, or until the pastry is golden and crisp. Drain on a paper towel, then, with a cloth over your hand for protection, gently slide the pastry flower off the mold. You may need to work it free with a knife.

Place on a baking sheet lined with a paper towel and keep warm in the oven while cooking the remaining batter. Place the warm pastries in a serving dish, drizzle with the honey, dust with confectioners' sugar and serve immediately.

THESE LITTLE LOGS OF FRUIT AND NUTS ARE THE SUCCESSORS TO THE SWEETMEATS THAT THE MOORS ENJOYED CENTURIES AGO. ALMONDS, FRUIT AND HONEY ARE ROLLED INTO THIN FINGERS, THEN BAKED. ENJOY THEM WITH COFFEE IN THE MORNING OR WITH A GLASS OF PEDRO XIMÉNEZ SHERRY IN THE EVENING, OR VICE VERSA — I AM NOT JUDGMENTAL. *ALFAJORES* CAN BE FOUND IN BAKERIES AROUND ANDALUSIA, BUT MY FAVORITE BAKERY IN CÁDIZ SELLS THEM IN A BOX, EACH ONE INDIVIDUALLY WRAPPED IN DECORATED WAX PAPER. WHEN YOU UNROLL THEM, THERE IS A SENSE OF ANTICIPATION — AND THEN YOU BITE INTO THE LIGHTLY SPICED PASTRY, SWEET WITH FRUIT AND HONEY.

ALFAJORES
SPICED FRUIT AND NUT COOKIES

30 COOKIES

2 cups all-purpose flour

³/₄ cup blanched almonds

9 tablespoons unsalted butter,
   at room temperature, chopped

I cup dried figs, finely chopped

¹/₂ cup golden raisins

¹/₃ cup honey

finely grated zest of ¹/₂ lemon

10 cloves, heads only, ground

¹/₂ teaspoon ground cinnamon

I tablespoon Pedro Ximénez sherry

³/₄ cup confectioners' sugar, sifted

Preheat the oven to 400°F.

Toast the flour by spreading it thinly over two baking sheets and bake it for 12 to 15 minutes, or until golden. Place in a large mixing bowl.

Spread the almonds on a baking sheet and bake for 8 to 10 minutes, or until toasted, then remove and let cool. Chop the cooled almonds in a food processor until a coarse meal forms, then combine with the flour. Rub the butter into the flour mixture for 1 minute, or until nearly combined, then add the dried fruit, honey, lemon zest, spices and sherry and combine just until the dough comes together. Place in a bowl, cover and let stand at room temperature for 20 minutes.

Meanwhile, reduce the oven temperature to 350°F.

Divide the mixture into 30 pieces. Roll each piece out on a lightly floured surface into a log approximately 3 ¹/₄ inches long and ⁵/₈ inch in diameter. Place on a lightly floured baking sheet and bake for 15 minutes, or until golden.

Remove from the oven and, while still warm, roll well in the confectioners' sugar. Let cool, then serve with coffee or anise liqueur. The cookies will keep in an airtight container for up to 6 days.

THE ROADS TO CÁDIZ ARE LINED WITH PINES. THE GREAT BELTS OF WINDSWEPT TREES THAT WHISPER QUIETLY IN THE ATLANTIC BREEZE HOLD TOGETHER THE SAND DUNES, SHELTER THE FIELDS AND PRODUCE CREAMY LITTLE PINE NUTS, WHICH ARE USED EXTENSIVELY IN ANDALUSIAN PASTRIES. LIGHTLY TOASTED, THE PINE NUTS ARE TRAPPED IN LAYERS OF SWEET GLAZE AND COVER SPONGE CAKES AND PUFF PASTRIES. FOR THIS RECIPE, YOU CAN USE READY-MADE PUFF PASTRY, BUT I HAVE INCLUDED A SIMPLE RECIPE FOR ROUGH PUFF. MAKING THE PASTRY IS TIME CONSUMING, BUT THERE'S SOMETHING MEDITATIVE ABOUT FOLDING AND ROLLING A GREAT CHUNK OF BUTTER INTO PASTRY DOUGH.

HOJALDRES DE PIÑÓNES CON MANZANA

PUFF PASTRY WITH APPLE COMPOTE COATED IN PINE NUTS

12 PIECES

ROUGH PUFF PASTRY

4 cups all-purpose flour, plus extra, to dust

1 teaspoon fine sea salt

1 tablespoon sherry vinegar

2½ tablespoons unsalted butter, at room temperature, plus

1½ cups cold unsalted butter

juice of 1 lemon

9 Granny Smith apples

7 tablespoons unsalted butter

1¾ cups superfine sugar

⅓ cup Spanish brandy

1 cinnamon stick

¾ cup pine nuts

3½ oz quince paste, finely chopped

To make the rough puff pastry: sift the flour and sea salt into a bowl. Add the vinegar, the 2½ tablespoons room-temperature butter and 1 cup water and combine very slowly until a smooth, elastic dough forms. Shape the dough into a ball on a lightly floured surface. Place in a bowl, cover with plastic wrap and refrigerate for 2 hours.

Meanwhile, put the lemon juice in a large bowl and fill with water. Peel, core and cut the apples into ½-inch dice, dropping them into the acidulated water as you go. Drain well, then place in a heavy-bottomed saucepan with the butter, 1 cup of the sugar, 3 tablespoons of the brandy and the cinnamon stick. Cook over high heat, stirring continuously, until the butter has melted. Reduce the heat to low, then cover and cook, stirring frequently, for 30 minutes, or until the mixture reaches a jam-like consistency. Remove from the heat.

Place the puff pastry dough on a cold, well-floured surface and roll out into a 12-inch square. Shape the 1½ cups cold butter into a 6-inch square and place in the center of the dough. Make a cut from each corner of the butter to each corner of the dough, then fold the outside edges of the dough over the butter to completely encase it.

Using a rolling pin, gently but firmly work the dough and butter into a 6 x 18 inch rectangle, keeping the butter in between the layers of dough. Measure the dough into thirds lengthways, then bring one end of the pastry to the far third mark, then fold the remaining third over this. Place the dough on a floured baking sheet, cover with plastic wrap and refrigerate for 25 minutes.

Place the pastry back on a cold, well-floured surface with the open end facing you. Roll it into another 6 x 18 inch rectangle, then fold over the ends as before. Place back on the floured sheet, cover and refrigerate for another 25 minutes. Repeat this process three more times, refrigerating for 25 minutes between each rolling.

Roll out the pastry on a lightly floured surface into a 12 x 16 inch rectangle, then place on a large, flat, well-floured baking sheet. Trim the pastry edges and prick the base all over with a fork. Cover with another baking sheet of the same size and refrigerate for 30 minutes.

Meanwhile, preheat the oven to 425°F.

Bake the pastry, still in between the two baking sheets, for 15 minutes, or until golden and crisp. Remove from the oven and reduce the oven temperature to 350°F.

Remove the top baking sheet, allow the pastry to cool slightly, then cover with the apple compote, leaving a 1/2-inch border around the edges. Scatter evenly with the pine nuts, then bake for another 15 to 18 minutes, or until the pine nuts are golden. Remove from the oven.

Meanwhile, place the remaining sugar in a small saucepan with 1/3 cup water. Stir over low heat until the sugar has dissolved, then boil for 2 minutes. Add the quince paste and remaining tablespoon of brandy, increase the heat to high and stir continuously until the quince paste has dissolved.

While the tart is still hot, carefully brush the quince glaze over the pine nuts and let cool. Cut into 12 pieces and serve at room temperature.

TABERNA CASA MANTECA

A CORNER BAR IN CÁDIZ

I wanted to give you a recipe for *mojama* (pictured on page 91), which is salty sun-dried tuna, sort of like the *jamón* of the sea, but it's too simple to justify a recipe. You take *mojama*, sliced painstakingly thin, and then you drizzle it with a little arbequina olive oil. You might eat it with a little ripe fig cut into quarters, but that's it. It's this simplicity that makes me yearn for Spain when I'm not there and revel in the culture of ordinary beauty when I am. I could go on about how the Spanish can turn anything, like an ordinary corner bar, into a personal expression of their existence. One of my favorites is Taberna Casa Manteca in Cádiz. It is owned by a young bloke, Tómas Ruiz Fabrellas. His dad was a famous baby-faced bullfighter and Tómas shares his father's love of adventure, sailing around the world and working as a local lifeguard. His bar has amazing vibrancy, serving finely sliced *jamón* and chorizo on pieces of waxed paper. The bar is actually an old general store, and tins of goods still line the shelves. Tómas buys the best preserved food from around Spain — they're so good that he opens them up in front of you and dishes them up. And he serves great *mojama*!

EL FENÓMENO DEL JAMÓN

THE JAMÓN PHENOMENON

★ ★ ★

A *JAMÓN* — PRONOUNCED HA-MON — IS NOT JUST A CURED HIND LEG OF PORK. IT IS FAR MORE THAN THAT. IT IS A FOOD IMBUED WITH THE TRADITIONS OF FAMILY, FRIENDSHIP, FAITHFULNESS AND FEASTING. *JAMÓN* IS SO APPRECIATED IT IS GIVEN AS A GIFT TO CURRY FAVOR OR AS A LOW-LEVEL BRIBE, AND IT HOLDS A PLACE IN THE SPANISH PSYCHE IN A WAY THAT IS PERHAPS UNIQUE.

Just south of the ancient city of Salamanca, perched on a high plateau, is Guijuelo — the "Detroit" of *jamón*. *Jamón* factories ring this town; there are factories on the roads leading into the main plaza, and right in the very heart of the town, wedged between old churches and *jamón* bars, are *jamón secaderos*, or drying rooms, that have been built to look like blocks of flats. Through an open window, where you'd expect to glimpse a private moment in someone's domestic life, there are, instead, hundreds of *jamones* hanging, slowly drying.

A *jamón*, depending on its quality, is dry-aged for between 7 and 40 months. During that period, the leg loses more than one-third of its weight, and develops a coating of fungus that transforms the flavor of the flesh. Some Spanish jokingly describe the process as somewhere between "mummification and transubstantiation." The bulk of *jamón* is Serrano — 90 percent of it in fact. Serrano *jamón* made from the back leg of run-of-the-mill white pigs and, in some regions, Duroc pigs. Serrano is reasonably priced and generally of good quality. Then there is *jamón* made from the native Ibérico pigs. These are black or reddish pigs found only on the Iberian Peninsula. *Jamón* made from these pigs is referred to as Ibérico. These pigs have a wonderful ability to create marbled flesh, and some are allowed to graze in open woodland under oak trees. The Spanish word for acorn is *bellota* — and an Ibérico pig that has been eating acorns makes the best and most expensive *jamón* of all.

In some factories in Guijuelo, the curing process is open to the street and one can see the legs of pork sitting under mountains of sea salt, where they remain for about 10 days. During this time, the salt begins to draw out the liquid from inside the legs. From here, they are rinsed and left hanging to slowly dry in the *secaderos*, with shuttered windows open to the air flowing down from the nearby sierra. In Guijuelo, as in other *jamón* towns such as Jabugo and Teruel, the winters are cool and wet and the summers hot and dry. These climatic variations allow the salt to migrate toward the center of the *jamón* and then migrate outward again. During this period, many things are happening. Enzymes are changing the flesh, and indigenous microflora — harmless penicillium and aspergillus molds — penetrate the flesh, giving a flavor that is unique to every Spanish region. These wild molds help develop flavors that range from earthy to cigar-box to floral. This is why you can cure pork anywhere in the world — but only in Spain can you make *jamón*.

On average, each Spaniard eats more than 11 pounds of *jamón* annually. It is eaten for breakfast, lunch and dinner and as a snack throughout the day and into the small hours of the morning. It is also used extensively in cooking.

These recipes explore the different ways and techniques used to imbue layers of flavor, seasoning, texture, richness and aroma to a dish by adding a little vitamin J — *jamón*!

FOR BREAKFAST IN SEVILLE, THIS IS THE ULTIMATE SANDWICH: A TOASTED BREAD ROLL RUBBED WITH GARLIC AND TOMATO, WITH A FEW SLICES OF *JAMÓN* AND OLIVE OIL. IT'S FANTASTIC!

BOCADILLO DE JAMÓN
TOASTED JAMÓN AND TOMATO ROLL

SERVES 6

6 small bread rolls — dinner rolls
   are perfect
1 garlic clove, unpeeled
⅓ cup extra virgin olive oil
3 ripe tomatoes, halved
12 slices of *jamón*

Cut the bread rolls in half and lightly toast on both sides — the bread should just begin to crisp up but not gain any color.

Cut the garlic clove in half. Rub the toasted surface of the bread with the garlic to impart a generous but not overwhelming flavor. Drizzle a little olive oil over each toasted side of the bread, then rub each roll with the cut side of one tomato half, leaving on a good amount of juice and pulp.

Place two slices of *jamón* on the bottom of each roll, then cover with the top half. Serve immediately and enjoy with gusto!

LAYING A FEW FINE SLICES OVER A FINISHED DISH IS A CLASSIC WAY IN WHICH *JAMÓN* IS USED TO ENRICH A DISH. THE RESIDUAL HEAT FROM THE COOKED POTATOES WARMS THE *JAMÓN*, ALLOWING ITS AROMA TO ENTICE THE DINER. THIS IS A HEARTY DISH TO SAY THE LEAST: DEEP-FRIED EGGS SERVED WITH POTATOES AND CHORIZO. THIS COULD BE A WINTER'S BREAKFAST, OR A LUNCH TO FEED THE WORKERS.

HUEVOS ROTOS
FRIED EGGS AND POTATOES

6 MEDIAS RACIONES

$^7/_8$ cup extra virgin olive oil

3 large roasting potatoes, cut into $^5/_8$-inch dice

10 $^1/_2$ oz fresh chorizo, cut into bite-size pieces

6 garlic cloves, unpeeled

$^1/_2$ teaspoon smoked paprika

1 teaspoon coarse sea salt

olive oil, for deep-frying

6 eggs

6 slices of *jamón*

Heat the extra virgin olive oil in a large heavy-bottomed frying pan over medium-high heat. Add the potatoes and cook, turning occasionally, for 15 minutes, or until lightly colored. Add the chorizo and the garlic cloves and cook for another 10 minutes, or until the potatoes are tender and the chorizo is cooked. Remove with a slotted spoon, drain on a paper towel and sprinkle with the paprika and sea salt.

Meanwhile, fill a deep fryer or large heavy-bottomed saucepan one-third full of oil and heat to 350°F, or until a cube of bread dropped into the oil browns in 15 seconds. Crack the eggs, one at a time, into a cup, then carefully slide into the hot oil and cook for 30 to 90 seconds, depending on how you like your eggs. Remove with a slotted spoon and drain on a paper towel.

Divide the potato mixture among six warm plates. Sit an egg on each and season to taste. Lay a slice of *jamón* over the top and serve immediately.

I CAN'T WALK PAST A BAR THAT DISPLAYS A HANDWRITTEN SIGN SAYING "*HAY CALDO*," OR "WE HAVE BROTH." INSIDE, THE BAR STAFF IS SERVING UP LITTLE GLASSES OF RICH STOCK LEFT OVER FROM THE *COCIDO*. TO MAKE A *COCIDO* IS SIMPLE, BUT IT TAKES GREAT PREPARATION AS IT IS A RICH, SLOW-COOKED STEW CONTAINING CHICKPEAS, VEGETABLES, MEATS, CHICKEN, SAUSAGES AND, OF COURSE, *JAMÓN*. THIS IS A SHORTCUT TO THE SAME RICH, LIP-SMACKING CLEAR SOUP THAT SOMETIMES I JUST CRAVE. FOR THIS SOUP, A PIECE OF *JAMÓN* IS ADDED TO THE POT TO SLOWLY RELEASE A LITTLE SALT, SOME RICH TEXTURE AND A LOT OF FLAVOR. NOTE THAT TO KEEP *CALDO* CLEAR, IT SHOULD BE BARELY SIMMERED AND NEVER BOILED. *CALDO* CAN BE USED TO START A MEAL, BE A MEAL IN ITSELF WITH THE ADDITION OF SOME PASTA, OR BE OF GREAT COMFORT WHEN YOU'RE NOT FEELING WELL. IT'S NO USE MAKING ANY LESS THAN ENOUGH FOR 12, BUT ANY EXCESS CAN EASILY BE STORED IN THE FREEZER FOR A MONTH. AFTER BEING USED TO MAKE THE *CALDO*, THE CHICKEN AND *JAMÓN* CAN BE SHREDDED AND MIXED WITH BÉCHAMEL SAUCE TO MAKE *CROQUETAS*.

CALDO
JAMÓN CONSOMMÉ

SERVES 12

3 1/2 lb whole chicken

5 1/2-oz piece of *jamón*

1 yellow onion, halved

4 bay leaves

1 leek, white part only,
  halved and washed

2 carrots

1 garlic bulb

4 whole black peppercorns

Rinse the chicken well and discard any giblets. Place in a large stockpot with the remaining ingredients. Cover with cold water, place over high heat and bring to just below a boil. Reduce the heat to low and simmer for 3 hours, skimming continuously. The stock should just simmer very gently and not boil.

Remove the chicken and *jamón* from the stock and reserve for *croquetas* if desired. Strain the consommé and ladle into warm bowls. Serve with a small glass of chilled amontillado sherry.

JAMÓN FAT HAS A SPECIAL PLACE IN THE SPANISH KITCHEN. IT IS TREASURED AS A SOURCE OF FLAVOR: EVERYTHING A PIG ATE IN ITS LIFE IS CONCENTRATED IN ITS FAT. IF THE PIG WAS LUCKY ENOUGH TO FEAST ON ACORNS, ITS FAT WILL HAVE A WONDERFUL NUTTINESS AND BE MOST SOUGHT AFTER. PARTICULARLY FATTY PIECES OF *JAMÓN* ARE PROCURED BY HOME COOKS FOR CERTAIN DISHES. THIS IS ONE OF THEM — A HEARTY SALAD THAT COMBINES THE SWEETNESS OF COOKED ONIONS, THE EARTHINESS OF POTATOES AND THE RICH NUTTINESS OF *JAMÓN* FAT.

PATATAS MEÑEADAS
WARM POTATOES WITH CRISPY LARDONS

6 RACIONES

$1/3$ cup extra virgin olive oil, plus extra, to drizzle

$3 1/2$ oz *jamón* fat, roughly chopped

1 large yellow onion, finely chopped

4 garlic cloves, finely chopped

coarse sea salt

$2 1/4$ lb roasting potatoes, peeled

6 oz pancetta, cut into lardons

2 teaspoons smoked paprika

Heat half of the olive oil in a large heavy-bottomed saucepan over medium-low heat. Add the *jamón* fat and cook for 10 to 15 minutes, or until rendered. Remove and discard any *jamón* pieces and reserve the fat in the pan. Add the onion and garlic, season with a pinch of sea salt, then reduce the heat to low. Cover and cook, stirring occasionally, for 30 minutes, or until the onion is very soft.

Cut the potatoes into large chunks by almost cutting through with a knife, then twisting the knife to break the potato apart. (This creates a rough surface on the potato that releases starch, giving a smooth texture to the dish.) Add the potatoes to the onion mixture with 1 cup water, then cover and simmer for 45 minutes, or until the potatoes are very tender, shaking the pan occasionally.

Meanwhile, heat the remaining olive oil in a frying pan, add the pancetta and cook over medium-low heat for 10 minutes, or until golden and crisp. Drain on a paper towel.

Sprinkle the paprika over the potatoes and roughly mash with a fork. Season with sea salt and drizzle with a little more olive oil. Transfer to a warm serving dish, scatter with the warm pancetta lardons and serve.

EL CORTADOR

THE CORTADOR

There is an art to cutting *jamón* properly, and the master of this art is called a *cortador*. *Cortadores* cut wafer-thin slices along the grain, creating pieces around 1¼ inches wide called *lonchas*.

In Spain, cutting *jamón* is a full-time position. *Cortadores* work in restaurants, in bars and for events companies; some beer companies may even have a full-time *jamón* cutter in their hospitality and promotions department. A while ago, a friend of mine attended his nephew's wedding, where there were 11 different *cortadores* cutting 11 different *jamones* for the 300 guests. One *cortador* I know travels the world with his knives packed in a violin case.

Pedro Nieto, a *jamón* maker from Guijuelo and a trained *cortador*, explains the process far more eloquently than I can.

"The thinner the slice of *jamón*, the better. This makes the fibers of meat thinner and you don't notice the meat. You taste the flavors of every part of the process: the acorns in the *dehesa*, the transformation of the drying, the effect of the local molds — not just the meat. It is important to cut right across the width of the *jamón*, as every muscle has a different flavor. The pieces should be large enough to be appetizing, but small enough to fit into the mouth. A slice can sit on the tongue and be warmed by the mouth, releasing the aromas before you eat it. This is the art of the *cortador*."

IN ZARAGOZA, THERE IS A SMALL SUBURBAN RESTAURANT OWNED BY A MAN WHO HAS SPENT HIS LIFE STUDYING *JAMÓN*. HE IS A BRILLIANT *CORTADOR* (SEE PREVIOUS PAGE), WHO JOKINGLY SAYS HE SOLD HIS SOUL TO THE DEVIL TO BE ABLE TO CUT *JAMÓN* SO WELL. ON ANY GIVEN DAY, HE WILL HAVE THREE DIFFERENT *JAMONES* FROM DIFFERENT REGIONS ON HIS BAR READY FOR SLICING. THIS IS ONE OF THE DISHES HE SERVED ME ONE DAY: BRILLIANTLY SOFT ARTICHOKES IN A DELICATE *JAMÓN* AND SHERRY-FLAVORED SAUCE.

ALCACHOFAS CON JAMÓN
ARTICHOKES WITH JAMÓN

6 MEDIAS RACIONES

juice of 1 lemon

8 artichokes

3 tablespoons olive oil

1 large yellow onion, finely chopped

2 garlic cloves, finely chopped

3 1/2-oz piece of *jamón*, finely chopped

2 bay leaves

1 tablespoon all-purpose flour

2 cups dry sherry

1 teaspoon fine sea salt

a small handful of parsley, finely chopped

12 slices of thiny sliced *jamón*, roughly torn

Add the lemon juice to a large bowl of water to stop the artichokes browning as you peel them. Working one at a time, and using a small sharp knife, slice off most of the stem and the top one-third to half of the artichoke tops. Pull off the tough outer leaves to reveal the soft, pale yellow inner leaves, then peel the stem and slice the artichoke lengthways into quarters. Using a teaspoon, scoop out and discard the hairy choke. Place in the acidulated water and repeat with the remaining artichokes. Bring a large saucepan of salted water to a boil over high heat. Add the drained artichokes and boil for 15 minutes, or until just tender. Drain again.

Meanwhile, heat the olive oil in a large heavy-bottomed saucepan over medium heat. Add the onion and sauté for 5 to 6 minutes, or until soft but not brown. Add the garlic, finely chopped *jamón* and bay leaves and sauté for another 5 minutes. Sprinkle in the flour and stir for 1 minute, then increase the heat to high, add the sherry and boil for 1 minute. Reduce the heat to medium-low and simmer for 20 minutes, or until reduced by half, stirring occasionally.

Add the cooked artichokes, 1³/₄ cups warm water and the sea salt. Combine gently and cook for another 15 minutes, or until the liquid has reduced by half. Stir in the parsley and transfer to a warm serving dish. Scatter the roughly torn *jamón* over the artichokes and serve.

A *MENESTRA* IS A BRAISE OF VEGETABLES IN A *JAMÓN*-INFUSED TOMATO SAUCE. IN SPAIN, IT IS EATEN AS A FIRST COURSE, PERHAPS BEFORE SOME MEAT. *MENESTRAS* ARE ALWAYS A SEASONAL DISH AND ARE MADE WITH WHATEVER VEGETABLES ARE PLENTIFUL, SO DON'T BE LIMITED TO THE ONES IN THIS RECIPE. FOR SOME VEGETABLES, THE COOKING TIMES MAY SEEM QUITE LONG — DON'T WORRY, THEY ARE CORRECT. THAT'S SIMPLY THE NATURE OF SOME SPANISH COOKING. (I BELIEVE WE HAVE SWUNG THE OTHER WAY AND NOW ACTUALLY UNDERCOOK OUR VEGETABLES!) THE TANG OF THE TOMATO SAUCE BRINGS EVERYTHING TOGETHER, MARRYING THE EARTHY FLAVOR OF THE VEGETABLES WITH THE RICHNESS OF THE OIL AND *JAMÓN*.

MENESTRA DE VERDURAS
SEASONAL VEGETABLES WITH GARLIC, TOMATO AND JAMÓN

6 MEDIAS RACIONES

Bring a large saucepan of lightly salted water to a boil. Cook the vegetables separately, beginning with the artichokes for 15 minutes, then the potato, Brussels sprouts, carrots and turnips for 10 minutes each, and 5 minutes for the beans. Remove the vegetables each time with a slotted spoon, drain well and spread out on a baking sheet to cool.

Meanwhile, place the tomatoes, garlic cloves and 1 teaspoon of the sea salt in a food processor and blend until roughly puréed.

Place the chopped *jamón* fat and 3 tablespoons of the olive oil in a small saucepan and cook over low heat for 15 minutes, or until the fat has rendered. Remove and discard any *jamón* pieces and reserve the fat. Place the drained vegetables, tomato purée and chopped *jamón* in a large heavy-bottomed saucepan and simmer over medium heat for 15 minutes. Pour in the remaining olive oil and cook for another 15 minutes, or until the flavor and texture of the vegetables are well integrated and the edges of the vegetables are just starting to break down.

Stir the melted *jamón* fat, remaining sea salt and the chopped parsley into the vegetables. Place on a warm serving dish, drizzle with extra virgin olive oil and serve hot, with crusty bread.

5 artichokes, halved and stems removed (see preparation instructions on page 124)

1 large roasting potato, peeled and cut into 1-inch chunks

1 lb Brussels sprouts

2/3 lb baby carrots, peeled and trimmed

2/3 lb baby turnips, peeled, trimmed and halved

1/2 lb large green beans (see page 47), trimmed and cut into 1 1/2-inch lengths

6 ripe tomatoes

2 garlic cloves, peeled

2 teaspoons fine sea salt

1 1/2 oz (about 3 tablespoons) *jamón* fat, finely chopped

1/3 cup olive oil

3 1/2 oz piece of *jamón*, finely chopped

3 tablespoons roughly chopped parsley

extra virgin olive oil, to drizzle

crusty bread, to serve

AS I SAT IN HER KITCHEN, CONCHA BARRADO REELED OFF DOZENS OF *JAMÓN* RECIPES. HER HUSBAND'S FAMILY HAVE BEEN MAKING *JAMÓN* IN GUIJUELO FOR GENERATIONS AND SHE KNOWS A *JAMÓN* RECIPE FOR EVERY OCCASION AND TO GO WITH ALMOST EVERY FOOD KNOWN TO MAN. ONLY WHEN IT CAME TO DESSERTS DID SHE FAIL TO COME UP WITH ONE. THIS IS ONE OF HER FISH RECIPES THAT STRUCK ME AS BEING PARTICULARLY DELICIOUS — BAKED BABY HAKE WRAPPED AROUND *JAMÓN*, THEN GRILLED AND TOPPED WITH A GOOD DOLLOP OF *ALIOLI*.

PESCADILLA
BAKED HAKE WITH JAMÓN AND GARLIC MAYONNAISE

6 RACIONES

ALIOLI
at least 2 peeled garlic cloves,
  or to taste
2 pinches of coarse sea salt
2 egg yolks
I tablespoon Dijon mustard
2/3 cup extra virgin olive oil
2/3 cup sunflower oil
2 tablespoons lemon juice

6 hake or whiting or cod, 10½ oz each
I tomato
2 garlic cloves
2 bay leaves
I leek, white part only, chopped
1/3 cup white wine
18 new potatoes, washed
  but not peeled
coarse sea salt
12 slices of *jamón*
extra virgin olive oil, to drizzle
I tablespoon roughly chopped parsley

To make the *alioli*: put the garlic cloves on a wooden cutting board, chop roughly, then sprinkle with the sea salt. Crush to a smooth paste using the flat part of the knife. Place a bowl on a wet cloth that has been folded into quarters — this stops the bowl flying off the surface. Add the egg yolks to the bowl with the mustard and garlic paste and gently blend together using an egg whisk. Add the oils, a few drops at a time, whisking continuously, ensuring the mixture is emulsified before adding more oil. Slowly whisk in the remaining oils, little by little, until you have a thick mayonnaise. Check for seasoning — dissolve some extra sea salt in the lemon juice if necessary before mixing the lemon juice into the mayonnaise. Finally, whisk in I tablespoon warm water so the *alioli* stays emulsified. Cover and refrigerate until needed. This recipe makes more *alioli* than you need, but the remaining *alioli* will keep in the refrigerator for 2 to 3 days.

Fillet the fish, leaving the skin on and reserving the bones. Place the fish bones, tomato, garlic cloves, bay leaves, leek and wine in a large saucepan. Add enough water to just cover, then cook over high heat until just below a boil. Reduce the heat to low and simmer very gently for 25 minutes, skimming the surface regularly. Strain, discard the solids and pour the stock into a large clean saucepan. Add the potatoes and cook for 20 minutes, or until tender. Remove the pan from the heat and keep the potatoes warm in the stock.

Preheat the oven to 350°F. Season the fish fillets with some sea salt, then place a slice of *jamón* on each fillet. Starting from the tail end, roll up each fillet and secure with a toothpick. Place the fish rolls on a baking sheet, drizzle with a little olive oil and bake for 5 to 10 minutes, or until the fish is just cooked through.

Meanwhile, preheat the broiler to high. Put a tablespoon of *alioli* on top of each fish roll and broil for I minute, or until golden.

To serve, divide the fish and warm potatoes among six small warm plates. Pour a tablespoon of the stock over the potatoes, sprinkle with a little parsley and serve immediately.

JAMÓN HAS MANY GUISES AND CAN SERVE MORE THAN ONE PURPOSE IN A DISH. IN THIS SIMPLE WAY OF COOKING FRESH TROUT, THE *JAMÓN* SLICES ARE FIRST GENTLY FRIED TO RENDER OUT SOME FAT IN WHICH TO COOK THE FISH. THOSE SLICES ARE THEN PLACED INSIDE THE FISH TO ADD SUCCULENCE, FLAVOR AND SALT. FINALLY, SOME SLICES ARE LAID OVER THE TOP, OFFERING A CONTRAST IN FLAVOR AND TEXTURE TO THE MILDER, EARTHIER AND QUITE MOIST TROUT UNDERNEATH.

TRUCHA CON JAMÓN
PAN-FRIED TROUT WITH JAMÓN

2 RACIONES

3 tablespoons extra virgin olive oil

10 thin slices of *jamón* Serrano

2 rainbow trout

coarse sea salt

2 teaspoons thyme leaves

seasoned all-purpose flour, to dust

5 tablespoons butter

1 lemon, halved

Preheat the oven to 350ºF.

Heat the olive oil in a large ovenproof frying pan over medium heat. Add the *jamón* slices and cook for 2 to 3 minutes, or until some of the fat has rendered and the meat is a little crisp. Remove, drain on a paper towel and reserve the pan.

Rinse and pat dry the fish with a paper towel. Using kitchen scissors, trim off all the fins. Season the fish inside and out with the sea salt. Sprinkle the thyme leaves inside the fish, then place three slices of *jamón* inside each fish. Place the seasoned flour on a large plate and dust each fish with the flour. Heat the butter in the reserved frying pan over high heat. When the butter starts to foam but not burn, add the fish and cook for 30 seconds, then reduce the heat to medium. Season with more sea salt and cook for another 2 minutes, then turn the fish. Season again and cook for another 2 minutes.

Squeeze the lemon juice over the fish, then transfer the pan to the oven and bake for 6 to 8 minutes, or until just cooked through. Drain on a paper towel, then place on warm plates. Top with the remaining *jamón* slices and serve immediately.

LA DEHESA

THE PIGS' PADDOCK

The hallmark *jamón* is *jamón Ibérico de bellota* (*bellota* is Spanish for acorn). When they are around a year old, Iberian pigs are moved onto the *dehesa*, the holm oak forests that cover 6 million acres of southwest Spain. For a four-month period called *montanera*, the pigs lead a supervised free-range existence consuming up to 22 pounds of grass, acorns, insects and other small wildlife a day. The herds can wander up to 3½ miles each day. This combination of an oil-rich acorn diet and exercise helps the fat interlace the flesh and gives a distinctive nutty flavor and a texture that can range from overtly rich and luscious to lean, minerally and silky. There is an argument that huge tracts of Spain covered in beautiful open woodland have not been cleared because of the beautiful *jamón* they help produce. So save the forests and eat *jamón*!

LA COMIDA ROJA

RED FOOD

★ ★ ★

EVERY AUTUMN IN THE VALLE DEL TIETAR, THE LITTLE TOWN OF VALDEIÑIGOS IS CLOAKED IN A RICH, SWEET SMOKE. TO USE THE WORD *SMOKE* IS A LITTLE HARSH — IT'S MORE LIKE A SUBTLE AROMATIC HAZE. AT THE HEART OF THE TOWN IS A BRICK-AND-CONCRETE CHURCH SURROUNDED BY NEAT WHITEWASHED BRICK-AND-CONCRETE HOMES. BEYOND THEM EXTEND HUNDREDS OF ACRES OF FIELDS COVERED IN LITTLE BUSHES LADEN WITH RIPE RED PIMIENTO PEPPERS. THIS IS LA VERA, THE SMALL REGION IN THE NORTH OF EXTREMADURA WHERE LA VERA *PIMENTÓN* IS MADE. *PIMENTÓN* IS KNOWN IN ANGLO COUNTRIES AS SPANISH PAPRIKA AND IS AS INTEGRAL TO THE SPANISH KITCHEN AS SALT AND PEPPER IS ELSEWHERE.

At this time of the year, grower José Recio Martín is very busy. When he is not supervising the picking of the ripe pimientos, he is managing the *secaderos* — wood-fired kilns built for drying peppers. Every night he wakes and drives from his home to stoke the fires of the *secaderos*. "It takes between 10 to 15 days to completely dry the peppers," he says, carefully turning them over with what looks like a garden fork. It has tines with blunt tips so they don't pierce the skins. "One wet or even humid day can set back the drying time by days."

It is the unpredictable weather that made La Vera the capital of smoked paprika. In Murcia in the south of Spain, *pimentón* is made by sun-drying peppers, but in La Vera, the clouds that develop around the sierra bring a lot of dark and rainy days. The locals responded by using some of the disused tobacco kilns to dry their peppers over the smoke from oak log fires.

The *agridulce*, or bittersweet *pimentón*, is much loved in these parts. On some days in the local bar in Valdeiñigos, the only tapas served are little plates of pig skin boiled in salted water flavored with garlic, bay leaves and *agridulce pimentón*. "The brighter *pimentón* from Murcia is like the enticing girl you fall for straight away, but she has no depth," says José. "So you end up getting tired of her. But our more intense *pimentones* are like the woman you don't get along with at first, then you realize how truly beautiful she is and you fall in love with her forever."

Extremadura is one of the least populous and under-exploited parts of the nation. Here *pimentón* is used in countless savory dishes, and the red color it imparts to the food has earned the local cuisine the nickname *la comida roja* — "red food." All of the following dishes come from Extremadura, and characteristically, most call for *pimentón*.

THE TOWN OF TRUJILLO SITS ON TOP OF A SOLITARY HILL DOMINATING THE LONELY PLAINS BELOW. IN THE TOWN SQUARE, UNDER THE BELL TOWERS TOPPED WITH STORK NESTS PERCHED ON THE BLUE AND WHITE TILED ROOFS, STANDS A STATUE OF LOCAL HERO FRANCISCO PIZARRO. HE WAS A CONQUISTADOR WHO, ALONG WITH CORTÉS AND OTHER SPANIARDS, WAS RESPONSIBLE FOR CONQUERING THE PEOPLE OF THE AMERICAS. WHILE THE LAST OF THE INCA GOLD WAS SPENT BUILDING SPANISH CHURCHES AND PALACES LONG AGO, EVERY DAY, IN EVERY KITCHEN ACROSS SPAIN, COOKS STILL USE OTHER TREASURES THE CONQUISTADORS BROUGHT BACK FROM THE AMERICAS: TOMATOES AND BELL PEPPERS, WHICH TRANSFORMED THE WAY THE SPANISH COOKED AND ATE. FROM THE HOME OF PIZARRO COMES THIS FRESH AND LIGHTLY SPICED SOUP. IT IS MADE WHEN TOMATOES ARE AT THEIR MOST BOUNTIFUL — IN OTHER WORDS, IT'S A WAY OF USING UP REALLY RIPE TOMATOES.

SOPA DE TOMATE AL COMINO
TOMATO AND CUMIN SOUP

6 MEDIAS RACIONES

3 tablespoons extra virgin olive oil

I red onion, roughly chopped

I large red bell pepper, seeded and
   ribs removed, roughly chopped

2 garlic cloves, finely sliced

2¼ lb ripe tomatoes, peeled (see
   glossary) and roughly chopped

I teaspoon cumin seeds, roasted
   and ground

2 teaspoons superfine sugar

2 teaspoons smoked paprika

2 teaspoons fine sea salt

6 eggs

toasted bread, to serve

Heat the olive oil in a large heavy-bottomed saucepan over medium heat. Add the onion and a pinch of salt and cook for 5 minutes, or until soft and translucent. Add the bell pepper and garlic and reduce the heat to medium-low. Cover and cook, stirring occasionally, for 40 minutes, or until the mixture has a jam-like consistency.

Stir in the tomatoes and 3 cups water and simmer for 25 minutes, or until the mixture has a soupy consistency. Add the cumin, sugar, 1½ teaspoons of the paprika and the sea salt and combine well.

Crack the eggs, one at a time, into a cup, then gently slide them into the soup around the edges. Cover and simmer gently for 3 minutes for soft eggs, or 5 to 6 minutes for well-done eggs.

Gently divide the cooked eggs and soup among warm bowls. Sprinkle with the remaining paprika and serve with toasted bread.

THE *MATANZA* IS THE NAME SPANIARDS GIVE TO THE DAY THEY KILL THE FAMILY PIG. IT IS A MUCH CELEBRATED DAY, ALBEIT A SAD ONE FOR ANY CHILDREN WHO BEFRIEND THE PIG. IN PLASENCIA, THERE IS A BUTCHER'S SHOP DECORATED WITH ART CELEBRATING THE *MATANZA*. WHEN THEY KILL THE PIG, THE SPANIARDS MAKE CHORIZO SAUSAGES, FLAVORED WITH LOTS OF *PIMENTÓN*, WHICH ARE THEN HUNG IN THE RAFTERS TO DRY AND ARE EATEN OVER WINTER. ON THE DAY OF MAKING THE SAUSAGES, A MEMBER OF THE PARTY FRIES UP A QUANTITY OF THE SAUSAGE MIXTURE TO FEED THE FAMILY. THIS DISH IS CALLED *PICADILLO* (MEANING "CHOPPED"). *PICADILLO* CAN NOW REFER TO MANY DIFFERENT DISHES. THIS VERSION USES BEAUTIFUL FRESH FISH MARINATED IN PAPRIKA, HERBS AND WHITE WINE. IT HAS A LOVELY TEXTURE AND DRY SWEET FINISH.

PICADILLO DE ATÚN
PAN-FRIED TUNA WITH SMOKY PAPRIKA

6 RACIONES

2¼ lb skinless tuna fillets, cut into 1-inch chunks
1 tablespoon smoked paprika
2 teaspoons fennel seeds, toasted and roughly chopped
1 tablespoon oregano leaves
3 garlic cloves, finely chopped
2 tablespoons finely chopped parsley
¾ cup dry white wine
⅔ cup extra virgin olive oil
coarse sea salt

Put the tuna, paprika, fennel seeds, oregano, garlic and parsley in a bowl with ½ cup of the wine. Mix well, then cover with plastic wrap and marinate in the refrigerator overnight.

Heat half of the olive oil in a large heavy-bottomed frying pan over medium-high heat. Add half of the tuna, season to taste with sea salt and cook for 1 minute, or until golden. Add 2 tablespoons of the remaining wine, turn the tuna and cook the other side for another minute, then place on a warm serving plate — the idea is to cook and color the tuna, but not overcook it.

Wipe the frying pan clean with a paper towel and repeat with the remaining olive oil, tuna and wine. Allow to cool a little before serving.

PIMENTÓN AHUMADO (SMOKY SPANISH PAPRIKA) IS REGARDED AS A NATURAL FOOD PRESERVATIVE BY MANY SPANIARDS. THEY SAY A COMBINATION OF THE NATURAL CHEMICALS INFUSED INTO THE PEPPERS AS THEY DRY OVER THE FIRE AND SOME COMPOUNDS IN THE PEPPERS THEMSELVES ACT AS ANTIBACTERIAL AGENTS. THAT IS WHY SO MANY SPANISH *EMBUTIDOS* (SAUSAGES AND CURED MEATS) ARE MADE WITH *PIMENTÓN AHUMADO*. *MORCILLA DE CALABAZA* IS TRADITIONALLY A PUMPKIN AND PORK SAUSAGE MADE WITH A LOT OF SALT, STUFFED INTO SAUSAGE SKINS AND HUNG TO CURE FROM THE RAFTERS. WE'VE CHANGED THIS RECIPE EVER SO SLIGHTLY TO MAKE A RICH, SWEET AND SPICED PÂTÉ THAT IS DELICIOUS ON TOASTED BREAD AND OFFERS A REAL TASTE OF THE FOOD FROM EXTREMADURA.

MORCILLA DE CALABAZA
SPICY PORK AND PUMPKIN PÂTÉ

30 TAPAS

3 1/2 lb pumpkin or kabocha squash, seeded and peeled, cut into 2-inch chunks
2 yellow onions, roughly chopped
I garlic bulb
I tablespoon fine sea salt
10 1/2 oz pork back fat, chilled
I tablespoon dried oregano
I 1/2 tablespoons smoked paprika
30 cloves, heads only, ground
toasted bread or crackers, to serve

Put the pumpkin, onions and garlic bulb in a heavy-bottomed saucepan, add 7/8 cup water, then cover and cook over low heat for I hour. Remove the lid and cook for another 20 minutes, or until most of the liquid has evaporated. Remove from the heat and drain off any remaining liquid.

When cool enough to handle, remove and finely chop the onions, then place in a bowl. Squeeze the cooked garlic cloves out of their skins into the same bowl, add the pumpkin and I teaspoon of the sea salt and combine well. Place a double-layered square of cheesecloth in a bowl, pour in the pumpkin mixture and tie the cloth up with string. Hang it in the refrigerator overnight, suspended over a bowl. The mixture should yield just under 2 1/4 lb of pumpkin pulp.

Using the steel blade of your food processor or a hand grinder, grind the chilled back fat.

Combine the drained pumpkin mixture, oregano, paprika, cloves and remaining sea salt in a bowl. Add the minced back fat and mix together well. Place the mixture in a serving bowl or dish, such as an earthenware *cazuela* (see glossary). Cover tightly with plastic wrap and refrigerate for 24 hours.

To serve, spread a little on toasted bread or crackers and enjoy with beer or light red wine.

IT'S AMAZING WHAT IS SOLD IN GAS STATIONS AND WHAT THAT SAYS ABOUT A SOCIETY. WHEN PEOPLE VISIT ANOTHER REGION OF SPAIN, THEY LIKE TO TAKE WITH THEM A SOUVENIR OF THEIR TRAVEL. THAT'S WHY GAS STATIONS AND ROADSIDE RESTAURANTS OFTEN HAVE GREAT LOCAL PRODUCE. SO ONE DAY WHEN I STOPPED TO REFUEL IN EXTREMADURA, I FOUND, AMONG THE TRUCKERS' MAGS, BAGS OF SWEETS AND OIL FILTERS, A SMALL PYRAMID OF CANNED *PERDIZ EN ESCABECHE* (MARINATED PARTRIDGES). THE TRADITIONAL EXTREMEÑAN WAY OF PRESERVING MEAT INVOLVES BOILING VINEGAR WITH WINE AND SPICES TO PRODUCE A LIQUID TOO ACIDIC FOR ANY BUGS TO SURVIVE IN. UNDER CERTAIN CONDITIONS, GAME OR FISH COULD LAST FOR WEEKS IN *ESCABECHE*. WITH REFRIGERATION, HOWEVER, *ESCABECHE* BECAME LESS ACIDIC AND MORE A FLAVORING THAN A PRESERVATIVE. YOU CAN USE PARTRIDGE FOR THIS RECIPE, BUT AS THEY ARE SEASONAL AND A LITTLE HARD TO COME BY, I HAVE USED QUAIL — BUT PLEASE FEEL FREE TO USE ANY GAME BIRD YOU CAN GET YOUR HANDS ON.

CODORNIZ EN ESCABECHE

MARINATED QUAIL

6 MEDIAS RACIONES
4 RACIONES

$2/3$ cup extra virgin olive oil
I red onion, finely sliced
fine sea salt
I large carrot, peeled and cut into very thin rounds
3 garlic cloves, finely sliced
4 bay leaves
IO peppercorns
a few thyme sprigs
I cup white wine
I cup good-quality chardonnay vinegar
6 quails
I cup all-purpose flour
3 tablespoons finely chopped parsley

Heat $1/3$ cup of the olive oil in a large heavy-bottomed saucepan over medium-high heat. Add the onion and a pinch of salt, then cover and cook for 5 minutes, or until soft. Add the carrot, garlic, bay leaves, peppercorns and thyme sprigs and cook, uncovered, for another 5 minutes. Add the wine, increase the heat to high and boil for 2 to 3 minutes, then reduce the heat to medium, add the vinegar and I$1/4$ cups warm water and simmer for IO minutes.

Meanwhile, using a pair of kitchen scissors, cut the last two segments off each quail wing, leaving just the first small bone attached to the breast. Bone each quail by running the tip of a sharp knife to one side of the breastbone and cutting away the flesh from the ribcage right down to the spine. Repeat on the other side, cutting through the skin near the spine to give you two breast and thigh portions. Cut the skin joining the breast and thigh.

Mix the flour with I teaspoon sea salt on a large plate. Dust the quail pieces in the flour. Heat the remaining olive oil in a large heavy-bottomed frying pan over high heat. Working in batches, cook the quail pieces for 3 minutes on each side, or until golden, then remove and drain on a paper towel.

Add the browned quail pieces to the *escabeche* mixture, then cover and simmer over medium-low heat for I5 minutes. Stir in the parsley. Serve hot, or allow to cool, then cover, refrigerate and serve the following day.

EVERY REGION OF SPAIN HAS A PEPPER SALAD AND, FROM AN OUTSIDER'S PERSPECTIVE, THERE MAY NOT SEEM A LOT OF DIFFERENCE BETWEEN THEM. BUT THIS EXTREMEÑAN VERSION IS PROBABLY ONE OF THE MOST ROBUST OF THEM ALL. IT INVOLVES HAND-ROASTING BELL PEPPERS OVER A GAS FLAME USING A PAIR OF KITCHEN TONGS. THE PROCESS IS INTENSE BUT SHORT, REALLY SEARING THE SKIN AND OUTSIDE LAYER OF THE FLESH, BUT LEAVING THE INTERIOR FIRM. THE SKIN IS PEELED AWAY — A JOB THAT CAN BE A LITTLE TIME CONSUMING — LEAVING A VERY LOVELY SMOKY FLESH. COMBINED WITH THE ACID OF THE TOMATO AND FLAVOR HIT FROM THE *PIMENTÓN*, IT IS A VERY WONDERFUL DISH. IT'S GOOD ON TOASTED BREAD, BY ITSELF OR AS AN ACCOMPANIMENT TO MEATS.

ZARANGOLLO EXTREMEÑO
ROASTED PEPPER AND TOMATO SALAD

6 MEDIAS RACIONES

3 red bell peppers
3 green bell peppers
3 garlic cloves, roughly chopped
I teaspoon coarse sea salt
6 tomatoes, peeled, seeded (see glossary) and cut into thin wedges
a handful of parsley, roughly chopped
I teaspoon smoked paprika
½ cup extra virgin olive oil
¼ cup sherry vinegar

Place the bell peppers directly on the flames of a gas stovetop or a grill pan and cook, turning frequently with a pair of metal kitchen tongs, for 10 to 15 minutes, or until the skins blacken and begin to peel off. The flesh should still be quite firm. Place in a heatproof bowl until cool enough to handle, then peel off and discard the skins. This is a rustic dish, so don't worry if there are black bits or a little skin still left on. Cut the peppers in half, then remove and discard the stems, seeds and ribs. Cut the flesh into strips 1¼ inches wide and place in a bowl.

Place the garlic on a cutting board, sprinkle with the salt and chop together to form a very rough paste. Add the garlic paste to the peppers with the remaining ingredients. Toss to combine well and serve while the peppers are still warm.

THERE IS A SIMPLE TECHNIQUE USED RIGHT ACROSS SPAIN CALLED *REFRITO*. IT IS BASICALLY HEATING A FLAVORSOME INGREDIENT LIKE GARLIC IN SOME OIL, THEN POURING THE OIL OVER A DISH JUST BEFORE IT IS SERVED. (IN ONE VISIT TO A BUDGET GRILLED-FISH HOUSE IN THE BASQUE COUNTRY, I SUSPECTED THEY WERE USING A GARLIC *REFRITO* TO COVER UP SOME RATHER SMELLY OLD FISH.) THIS IS A VERY SIMPLE VEGETABLE DISH THAT IS DRESSED WITH A SLIGHTLY UNUSUAL *REFRITO*. IN THIS VERSION, SMOKED PAPRIKA IS ADDED TO OLIVE OIL AND QUICKLY HEATED BUT NOT FRIED, AS FRYING WOULD ALTER THE TASTE OF THE *PIMENTÓN*. THE HEATING RELEASES FLAVOR AND COLOR INTO THE OIL, WHICH IS ALLOWED TO COOL SLIGHTLY IN A JUG; THE PAPRIKA THEN SINKS TO THE BOTTOM OF THE JUG AND THE FLAVORED OIL IS SPOONED OFF THE TOP, LEAVING THE POWDER TO SETTLE AND BE DISCARDED. RATHER CLEVER, I THINK.

ALCACHOFAS CON JUDÍAS EN REFRITO
ARTICHOKES AND GREEN BEANS WITH PAPRIKA SAUCE

6 MEDIAS RACIONES

6 artichokes (see page 124 for
  preparation instructions),
  quartered
12 oz large green beans
  (see page 47), trimmed and
  cut into 1-inch lengths
coarse sea salt
3/4 cup extra virgin olive oil
3 garlic cloves
2 teaspoons smoked paprika

Bring two large saucepans of salted water to a boil. Add the artichokes to one and the beans to the other. When the water returns to a boil, cook the vegetables for 15 minutes, or until tender. Drain well, place together on a warm serving plate and season to taste with sea salt.

Meanwhile, heat the olive oil in a heavy-bottomed frying pan over medium-high heat. Add the garlic cloves and cook for 30 to 60 seconds, or until light golden but not brown. Remove from the heat and allow the oil to stand for 2 to 3 minutes, or until slightly cooled. Stir the paprika into the oil, then pour into a heatproof jug and let stand for 1 minute, or until the paprika settles to the bottom.

Spoon the warm oil over the warm vegetables, being careful not to disturb the layer of settled paprika. Serve immediately.

THE MARKET HAD FINISHED FOR THE DAY IN THE MAIN SQUARE IN PLASENCIA AND SOME OF THE VENDORS WERE DOWNING A FEW DRINKS IN THE CAFÉ ESPAÑA. *CALDERETA DE CABRITO* — KID HOT POT — WAS ON THE SPECIALS MENU AND THE VENDORS WERE ORDERING AN EARLY LUNCH. I COULD SMELL SOMETHING WONDERFUL COMING FROM THE KITCHEN, AND THE GRUNTS OF APPROVAL UTTERED BY THE DINERS WERE A GOOD INDICATION THAT IT SHOULD BE TRIED. WOW! IT WAS A WONDERFUL SLOW-COOKED WET DISH THAT HAD BEEN THICKENED WITH FINELY CHOPPED LIVER, PROBABLY FROM THE BABY GOAT. IT REALLY ADDED ANOTHER DIMENSION OF FLAVOR AND A LOVELY TEXTURAL ELEMENT THAT PARTICULARLY LENT ITSELF TO RED WINE. I'VE USED CHICKEN LIVER IN THIS VERSION AS IT IS EASIER TO OBTAIN — BUT IT IS JUST AS GOOD. KID IS AVAILABLE IN SPECIALTY MARKETS; IF YOU KNOW A MEDITERRANEAN OR VIETNAMESE BUTCHER, TELL HIM WHAT YOU ARE COOKING AND HE SHOULD KNOW HOW TO PREPARE THE MEAT FOR YOU.

CALDERETA DE CABRITO
MILK-FED GOAT HOT POT

6 RACIONES

9 lb goat forequarter, cut into
  2- to 2½-inch chunks
sea salt
½ cup extra virgin olive oil
10½ oz chicken livers, trimmed
I large yellow onion, finely chopped
4 garlic cloves, finely chopped
3½ cups dry white wine
3 tablespoons smoked paprika

Season the goat to taste with sea salt. Heat ⅓ cup of the olive oil in a *perol* (see glossary) or very large heavy-bottomed saucepan over high heat. Cook the meat in batches for at least 5 minutes on each side, or until very well browned. Remove and set aside, then add the livers to the pan and cook for 3 minutes, or until browned and cooked through. Remove and set aside.

Add the remaining olive oil to the pan and sauté the onion over medium heat for 8 to 10 minutes, or until caramelized. Add the garlic and a pinch of salt and sauté for another 5 minutes. Stir in ½ cup of the wine using a wooden spoon, scraping up any cooked-on bits from the bottom of the pan. Stir in the remaining wine, increase the heat to high and bring to a boil.

Add the browned goat pieces and 8 cups water. Bring to a boil, then add the paprika and season to taste. Reduce the heat to medium-low and simmer for 3 hours, or until the meat is nearly tender.

Finely chop the browned livers, add to the pan and cook for another 20 minutes, or until the goat is very tender.

TO GET AN IDEA OF THE INTENSITY AND ENERGY OF THE SPANISH *FERIA* OR FAIR, IMAGINE THE SIDESHOWS FROM THE AGRICULTURAL SHOW YOU WENT TO AS A KID AND MULTIPLY THAT BY A HUNDRED. THOUSANDS OF COLORED LIGHTS; CRAZY, CRAZY RIDES; HORDES OF RAMPAGING TEENAGERS; A CACOPHONY OF POP MUSIC FROM SCORES OF DIFFERENT *CASETAS* (LARGE TENTS RUN BY LOCAL SOCIAL OR POLITICAL ORGANIZATIONS) — THAT IS THE *FERIA*. IT'S AN EARLY-SUMMER INSTITUTION IN ALMOST EVERY DECENT-SIZE TOWN. SOME OF THE *CASETAS* HAVE A PORTABLE KITCHEN AND MANY SERVE SKEWERS OF GRILLED MEAT MARINATED IN *ADOBO* — THE CLASSIC MARINADE OF HERBS AND *PIMENTÓN*. LAST TIME I WAS IN CÁCERES, THE TOWN WAS EMPTY; IT SEEMED THEY WERE ALL AT THE *FERIA* — ALL 82,500 OF THEM. THERE, I HAD ONE OF THE BEST *PINCHOS* I HAVE EVER HAD. IT WAS A SKEWER OF LAMB, SLIGHTLY CHARRED ON THE OUTSIDE, MOIST IN THE MIDDLE AND REDOLENT OF GARLIC, CUMIN, OREGANO AND LOADS OF SWEET SMOKY PAPRIKA. HERE WE ARE USING CHICKEN, BUT YOU CAN JUST AS EASILY SUBSTITUTE LAMB, BEEF OR PORK.

ADOBO DE POLLO

CHICKEN SKEWERS MARINATED WITH PAPRIKA AND OREGANO

12 TAPAS

6 RACIONES

2¼ lb skinless chicken thigh meat, cut into 1-inch chunks

2 tablespoons smoked paprika

1 tablespoon cumin seeds, roasted and ground

3 garlic cloves, finely chopped

3 tablespoons finely chopped parsley

1 teaspoon dried oregano

½ teaspoon saffron threads

1 teaspoon fine sea salt

½ cup extra virgin olive oil

Combine all of the ingredients in a large bowl, cover with plastic wrap and marinate in the refrigerator overnight.

Thread the chicken meat onto 12 metal skewers. Heat a charcoal grill or grill pan to high. Cook the chicken skewers for 5 minutes, or until cooked through, turning regularly. Allow to cool slightly, then serve.

PIMENTÓN

SPANISH PAPRIKA

Since I can remember, we have always had little tins of *pimentón* in the kitchen. Some had pictures of newlyweds dressed in 1960s "mod" gear, some had images of blazing saints, others bore pictures of flowers. *Pimentón* is ubiquitous to much of Spanish cooking; it is a cornerstone flavor. When used at the start of a dish, such as an *estofado* (stew), the flavor is well cooked through and mellows out. Where it is added in the middle of cooking, the flavor is more pronounced. Dusted on a dish just before serving, it adds a sharp hit of earthiness, almost astringency. I like to compare it to Japanese dashi: it is so often there in the food, not taking center stage, just sitting in the background helping all the other flavors come together while adding its own special notes.

THE VARIETIES

Pimentón production is mainly divided between the two *Denominación de Origen* (DO) regions of La Vera near Cáceres in Extremadura, and Murcia in the southeast, with some production in Navarra. *Pimentón* from the La Vera DO is, by regulation, dried over oak fires, and is therefore smoked. It adds a subtle, rich smokiness to dishes and should be handled gently. *Pimentón* from the hot, dry region of Murcia is generally sun-dried, but some brands are now air-dried. It has a sharper, brighter flavor, but some think it lacks the depth of La Vera *pimentón*. *Ahumado* on the label indicates the *pimentón* has been smoked, despite its origin.

    Pimentón dulce is sweet paprika made from *jarnade* peppers and gives food a lovely round flavor. *Pimentón agridulce* is bittersweet paprika made from *jarita* peppers and adds a deep pepper flavor with a hit of bitterness. *Pimentón picante* can be made from a variety of peppers and has a sharp little kick.

THERE IS A SHEEP'S MILK CHEESE THAT IS NOT SET WITH ANY RENNET, MADE IN A TOWN CALLED CASAR DE CÁCERES. AN INFUSION OF A LOCAL THISTLE IS POURED INTO THE RAW MILK AND AN ENZYME IN THE THISTLE SETS THE CURD. THIS CHEESE, CALLED *TORTA DEL CASAR*, IS SERVED BY CUTTING OFF THE TOP AND SCOOPING THE THICK, CREAMY INTERIOR ONTO BREAD. IN EXTREMADURA, A TRADITIONAL DESSERT IS MADE BY BLENDING THIS CHEESE WITH QUINCE. AS THIS CHEESE IS HARD TO COME BY, WE'VE TESTED THIS DISH WITH SHEEP'S FROMAGE FRAIS AND GIVEN IT A TWEAK BY MIXING IN SOME ITALIAN MERINGUE. THIS RECIPE MAKES A LITTLE EXTRA MERINGUE BECAUSE IT'S HARD TO MAKE IN SMALLER QUANTITIES — PERHAPS SPOON THE LEFT-OVER MERINGUE ONTO A LITTLE TART AND FLASH IT UNDER A BROILER.

MOUSSE DE QUESO DE OVEJA CON MEMBRILLO

SHEEP'S CHEESE MOUSSE WITH QUINCE

SERVES 6

2 quinces, peeled, cored and cut into 8 wedges

¼ cup Calvados (apple brandy)

I cinnamon stick

I⅓ cups superfine sugar

finely grated zest of 2 lemons

10½ oz sheep's fromage frais

I cup whipping cream

½ cup slivered almonds, toasted

ITALIAN MERINGUE

4 egg whites

I cup superfine sugar

Preheat the oven to 300ºF.

Place the quince wedges in a baking dish with the Calvados, cinnamon stick, ⅓ cup of the sugar, ¼ cup water and half of the lemon zest. Cover tightly with foil and bake for I hour. Remove the foil, add another ¼ cup water and turn the quince wedges over. Cover again and bake for another 30 minutes, or until tender. Remove from the oven and let cool.

Place 9¼ oz of the cooled quince wedges and ⅓ cup of the cooking liquid into a blender with the remaining sugar, remaining lemon zest and the fromage frais. Process until smooth and set aside.

To make the Italian meringue: whisk the egg whites using an electric mixer until soft peaks form. Meanwhile, place the sugar and I cup water in a small saucepan and stir over high heat until the sugar has dissolved. Bring to a boil, then remove from the heat. With the mixer on low speed, slowly pour the hot syrup into the beaten egg whites in a slow steady stream. Do not pour the syrup on the moving whisk as it will spray hot liquid — and also be careful not to pour it down the side of the bowl as it will not integrate. When all of the syrup has been added, continue whisking for another 2 to 3 minutes, or until the meringue is cool, thick and glossy.

Whisk the cream until firm peaks form. Gently fold I cup of the whipped cream and I cup of the meringue into the cheese and quince mixture. Divide the mixture among six bowls, cover with plastic wrap and refrigerate for 2 to 3 hours, or until chilled. To serve, sprinkle with toasted almonds.

THIS CLASSIC EXTREMEÑAN DESSERT REFLECTS A TRADITIONALLY CONSERVATIVE ATTITUDE TO KITCHEN MANAGEMENT — MAKE USE OF EVERYTHING, AND USE YOUR SKILL TO TRANSFORM THE MOST BASIC INGREDIENTS INTO SOMETHING MUCH GREATER THAN THE SUM OF ITS PARTS. IN EXTREMADURA, *REPÁPALOS* CAN ALSO MEAN "MEATBALLS," BUT IN THIS RECIPE, IT REFERS TO SOFT LITTLE BREAD DUMPLINGS SITTING IN A BOWL OF COLD, SWEET MILK SPICED WITH CINNAMON AND MINT — A PERFECT SUMMER DESSERT.

REPÁPALOS CON LECHE

MILK SOUP WITH CINNAMON BREAD DUMPLINGS AND MELON

SERVES 6

10 3/4 cups milk

zest of 2 lemons, cut into large strips

2 cinnamon sticks

4 mint sprigs, plus extra sprigs,
   to serve

3 3/4 cups superfine sugar

1/4 cup anise liqueur (see glossary)

8 slices two-day-old bread,
   crusts removed

I honeydew melon

olive oil, for deep-frying

5 eggs, lightly beaten

ground cinnamon, to sprinkle

Place the milk, lemon zest, cinnamon sticks, mint, sugar and anise in a large heavy-bottomed saucepan and stir over medium heat until the sugar has dissolved. Simmer for 30 minutes, then remove from the heat and let cool. Strain, then measure out 4 1/3 cups milk and refrigerate until chilled.

Pour the remaining milk into a bowl. Break the bread into rough chunks about 1 1/2 inches in size and soak in the milk for 2 to 3 minutes.

Cut the melon in half, then scoop out and discard the seeds. Using a melon baller or small spoon, scoop out balls or round shapes, placing them in a bowl. Cover and refrigerate until needed.

Heat the olive oil in a deep fryer or large heavy-bottomed saucepan to 375°F, or until a cube of bread dropped into the oil browns in 10 seconds.

Carefully lift the bread out of the milk, one piece at a time, and dip in the beaten eggs, allowing the excess to drain off. Deep-fry the bread chunks for I minute, or until golden, turning several times. Drain on a paper towel and repeat with the remaining bread chunks and beaten eggs.

Place the warm bread dumplings and melon balls in chilled bowls. Pour the reserved chilled milk over and serve scattered with a few torn mint leaves and a sprinkling of ground cinnamon.

LAS
CONSERVAS

PRESERVING FOOD

★★★

IT WAS A FRIDAY NIGHT IN THE OLD TOWN OF CÁDIZ. THE ROUGH STONE BUILDINGS STILL PULSED HEAT OUT INTO THE TINY STREETS LONG AFTER THE SUN HAD GONE DOWN. AMONG THE SMOKE AND THE SHOUTING I FOUND A SPACE AT THE BAR. I ORDERED A BEER AND LOOKED AT THE MENU. THERE WASN'T A PIECE OF FRESH FOOD TO BE SEEN — YET THIS BAR WAS PUMPING. A GREAT MIX OF YOUNG AND OLD, MEN AND WOMEN; THE LITTLE ROOM RINGING WITH LAUGHTER. A SHEET OF WAXED PAPER WAS PLACED ON THE MARBLE BAR IN FRONT OF ME AND A PACKET OF CHIPS WAS OPENED AND POURED ONTO THE PAPER: PERFECT SLIVERS OF POTATO COOKED IN FRESH SUNFLOWER OIL. NEXT CAME A BOWL OF LITTLE GREEN OLIVES. WONDERFUL. THEN A CAN OF MUSSELS: THE BARTENDER RIPPED OFF THE LID AND THE RED PIMENTÓN-INFUSED OIL DRIBBLED DOWN HIS HAND LIKE BLOOD. STUNNING. THE MEN WHO OWNED THE BAR LOVED GOOD FOOD BUT WERE NOT COOKS — SO THEY SIMPLY BOUGHT THE BEST PRESERVED FOOD FROM ALL AROUND SPAIN AND OPENED UP THE CANS, JARS OR BAGS. IT IS ONE OF THE BEST BARS IN ANDALUSIA.

The Spanish, you see, are not snobs about preserved food, because nothing goes into a can or a jar unless it's the best — the best mussels, anchovies, clams, sardines, tuna, asparagus, beans, bell peppers, peaches and apricots. The best of the season is put under glass or into a can for the rest of the year. Safely secured from deterioration, the goods are traded across Spain, as they have been since preserving was invented. Galician clams are harvested in the north and served in Cádiz in the south. Cantabrian anchovies are cured on the Bay of Biscay and eaten across Spain. In Navarra, there are entire towns in the Ebro Valley where particular varieties of fruit and vegetables are grown specifically for the preserving industry. I once met a market gardener in the Basque country who supplied the many Michelin-star restaurants around San Sebastián. Interestingly, he held some of his best produce back for preserving. His was a relatively small operation, no bigger than a large garage, set up on the banks of a creek under a copse of beech trees. One lunchtime, he opened a jar of his fava bean confit in olive oil. He gently heated them in a small saucepan, then poured them into a flat ceramic dish. With a little sausage and some bread, these made a meal. A very good meal — the flavors of the beans having developed and concentrated. Hand-picked, hand-peeled, hand-cooked and hand-packed, they had been changed completely by the process. And so had the price: they were around 18 dollars for a small jar! Spaniards will pay a good price for good *conservas*;

for some, they are a kind of fast food. With the main meal being taken in the middle of the day, some people work late or go out and want to eat later at night. Instead of cooking, they will open a can or jar of *conservas* as a snack.

The basis of preserving is to knock out the bacteria and to create a sterile environment in which bacteria cannot survive. This means sterilizing using heat, and making the food itself too acidic, too salty or too sweet for bacteria to live in. We start the process by sterilizing jars, lids and seals. Jars can be sterilized in the oven by placing them slightly apart in a cold oven and heating the oven to 225ºF and holding the temperature for 15 minutes. Then turn the oven off and leave the jars until cool enough to handle. Never shock glass by putting hot things into a cold jar or cold things into a hot jar. I handle jars with a clean cloth and never touch their interior. Seals and lids can be sterilized by boiling them for 10 minutes. The food itself is cleaned to remove bacteria-carrying dirt, then blanched to kill germs on the outside of the food. Some bacteria spores can survive this process, so the food is then pasteurized — cooked at a set temperature, in this case 175ºF, and held long enough for the core temperature of the food in the jar to reach this temperature. During this period, the air expands and is forced out of the jar, creating a vacuum seal. Your *conservas* should then be stored in a cool, dry place out of direct sunlight.

The use of a cooking thermometer is important for successful preserving. These are inexpensive and can be bought from cooking equipment shops, as can high-quality cooking jars, heavy preserving jars, rubber seals and lids.

The Spanish make a lot of *conservas* in glass. They like to see the quality of the food they are buying and later eating. Take a leaf from their book and never eat any food that looks discolored — and certainly never eat food that is "bubbling," or food from a jar with a distended or blown lid, or if a surge of gas comes out of the jar when the lid is opened.

My family has been preserving food for years and I have included a handful of recipes to get you going. We have erred on the side of caution and included increased times and temperatures for safety. We have also included quite salty brines or overly sweet syrups to ensure the liquid will be unsuitable for bacteria to "thrive" in. You can use the preserves right away, but normally one uses them when the food is out of season.

Remember to use only the best produce available — it looks better, lasts longer and, most of all, tastes great.

A SPANISH KITCHEN IS NOT COMPLETE WITHOUT A JAR OF THESE. ROASTED AT HIGH HEAT, THEN PEELED AND FOLDED ONE ON TOP OF THE OTHER, THEY ARE REALLY QUITE BEAUTIFUL. IN BARS AROUND SPAIN, LITTLE RED BELL PEPPERS, WHICH REMIND ME OF A JESTER'S SHOE, ARE STUFFED WITH COD AND DEEP-FRIED. BIGGER RED PEPPERS, *PIMIENTOS MARRONES*, ARE MORE LIKELY TO BE USED IN THE HOME. THEY MAY BE TORN LENGTHWAYS AND LAID ACROSS A RICE DISH TO FINISH IT; THEY CAN BE CHOPPED UP AND MIXED WITH MAYONNAISE AND COOKED POTATO TO MAKE A RUSSIAN SALAD. I ALWAYS FIND JARS OF RED PEPPERS SO ATTRACTIVE — SO DEEP RED, ALMOST VERMILLION, WITH A GLISTEN AND A SHEEN THAT IS QUITE BEAUTIFUL.

PIMIENTOS
RED PEPPERS

FILLS ONE 1-QUART JAR

8 red bell peppers
coarse sea salt, to sprinkle
olive oil, to drizzle
3 tablespoons malt vinegar

Preheat the oven to 400°F. Wash and sterilize a 1-quart preserving jar and its seal and lid (see page 163).

Place the peppers in a roasting pan, sprinkle with sea salt and a drizzle of olive oil and bake for 45 to 50 minutes, or until the skins are blackened and blistered. Remove the peppers from the roasting pan, place in a bowl and cover with plastic wrap.

When cool enough to handle, remove and discard the skins, ribs and seeds, but do not rinse. Place the flesh in a bowl with the vinegar and sea salt and mix together well.

Layer the peppers in the jar, fill the jar almost to the top with any of the leftover liquid, then seal.

Place an old plate on the bottom of a large heavy-bottomed saucepan so the jar is not in direct contact with the base of the pan. Place the jar on the plate and transfer to the stovetop. Fill with enough cold water to cover the jar and turn the heat to high. When the temperature reaches 175°F, reduce the heat and adjust it to keep the temperature at roughly 175°F for 30 minutes.

Carefully remove the jar from the water and allow to cool. Store in a cool, dry place for up to 6 months. Once opened, the peppers will keep, refrigerated, for 2 to 3 days.

WATCHING ROGER FELIP IBARS FROM MAS TRUCAFORT IN TARRAGONA MAKING A PAELLA FROM SCRATCH WAS INSPIRATIONAL (SEE PAGES 298 TO 303). EVEN BETTER, HE MADE IT WITH A JAR OF PRESERVED ARTICHOKES FROM HIS OWN CELLAR, WHICH HE HAD PREPARED FROM THE ARTICHOKES GROWN IN HIS OWN GARDEN. IN THE SPANISH HOME KITCHEN, THE USE OF PRESERVED FRUIT AND VEGETABLES IS ALWAYS COUNTER-SEASONAL. IF THE ASPARAGUS ARE GOOD IN SPRING, YOU'LL BE EATING THE PRESERVED ONES IN SUMMER AND AUTUMN. IF THERE ARE QUINCES IN THE AUTUMN, YOU'LL BE EATING *MEMBRILLO* OVER WINTER. THOSE WITH A VEGETABLE GARDEN WILL KNOW THAT WHEN VEGETABLES ARE IN THEIR FULL FLUSH, YOU HAVE SO MANY YOU JUST DON'T KNOW WHAT TO DO WITH THEM. PRESERVING MAKES THE MOST OF THE BOUNTY AND, IN YEARS GONE BY, WAS A WAY OF GETTING THROUGH THE LEAN MONTHS OF WINTER.

ALCACHOFAS
ARTICHOKES

FILLS TWO I-QUART JARS

about 2 tablespoons fine sea salt

juice of 2 lemons

15 large artichokes

Wash and sterilize two I-quart preserving jars and their lids and seals (see page 163).

Dissolve the sea salt in ½ cup boiling water and add this to 4 cups cold water. Stir in the lemon juice and set aside.

Bring a large saucepan of lightly salted water to a boil. Meanwhile, trim the stems and cut off the top one-third to half of the artichokes. Snap off the tough outer leaves until you start to see leaves with a tender, yellowy base. Trim the stems around the base, then cut the artichokes lengthways into quarters. Using a teaspoon, scoop out and discard any hairy choke. Rinse in cold water, then drop the artichoke quarters into the boiling water in two batches and cook for 2 minutes. Drain well. Layer the artichokes in the jars, cover with the salted lemon water and seal.

Place an old plate on the bottom of a large heavy-bottomed saucepan so the jars are not in direct contact with the base of the pan. Place the jars on the plate and transfer to the stovetop. Fill with enough cold water to cover the jars, then turn the heat to high. When the temperature reaches 175°F, reduce the heat and adjust it to keep the temperature at roughly 175°F for 30 minutes.

Carefully remove the jars from the water and allow to cool. Store in a cool, dry place for up to 6 months. Once opened, the artichokes will keep, refrigerated, for 2 to 3 days.

PRESERVED TUNA BELLY IS REMARKABLY POPULAR ACROSS SPAIN. AGAIN, THE VERY BEST PART OF THE CATCH — THE RICH, FAT BELLY FLESH — IS COOKED IN VERY, VERY SALTY WATER, PLACED IN OIL AND THEN PASTEURIZED. IT IS DELICIOUS BUT HIGHLY EXPENSIVE. FRESH TUNA BELLY, OR *VENTRESCA* AS IT IS KNOWN IN SPAIN, CAN BE VERY DIFFICULT TO COME BY, SO I USE A LARGE FILLET AND TRIM AWAY THE DARK BLOODLINES. THIS RECIPE WAS FIRST TOLD TO ME BY A WINEMAKER IN THE BASQUE COUNTRY WHO WAS SERVING HIS HOME-MADE PRESERVED TUNA WITH HIS SUPER-FRESH, WONDERFULLY ACIDIC *TXACOLI* WHITE WINE. THE TUNA WAS INCREDIBLY RICH AND MOUTH-FILLING AND PERFECTLY SALTY.

ATÚN
TUNA

FILLS TWO 1-QUART JARS

4½-lb piece of yellowfin tuna

1¾ cups fine sea salt

4 cups mild extra virgin olive oil

Wash and sterilize two 1-quart preserving jars and their seals and lids (see page 163).

Using a sharp knife, remove the skin, bloodlines and any bone or tough flesh from the tuna. Cut the tuna into pieces about an inch shorter than the jars. Place a plate on the bottom of a large saucepan and lay the tuna on the plate. Pour the salt over and cover with water. Bring to a boil over high heat, then reduce the heat to very low, cover and allow to barely simmer for 2 hours. Carefully remove the tuna and let cool.

Place the tuna upright in the jars, cover with the olive oil and seal.

Place an old plate on the bottom of a large heavy-bottomed saucepan so the jars are not in direct contact with the base of the pan. Place the jars on the plate and transfer to the stovetop. Fill with enough cold water to cover the jars and turn the heat to high. When the temperature reaches 175ºF, reduce the heat and adjust it to keep the temperature at roughly 175ºF for 30 minutes.

Carefully remove the jars from the water and allow to cool. Store in a cool, dry place for up to 6 months. Once opened, the tuna will keep, refrigerated, for 2 to 3 days.

ANCHOAS

ANCHOVIES

Santoño is a little factory town in Cantabria. The entire waterfront is filled with the aroma of curing anchovies. When anchovies are cured, however, they don't smell like fish. They have a sweet meaty smell, described by some as a cross between lilies and *jamón*. The tiny little fish are cleaned, beheaded and left to mature in drums of a super-salty, ochre-colored solution for around six months. During this time, the flesh loses moisture and becomes denser and firmer. Like *jamón*, it undergoes a transformation, aided by bacteria and enzymes, that changes its flavor completely. Once the curing process is complete, each anchovy is washed, spun dry, hand-cleaned, hand-filleted, then packed in a can with neutral olive oil. Anchovies are one of the cornerstones of Spanish tapas: a single perfect anchovy will be laid across a beautiful plate and served as is. Great anchovies are celebrated for their mouth-filling smoothness, hit of salt and lingering aroma. Most Spanish anchovies are very good to excellent — they are one of the first things I order in a bar when I am in Spain. After olives. Oh, and beer.

WHEN KING JUAN CARLOS OF SPAIN SPEAKS, EVERYBODY LISTENS. HE IS BOTH MAJESTIC AND DOWN TO EARTH, AND SO LOVED ON THE IBERIAN PENINSULA THAT EVEN ONE IN THREE PORTUGUESE WANT HIM AS THEIR KING. HIS FRIENDSHIP WITH MOROCCANS HAS EASED DIPLOMATIC TENSIONS — AND HE HAS TOLD SOUTH AMERICAN PRESIDENTS TO "SHUT UP!" HE LOVES TO RIDE HIS MOTORBIKE INCOGNITO THROUGH THE COUNTRYSIDE, AND MANY SPANIARDS HAVE A STORY OF MEETING HIM IN A SMALL TOWN, DRESSED IN HIS LEATHERS, HAVING A BITE TO EAT. ONE STORY GOES THAT WHEN KING JUAN CARLOS TASTED SOME CANNED ASPARAGUS, HE VOICED HIS APPRECIATION IN QUITE AN EARTHY MANNER. "THESE ASPARAGUS," HE PROCLAIMED, "ARE THE BALLS!" THAT BRAND OF CANNED WHITE ASPARAGUS HAS BEEN CALLED *COJONUDOS* EVER SINCE. EVERY TIME I SEE A CAN OF ASPARAGUS LABELLED *COJONUDOS*, I AM REMINDED WHY I LOVE SPAIN SO VERY MUCH.

ESPÁRRAGOS

ASPARAGUS

FILLS ONE 1-QUART JAR

2¼ lb fresh white asparagus
⅓ cup plus 1 tablespoon fine sea salt
juice of 1 lemon

Wash and sterilize a 1-quart preserving jar and its lid and seal (see page 163).

Wash the asparagus spears and peel the stems. Measure the depth of the jar and trim the spears so they fit ¾ inch beneath the lid to allow enough preserving liquid to cover them.

Dissolve the sea salt in ½ cup boiling water. Add this to 3⅞ cups cold water, then stir in the lemon juice and set aside.

Cook the asparagus in two batches in a large saucepan of boiling salted water for 2 to 3 minutes, or until nearly tender. Refresh the asparagus in iced water, then drain and arrange upright in the sterilized jar. Cover with the salted lemon water and seal.

Place an old plate on the bottom of a large heavy-bottomed saucepan so the jar is not in direct contact with the base of the pan. Place the jar on the plate and transfer to the stovetop. Fill with enough cold water to cover the jar, then turn the heat to high. When the temperature reaches 175°F, reduce the heat and adjust it to keep the temperature at roughly 175°F for 30 minutes.

Carefully remove the jar from the water and allow to cool. Store in a cool, dry place for up to 6 months. Once opened, the asparagus will keep, refrigerated, for 2 to 3 days.

IT WAS JUST BEFORE LUNCHTIME IN A BIG *CONSERVAS* FACTORY IN NAVARRA AND THE WOMEN ON THE ASPARAGUS LINE WERE WAITING FOR THE BELL. WITH HANDS LIKE LIGHTNING THEY CLEANED, TRIMMED, STACKED AND PACKED SCORES OF DIFFERENT TYPES OF CANS AND JARS OF WHITE ASPARAGUS. THE BIG SPEARS WENT INTO THE BIG CANS AND THE LITTLE ONES STOOD UP IN GLASS JARS. SEEING THE WOMEN STANDING IN THE STEAM WITH THEIR GLOVES AND HATS, I COULDN'T HELP THINKING OF *LAVERNE & SHIRLEY*. THE WAREHOUSE WAS LIKE A GALLERY: ROWS OF HAND-MADE PIECES OF ART. BUT IT WAS THE CONSERVED MIXED VEGETABLES THAT REALLY GOT ME. CAREFULLY LAID OUT IN ROWS AND LAYERS, THE JARS LOOKED MORE LIKE ENTRIES IN THE LOCAL AGRICULTURAL SHOW THAN COMMERCIAL PRODUCTS. IT WAS EXPLAINED TO ME THAT THEY WERE INDEED DESTINED FOR DISPLAY, ALBEIT IN RETAIL SPACES — AND, NOT SURPRISINGLY, THEY ALSO TASTED VERY GOOD.

MENESTRA
MIXED VEGETABLES

FILLS TWO 1-QUART JARS

juice of 3 lemons
2 1/4 lb baby artichokes
1 cup green beans
1 1/2 bunches baby carrots
1 1/2 bunches asparagus
1 cup fresh peas
(14 oz peas in the pod)
1/3 cup fine sea salt

Wash and sterilize two 1-quart preserving jars and their seals and lids (see page 163). Wash the vegetables carefully.

Pour the juice of one lemon into a large bowl of water. Working with one artichoke at a time and using a small sharp knife, slice off most of the stem and the top one-third to half of the top. Pull off the tough outer leaves to reveal the soft, pale yellow inner leaves, then peel the stem and slice the artichoke lengthways into quarters. Using a teaspoon, scoop out and discard the hairy choke. Place in the acidulated water and repeat with the remaining artichokes.

Working from the top, cut the green beans so they come to about 3/4 inch below the lids of the jars. Peel and trim the green tops from the carrots and cut the carrots lengthways into quarters. Peel the asparagus, then trim the spears so they stand 3/4 inch from below the lids.

Dissolve the salt in 1/2 cup boiling water. Add this to 3 7/8 cups cold water, then stir in the remaining lemon juice and set aside.

Cook the vegetables, including the peas, in batches in a large saucepan of boiling salted water until just tender. Drain, then refresh in iced water and drain again. Lay the jars on their sides and arrange the vegetables so they will be upright when the jars are standing up. Cover with the salted lemon water, then place a small plastic insert on top of the vegetables to keep them submerged. Seal the jars.

Place an old plate on the bottom of a large heavy-bottomed saucepan. Place the jars on the plate and transfer to the stovetop. Fill with enough cold water to cover the jars, then turn the heat to high. When the temperature reaches 175°F, reduce the heat and adjust it to keep the temperature at roughly 175°F for 30 minutes.

Carefully remove the jars from the water and allow to cool. Store in a cool, dry place for up to 6 months. Once opened, the vegetables will keep, refrigerated, for 2 to 3 days.

YEARS AGO, I MET AN OLD BLOKE WITH A DONKEY RETURNING FROM HIS *HUERTA*, HIS BASKETS FULL OF GREEN BEANS. THE SUN WAS LOW IN THE SKY BUT STILL WARM. HE LIVED IN A GROUP OF SQUAT LITTLE STONE HOUSES NEAR A TOWN CALLED PIEDRAHÍTA, A FEW HOURS WEST OF MADRID. HIS SHED WAS LIKE A MUSEUM, WITH CARTS AND DONKEY HARNESSES AND PIECES OF EQUIPMENT THAT HAVEN'T BEEN USED FOR SO LONG THAT ONLY HE CAN REMEMBER WHAT THEY ARE CALLED. BUT HE HAD A PILE OF JARS IN A BOX IN HIS SHED THAT HE HAD SAVED FOR THE TWO WIDOWS WHO LIVED IN THE VILLAGE. HE SAID HE GAVE THEM THE JARS AND BEANS, AND THEY IN RETURN PRESERVED THEM FOR HIM. LATER THAT NIGHT, I ARRIVED IN MADRID AND CAUGHT UP WITH A FRIEND. YOUNG AND SINGLE, WE WENT OUT TO A CLUB, LOOKING FOR FUN. LATER, VERY HUNGRY, WE SAT DOWN AT A TABLE, SMOKING AND SHARING A LATE-NIGHT SNACK. FUNNILY ENOUGH, IT WAS A JAR OF PRESERVED BEANS! I RECKON THESE PARTICULAR BEANS ARE GREAT WITH A WINTER SALAD — A SPLASH OF GREEN ON A PLATE.

ALUBIAS
GREEN BEANS

FILLS FOUR 1-PINT JARS

$1/3$ cup fine sea salt
juice of 1 lemon
$3^1/2$ lb green beans

Wash and sterilize four 1-pint preserving jars and their lids and seals (see page 163).

Dissolve the sea salt in $1/2$ cup boiling water and add this to $3^7/8$ cups cold water. Stir in the lemon juice and set aside.

Working from the top, cut the beans to just under the height of the jar. Cook the beans in two batches in a large saucepan of boiling salted water for 2 to 3 minutes, or until nearly tender. Refresh in iced water, then drain and arrange upright in the sterilized jars. Cover with the salted lemon water and seal.

Place an old plate on the bottom of a large heavy-bottomed saucepan so the jars are not in direct contact with the base of the pan. Place the jars on the plate and transfer to the stovetop. Fill with enough cold water to cover the jars, then turn the heat to high. When the temperature reaches 175°F, reduce the heat and adjust it to keep the temperature at roughly 175°F for 30 minutes.

Carefully remove the jars from the water and allow to cool. Store in a cool, dry place for up to 6 months. Once opened, the beans will keep, refrigerated, for 2 to 3 days.

MY DAD ONCE COMBINED HIS WONDERFUL ATTRIBUTES OF LOVING FOOD, BEING A RETIRED ENGINEER, AND INCREDIBLE THRIFT. WHEN I WAS ABOUT TO THROW OUT A POWERFUL OLD COMMERCIAL MIXER, HE JUMPED ON IT AND SAID "I'LL TAKE THAT!" NEXT AUTUMN, I DISCOVERED HE HAD TRANSFORMED THE MACHINE INTO A *MEMBRILLO* MAKER. *MEMBRILLO* IS THE WORD FOR BOTH FRESH QUINCE AND QUINCE PASTE AND IT IS OFTEN SERVED WITH CHEESE — I THINK IT'S BRILLIANT WITH BLUE CHEESE. WHEN WE WERE GROWING UP, A SLIVER OF SUPER-SWEET *MEMBRILLO* WAS OUR DESSERT. DAD'S NEW CONTRAPTION SLOWLY MIXES THE SUGAR AND QUINCES, WHILE A SMALL GAS FLAME REDUCES THE MIX. HE SPOONS IT INTO AN OLD, GREASED OLIVE OIL CAN, AND EVERY NOW AND THEN HE SLIDES OUT A LITTLE BIT AND CUTS OFF A SLICE. HE IS BRILLIANT.

MEMBRILLO
QUINCE PASTE

MAKES ABOUT 3 LB

3½ lb quinces, peeled and cored

2 cups superfine sugar, approximately

extra virgin olive oil, to grease

Slice each quince into eight wedges and place in a large heavy-bottomed saucepan. Cover with cold water and bring to a boil over high heat, then reduce the heat to low and simmer for 50 minutes, or until tender. Drain the quince, then pass through a food mill. Weigh the quince and place in a heavy-bottomed saucepan.

Measure the equivalent weight of sugar and stir into the quince purée. Cook, stirring frequently, for 3 hours, or until the mixture is very stiff. When the mixture thickens enough that a spoon will stand upright in it, you will need to stir continuously to stop the mixture from scorching.

Lightly grease an 8 x 6 inch baking dish with olive oil. Line the dish with parchment paper and grease again. Spread the *membrillo* evenly into the dish and let cool. Cut into six equal portions, then seal each portion well in plastic wrap and refrigerate for up to 12 months.

JUST BEFORE THEIR LEAVES TURN THE COUNTRYSIDE A PIERCING SHADE OF BURNT ORANGE, THE CHESTNUT TREES IN SPAIN RELEASE THEIR NUTS. FROM INSIDE A COARSE PRICKLY CASE COME A FEW SHINY CHESTNUTS, THE LAST REAL CROP OF ABUNDANCE BEFORE WINTER. WALK THE STREETS OF SPAIN WHEN THE AIR BEGINS TO CHILL AND THERE IS A CONSTANT FRAGRANT NOTE — THE AROMA OF CHESTNUTS ROASTING. FAST STREET FOOD IS FUN, BUT CHESTNUTS ARE SERIOUS BUSINESS IN SPAIN. PRIOR TO THE ARRIVAL OF POTATOES, THEY WERE THE MAIN SOURCE OF WINTER STARCH, AND TO THIS DAY THE EXTRAMEÑANS AND GALICIANS STILL MAKE A SOUP OF CHESTNUTS AND PORK. PRESERVING CHESTNUTS IN SUGAR IS A WAY OF KEEPING THEM OVER THE WINTER. THIS RECIPE CREATES A LOVELY AROMATIC SYRUP THAT CAN BE SERVED WITH THE CHESTNUTS WITH CREPES (SEE RECIPE ON PAGE 250), WITH ICE CREAM OR STEWED FRUIT.

CASTAÑAS EN ALMÍBAR

CHESTNUTS IN SYRUP

FILLS TWO 1-QUART JARS

4 lb fresh chestnuts

2 1/2 cups superfine sugar

2 lemons

1 vanilla bean

Take each chestnut and, using a small sharp knife, make a cross-shaped incision in its flat side. Bring a large saucepan of water to a boil and blanch the chestnuts for 3 minutes. Remove from the heat and leave the chestnuts in the water. Wait for the chestnuts to become cool enough to handle, then, using the blade of the knife, remove the outer skin. Remove the inner skin using a knife, or wipe it off with a clean cloth — the ease of removing the skin will depend on the age and variety of chestnut. Discard the skins.

Put the sugar in a large saucepan with 4 1/4 cups water. Using a vegetable peeler, remove the lemon zest in wide strips and add these to the pan. Cut the vanilla bean in half lengthways, then scrape the seeds into the pan. Discard the vanilla bean (or reserve for making vanilla sugar, if desired).

Bring the liquid to a boil over high heat and cook for 5 minutes. Add the peeled chestnuts. When the liquid starts to boil again, reduce the heat to medium and simmer for 20 minutes.

Meanwhile, wash and sterilize two 1-quart preserving jars and their lids and seals (see page 163). Making sure the jars are still very warm, remove the chestnuts from the heat and transfer to the jars using a sterilized slotted spoon, filling the jars evenly. Pour in the syrup and seal while still hot. Allow to cool, then store in a cool, dry place for up to 3 months. Once opened, the chestnuts will keep, refrigerated, for 2 to 3 weeks.

I WAS HEADING SOUTH TO SEVILLE AND HAD PROMISED TO SEE MY AUNTY ANDREA WHO LIVES ON THE OUTSKIRTS OF MADRID. I COULD SMELL LUNCH FROM THE ELEVATOR WELL ON THE BOTTOM FLOOR OF HER APARTMENT BUILDING. SHE GREETED ME WITH THE USUAL AFFECTION AND SCANNED ME WITH HER ONE GOOD EYE. SHE KNEW SHE COULD KEEP ME THERE AS LONG AS SHE LADLED OUT THE *COCIDO*, THE RICH CHICKEN STOCK FLAVORED WITH *JAMÓN*, AROMATIC CHICKPEAS, MEATS AND SAUSAGES. I WOULD HAVE GONE STRAIGHT AFTER LUNCH HAD IT NOT BEEN FOR HER APRICOTS. LIKE SO MANY OTHER SPANISH HOUSEWIVES, SHE HAS CANS — OR EVEN BETTER, JARS — OF APRICOTS, EITHER BOUGHT OR HOME-MADE, SITTING ON THE SHELF PRESERVED IN A LIGHT SUGAR SYRUP. ACROSS THE NATION, HOUSEWIVES BOTTLE THEIR FRUIT, ESPECIALLY IN THE RURAL PARTS. HERE IS A GOOD RECIPE TO MAKE THE MOST OF THE BEST FRUIT OF THE SEASON.

ALBARICOQUES

APRICOTS

FILLS TWO 1-QUART JARS

2 cups superfine sugar

3$\frac{1}{2}$ lb perfect ripe apricots

Clean and sterilize two 1-quart glass preserving jars and their lids and seals (see page 163).

Place the sugar and 4$\frac{1}{4}$ cups water in a heavy-bottomed saucepan and stir over low heat until the sugar has dissolved. Increase the heat and boil for 2 minutes, then remove from the heat and let cool.

Rinse the apricots, place them in the jars and pour in the cooled syrup. Place a small plastic insert over the apricots to keep them submerged, then seal the jars.

Place an old plate on the bottom of a large heavy-bottomed saucepan so the jars are not in direct contact with the base of the pan. Place the jars on the plate and transfer to the stovetop. Fill with enough cold water to cover the jars, then turn the heat to high. When the temperature reaches 195°F, reduce the heat and adjust it to keep the temperature at roughly 195°F for 30 minutes.

Carefully remove the jars from the water and allow to cool. Store in a cool, dry place for up to 6 months. Once opened, the apricots will keep, refrigerated, for 1 week.

TRADICIONES CATALANES

CATALAN TRADITIONS

★ ★ ★

THE VINEYARD WORKERS SAT IN A CIRCLE IN THE SHADE OF A TREE EATING THEIR LUNCH, DRINKING THEIR COFFEE AND SMOKING THEIR CIGARETTES. SIMULTANEOUSLY. THERE WAS A TORTILLA WRAPPED IN A CLOTH, AND THIN LOAVES OF CRUSTY BREAD THAT THE WORKERS WOULD BREAK OFF, THEN RUB WITH A CLOVE OF GARLIC AND SMALL THICK-SKINNED TOMATOES. "*PA AMB TOMÀQUET*," SAID GERARD IN CATALAN: "BREAD WITH TOMATO, THIS IS OUR NATIONAL DISH."

Gerard Batllevell Simó and his family were working quickly, harvesting their grapes before the autumn rain clouds rolled in over the hills from the Mediterranean. Soon these would be drenching the stony soils of the Priorat, a once-great wine region to the southwest of Barcelona. Here the steep ground is covered in little flat stones that resemble fingernails and flat broken tiles. In this grow squat bush vines that cling to the steep hills. New terraced vineyards have been bulldozed into the hills, creating bands of green vines on otherwise bare brown slopes.

Vines have been planted here since ancient times. Carthusian monks built a priory at Scala Dei in the 12th century, and for following centuries, vast quantities of communion wine and spirits were shipped across Europe, with a direct trade route to London. When phylloxera reached these hills behind Tarragona in the early 20th century, the industry was decimated within a decade. Many slopes were replanted with nut trees and the area descended into almost a century of poverty and depopulation. In the 1980s, the area was "rediscovered" by a handful of winemakers who understood how to make high-quality wine from these low-yielding vines. Today, wines from Priorat are some of the most expensive in Spain, with celebrities such as Gérard Depardieu buying into the industry.

But I didn't travel to the Priorat just for the renaissance of the wine industry, as it has been described by some. I came for the food. The Catalans inhabit the northeast coast of Spain and have their own language, culture and, most importantly from my point of view, cuisine. Influenced by centuries of Roman occupation and later trade with France and Italy, Catalans are renowned for their seafood, wine, mushrooms and their sensitivity to seasonal produce.

The recipes I was after, however, were up in the hills and mountains above the Mediterranean, where the traditional food of the Catalans could be found not just in the homes but in the restaurants: rich, hearty food that reflects a time when nothing was wasted, when ingredients had to be stretched — without a hint of resentment — to feed a large family, and embrace at the same time any natural bounty as it ripened. Food that was ingeniously thrifty, yet warmly generous. These are the dishes that have lovingly fed the people from this part of Catalonia for generations — a cuisine based on beans, greens, salt cod, eggs, chicken and pastry.

For this chapter, I have used the Catalan spelling of recipes and ingredients as the recipes were given to me in Catalan, via an interpreter.

For generations, the housewives of Catalonia had a love-hate relationship with the *CUINA ECONÒMICA* – a charcoal-burning beast on which they cooked their meals and heated their water and in which they baked their *COCAS*. *COCAS* are leavened flatbreads that are cooked in a hot oven. Yes, they are similar to pizza, but never tell a Catalan that her *COCA* is a pizza! Topped with whatever was in season, savory or sweet, the *COCAS* soaked up the high heat of an oven with a freshly made fire. After the fire went down, the rest of the dough went in to make the daily bread. This is a summer version of *COCA*, so please feel free to incorporate your own topping of cooked seasonal vegetables.

COCA DE RECAPTE
CATALAN FLATBREAD

6 MEDIAS RACIONES

1/4 oz fresh yeast, or 2 teaspoons
  dried yeast

1/2 teaspoon superfine sugar

2 teaspoons extra virgin olive oil,
  plus 2 tablespoons

1/2 teaspoon fine sea salt, plus extra,
  to sprinkle

4 cups all-purpose flour

1/3 cup olive oil,
  plus extra, for brushing

I large yellow onion, thinly sliced

3 bay leaves

2 garlic cloves, finely sliced

I large red bell pepper, seeded and
  ribs removed, very thinly sliced

I large green bell pepper, seeded and
  ribs removed, very thinly sliced

I tablespoon coarse polenta

2 zucchini, very finely sliced

about I pint cherry tomatoes, halved

2 tablespoons chopped parsley

Put the yeast in a bowl, add 1 1/3 cups lukewarm water and stir until the yeast has dissolved. Add the sugar, the 2 teaspoons extra virgin olive oil and the sea salt and whisk together. Cover and let stand in a warm place for 30 minutes, or until bubbles start to appear.

Add the flour and stir to combine. Place in the bowl of an electric mixer fitted with a dough hook and knead on low speed for 12 minutes. Allow to rest for 5 minutes, then knead again for 5 minutes, or until smooth and elastic. Cover and let stand in a warm place for another 30 minutes.

Meanwhile, heat the 1/3 cup olive oil in a heavy-bottomed saucepan over medium heat. Add the onion and bay leaves and sauté for 5 minutes, or until slightly golden. Add the garlic and bell peppers, then cover and cook for 20 minutes, or until the peppers are soft, stirring regularly. Remove from the heat.

Preheat the oven to 425°F.

Divide the dough into six equal portions, then roll out on a lightly floured surface into 12-inch tongue-like shapes. Sprinkle two well-oiled baking sheets with the polenta, place the dough pieces on top, cover with a clean cloth and let stand in a warm place for 15 minutes.

Toss the zucchini in a bowl with a little salt and the 2 tablespoons extra virgin olive oil.

Brush the pizza bases lightly with olive oil, sprinkle with sea salt and divide the onion and pepper mixture among the bases, leaving a 1/2-inch border. Scatter the tomatoes, zucchini and parsley over the top, drizzle with a little more oil and season to taste. Bake for 10 to 12 minutes, or until the bases are golden and crisp. Serve immediately.

A WEDDING IN PRIORAT IS, GENERALLY, A VERY HAPPY OCCASION, WITH NO EXPENSE SPARED TO CELEBRATE THE DAY. THIS OFTEN INVOLVES KILLING A FEW HENS TO FEED THE WEDDING PARTY. AS USUAL IN CATALAN COOKING, NOTHING IS WASTED: EVEN THE UNLAID EGGS INSIDE THE POOR CHICKENS ARE TURNED INTO A FLAN — A FIRM SAVORY CUSTARD FLAVORED WITH JUST A SCRAPING OF NUTMEG, SITTING IN A CLEAR LIQUID FLAVORED WITH SHERRY. THE SECRET TO MAKING THIS CONSOMMÉ AS CLEAR AS WATER IS TO TAKE THE COOKING PROCESS VERY SLOWLY. THIS STOPS THE STOCK DRAWING OUT THE PROTEIN FROM THE CHICKEN. THE ADDITION OF THE POTATO — A PRIORAT TRADITION — ADDS BODY AND AN EARTHY BACKGROUND NOTE TO THE CONSOMMÉ.

CONSOMÉ DE POLLASTRE AMB FLAM

CHICKEN CONSOMMÉ WITH EGG CUSTARD

6 MEDIAS RACIONES

2 1/4 lb chicken bones
3 tablespoons olive oil
I carrot, cut into large chunks
I yellow onion, unpeeled, halved
I garlic bulb, halved
2 large floury potatoes, peeled and left whole
6-oz piece of *jamón*
I cup oloroso sherry

EGG CUSTARDS

6 egg yolks
1/4 cup whipping cream
1/4 teaspoon freshly grated nutmeg
sea salt

Preheat the oven to 350ºF. Place the chicken bones in a roasting pan and cook for 30 minutes, or until golden.

Heat the olive oil in a large heavy-bottomed saucepan over high heat. Add the carrot, onion and halved garlic bulb and sauté for 8 to 10 minutes, or until golden. Add the roasted chicken bones, potatoes, *jamón* and 5 quarts cold water. Bring to a boil, then reduce the heat to low and simmer for 3 hours, skimming the surface regularly.

Strain the consommé through a fine sieve and pour into a clean pan. Stir in the sherry and boil for 2 minutes, then strain again and pour into a large bowl or jug. Let cool, cover with plastic wrap and refrigerate overnight. The following day, carefully remove the solidified fat from the top of the consommé.

To make the egg custards: preheat the oven to 300ºF.

Combine the egg yolks, cream, nutmeg, I 3/4 cups of the cold consommé and a pinch of salt in a bowl. Place six lightly greased 1/2-cup dariole molds or ramekins in a baking dish. Divide the mixture among the molds, cover each mold tightly with foil and place in the oven.

Pour enough warm water into the baking dish to come halfway up the sides of the molds. Bake for 25 to 30 minutes, or until just set but still a little wobbly in the center. Remove the custards from their water bath and let stand at room temperature for at least I hour before serving.

To serve, reheat the remaining consommé until just hot. Run a small flat knife around the edges of the flans and invert onto warm soup plates. Pour the consommé around the flans and serve immediately.

THIS RECIPE TRANSLATES AS "TORTILLA WITH SAUCE." IN SPAIN, ANYTHING WITH A SAUCE INSTANTLY BECOMES A MAIN MEAL AS YOU NEED BREAD TO SOAK UP THE SAUCE. *TRUITA AMB SUC* IS A TRADITIONAL PRIORAT DISH — A WAY OF EXTENDING SOME EGGS, BEANS AND GREENS FROM A SNACK TO A MAIN MEAL. THIS IS REAL POVERTY FOOD AND WAS SHOWN TO ME BY ONE OF THE PRIORAT'S BEST CHEFS, TONI BRU FROM EL CELLER DE L'ÀSPIC. ALTHOUGH HE COOKS GREAT MODERN FOOD, HE ALSO CHAMPIONS THE ROOTS OF HIS CUISINE. HE TOOK TIME IN HIS RESTAURANT TO SHOW ME THIS LOCAL CLASSIC, FOR WHICH THERE ARE 16 DIFFERENT RECORDED RECIPES. HIS VERSION MAKES A REALLY GOOD MEAL AND WILL WORK WELL IN THE FAMILY HOME, PERHAPS AS A SUNDAY MEAL ON A RAINY DAY. I'VE SUGGESTED YOU FINISH THE DISH IN A *CAZUELA* (AN EARTHENWARE BAKING DISH), BUT ANY SIMILAR-SIZE HEATPROOF DISH WOULD BE GOOD.

TRUITA AMB SUC
SPINACH AND WHITE BEAN TORTILLA IN SAUCE

6 RACIONES

½ cup dried cannellini beans, soaked in
cold water for 2 hours, then drained

SAFFRON SAUCE
1 tablespoon extra virgin olive oil
2 garlic cloves, very thinly sliced
a small pinch of saffron threads
3¾ cups chicken stock
1 tablespoon cornstarch (see glossary)
1 teaspoon fine sea salt

1 bunch picked English spinach leaves
(about 7 oz), washed well and dried
sea salt
10 eggs
3 tablespoons extra virgin olive oil

Place the drained beans in a saucepan, cover well with cold water and bring to a boil over high heat. Reduce the heat to medium and simmer for 40 to 50 minutes, or until tender. Drain.

Meanwhile, to make the saffron sauce: heat the olive oil in a large heavy-bottomed saucepan over medium heat. Add the garlic and saffron and stir for 1 minute, or until the garlic is very lightly browned. Pour in the stock, bring to a boil, then simmer for 10 minutes. Mix the cornstarch and 2 tablespoons of cold water in a small bowl until smooth, then stir into the sauce. Add the sea salt and cook, stirring regularly, for 10 to 12 minutes, or until the cornstarch is cooked out and the sauce has thickened slightly. Remove from the heat.

Plunge the spinach into a large saucepan of boiling water for 20 seconds. Drain, refresh in cold water, then squeeze out the excess water and roughly chop. Add the spinach and a pinch of salt to the beans and mix together well.

Lightly beat the eggs in a large bowl. Add the spinach and bean mixture, season to taste and combine well.

Heat the olive oil in a 10-inch nonstick frying pan over high heat. Pour in the egg mixture and, using a wooden spoon, gently bring the mixture from the edges of the pan into the middle for the first 30 seconds. After 1 minute, reduce the heat to medium, cover with a flat baking sheet and cook for another 3 minutes. Invert the tortilla upside down onto the baking sheet, then slide it back into the pan. Cover with the baking sheet again and cook for another 3 minutes, or until firm but not solid.

Meanwhile, preheat a 10-inch *cazuela* or heatproof shallow earthenware dish over low heat for 5 minutes. Place the tortilla in the dish and increase the heat to medium. Pour the saffron sauce over (it should just cover the tortilla) and cook for 2 to 3 minutes, or until heated through. Remove from the heat and let stand for 20 minutes, to allow the tortilla to absorb some of the sauce. Serve warm.

I ONCE WATCHED A FOREIGN TOURIST ARGUE WITH A LOCAL WOMAN THAT THE PRIORAT WAS A GOOD PLACE TO GET FRESH SEAFOOD AND THAT HE HAD EATEN IT THERE IN THE PAST. THE LOCAL WOMAN, WHO SPOKE VERY GOOD ENGLISH, VERY POLITELY EXPLAINED TO HIM THAT ALTHOUGH THE PRIORAT IS ONLY A SHORT DISTANCE FROM THE MEDITERRANEAN, FRESH FISH WAS NOT TRADITIONAL AND PERHAPS HE MAY HAVE BEEN MISTAKEN AND WAS INSTEAD REFERRING TO *BACALAO* (SALT COD), FOR WHICH THE REGION IS FAMOUS. OR HAD HE MISTAKEN PRIORAT FOR THE COASTAL CITY OF TARRAGONA? SHE LATER EXPLAINED TO ME THAT TOURISTS, NOT JUST AT PRIORAT BUT ACROSS SPAIN, BROUGHT WITH THEM UNREASONABLE EXPECTATIONS AND FALSE ASSUMPTIONS ABOUT FOOD. SHE WISHED PEOPLE WOULD SIMPLY ACCEPT A REGION'S LOCAL FOOD FOR WHAT IT IS — A SENTIMENT THAT IS COMPLETELY UNDERSTANDABLE. THIS *SAMFAINA* IS A CLASSIC CATALAN SAUCE CLOSELY RELATED TO THE FRENCH *RATATOUILLE*.

BACALAO AMB SAMFAINA

SALT COD WITH RATATOUILLE

6 RACIONES

Drain the salt cod, then trim off any fins and dark or brown flesh. Run your hands along the flesh and cut out the bones as you find them. Cut the fish into six equal portions.

Heat ⅓ cup of the olive oil in a large heavy-bottomed saucepan over high heat and sauté the onion for 5 minutes, or until golden. Reduce the heat to medium, add the garlic and bay leaves and cook, stirring occasionally, for 5 minutes. Add the bell pepper and cook for 10 minutes, or until soft. Add the zucchini and cook for another 5 minutes, then stir in the tomatoes, cover and cook for 5 minutes, or until soft. Remove the pan from the heat and set aside.

Heat the remaining olive oil in a large frying pan over high heat and cook the eggplant for 5 minutes, or until golden and tender, turning regularly. Drain on a paper towel, then add the eggplant to the tomato mixture, mix gently and season with salt to taste. You now have *samfaina*!

Preheat the broiler to high. Place the salt cod pieces on a lightly oiled baking baking sheet and cook for 4 minutes on each side, or until golden and cooked through. Divide the warm *samfaina* among six warm plates and place one piece of salt cod on top. Drizzle with a little extra virgin olive oil and serve.

- 2¼ lb salt cod, soaked in cold water for 48 hours, changing the water four times
- ½ cup extra virgin olive oil, plus extra, to drizzle
- 1 yellow onion, cut into ½-inch dice
- 2 garlic cloves, finely chopped
- 2 bay leaves
- ½ red bell pepper, seeded and ribs removed, cut into ½-inch dice
- 2 zucchini, cut into ½-inch dice
- 4 ripe tomatoes, peeled, seeded (see glossary) and cut into ½-inch dice
- 4 small slender eggplants, cut into ½-inch dice
- sea salt

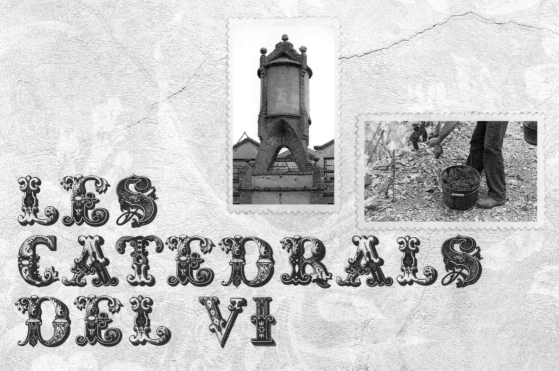

LES CATEDRALS DEL VI

THE CATHEDRALS OF WINE

It was vintage time in Falset and old pickups and tiny flatbed trucks were coming down from the hills, a few plastic crates of grapes in the back of each. They made their way to the rear of the old cooperative buildings in the heart of town, where they unloaded their harvest. The cooperative cellar dates back to the beginning of the 20th century. It was built in the modernist style, but looks like a medieval cathedral made entirely of concrete and brick. Designed by Cèsar Martinell, a disciple of Catalan architect Antoni Gaudí, it and the other buildings he designed around Catalonia are known as "the cathedrals of wine." With great towering vaulted ceilings and shafts of natural light beaming through the narrow windows, the cooperative felt like an ancient building — but the flurry of activity with great vats of wine being pumped from tank to tank and the constant flow of farmers and their grapes made it more industrious than holy. One of the managers told me to follow him to the flat roof. It was covered in ancient glass demijohns half full of wine. "This is how we make the *vi ranci*," he said. "It sits in the sun for six months and over this time it oxidizes. We have a system similar to the solera system where old wine is mixed with new wine." Although *vi ranci* translates as "rancid wine," the liquid he showed me was far from it. Oxidized and deep in color, it was not dissimilar to oloroso sherry, but yet in many ways was quite different. "This wine we use for special occasions," he explained, lifting up his glass. "*Salut!*"

I WAS WALKING THROUGH A VINEYARD WHEN THE SILENCE WAS BROKEN BY A CLATTERING OF HOOVES AS A GOATHERD PUSHED HIS GOATS THROUGH AN ALMOND GROVE IN THE VALLEY BELOW. THE SOUND OF ANIMALS GAVE WAY TO A DEEPER HUM. OVER A LITTLE HILL WAS A TRACTOR WITH WHAT APPEARED TO BE A PAIR OF BAT'S WINGS ABOVE A DRUM ATTACHED TO POWERFUL VIBRATING MECHANICAL ARMS. THE TRACTOR DRIVER BACKED THE MACHINE NEXT TO AN ALMOND TREE AND THE WINGS SPREAD UNDER THE BRANCHES. THE TREE WAS SHAKEN AND THE ALMONDS DROPPED ONTO THE WINGS AND THEN THE DRUM BELOW. "IF WE ONLY HAD A MACHINE WE COULD TAKE TO MADRID AND SHAKE THE POLITICIANS," SAID THE FARMER. TRADITIONALLY, ALMONDS ARE USED IN MANY DISHES FROM THE PRIORAT. SOMETIMES THEY ARE POUNDED TO MAKE A *PICADA* THAT COULD BE STIRRED THROUGH A SLOW-COOKED DISH OF RABBIT OR GARLICKY SALT COD. THIS RECIPE MAKES LOVELY MOIST MEATBALLS WITH A RICH, VISCOUS SAUCE THICKENED WITH EGGPLANT AND DOTTED WITH GOLDEN ALMONDS.

MANDONGUILLES AMB AUBERGÍNIA

PORK AND VEAL MEATBALLS WITH A FRIED ALMOND AND EGGPLANT SAUCE

6 RACIONES

Soak the bread in the milk for 20 minutes. Squeeze out the milk and break the bread into rough pieces into a large bowl. Add the veal, pork, *jamón*, eggs, nutmeg, sea salt and half of the parsley and mix together well using your hands. Shape the mixture into 36 golf ball–size rounds and place on a baking sheet lined with parchment paper. Cover and set aside.

Heat 1/3 cup of the olive oil in a very large frying pan over high heat. Add the almonds and stir constantly until golden. Remove the almonds with a slotted spoon, reserving the oil in the pan, and drain on a paper towel. Add another 3 tablespoons olive oil to the pan and cook the eggplants over high heat for 5 minutes, or until browned. Season to taste, then remove using a slotted spoon and drain on a paper towel.

Heat the remaining olive oil in the pan. Cook the meatballs in batches over high heat for 2 to 3 minutes, or until browned all over, then remove from the pan. Add the onion, bay leaves and garlic to the pan, reduce the heat to medium and sauté for 15 minutes.

Sprinkle the flour over the mixture and stir for 1 minute, then pour in the wine, 2 cups water and the remaining parsley and bring to a boil. Return the meatballs to the pan, reduce the heat to low and simmer for 10 minutes. Add the almonds and cook for another 20 to 30 minutes, or until the sauce begins to thicken. Add the eggplant and stir through for 1 minute, or until warmed through. Serve hot.

- 3 slices two-day-old bread, crusts removed
- 1 1/8 cups milk
- 1 1/2 lb ground veal
- 1 1/2 lb ground pork
- 3 1/2-oz piece of *jamón*, chopped
- 3 eggs, lightly beaten
- 1 teaspoon freshly grated nutmeg
- 1 teaspoon fine sea salt, plus extra as needed
- a large handful of finely chopped parsley
- 1 cup extra virgin olive oil
- 2/3 cup blanched almonds
- 4 slender eggplants cut into strips 1/2 inch wide
- 1 large yellow onion, finely chopped
- 2 bay leaves
- 3 garlic cloves, finely chopped
- 1 tablespoon all-purpose flour
- 1 1/8 cups white wine

SO WHY ON EARTH IS THERE AN ITALIAN DISH IN A BOOK ON SPANISH FOOD? IT HAS BEEN EXPLAINED TO ME THAT ON CHRISTMAS DAY, IN PARTS OF CATALONIA, IT IS TRADITIONAL TO COOK A CAPON — AN EMASCULATED ROOSTER, KNOWN LOCALLY AS "A COCK WITHOUT A CROW." WITH THE CAPON, THE CATALANS MAKE A SOUP CALLED *SOPA DE GALETS*. *GALETS* ARE LARGE PASTA SHELLS ALMOST THE SIZE OF THE PALM OF A CHILD'S HAND, WHICH ARE SERVED WITH MEATBALLS COOKED IN THE SOUP. ON THE FOLLOWING DAY, THE LEFTOVER MEAT IS SHREDDED AND MIXED WITH A *SOFRITO* OF ONIONS, GARLIC AND RED BELL PEPPER UNTIL SMOOTH, THEN STUFFED INTO CANNELLONI. AS FOOD KNOWS NO BORDERS, AND BARCELONA IS ONE OF THE BUSIEST PORTS IN THE MEDITERRANEAN, IT IS ONLY NATURAL THAT CATALANS PICKED UP ONE OF ITALY'S GREAT DISHES AND MADE IT THEIR OWN.

CANELONS D'ÀNEC
CANNELLONI FILLED WITH DUCK

4 MEDIAS RACIONES

2 teaspoons fine sea salt
I teaspoon ground juniper
I teaspoon ground coriander
4½ lb duck or capon

PASTA
2 cups all-purpose flour
2 cups fine semolina
5 eggs, lightly beaten
I teaspoon fine sea salt

BÉCHAMEL SAUCE
5 tablespoons butter
⅔ cup all-purpose flour
5¼ cups milk
I yellow onion, studded with
    3 bay leaves and 6 cloves
sea salt

Preheat the oven to 400°F.

Sprinkle half of the sea salt and half of the ground juniper and coriander inside the duck cavity, then rub the breast with the remaining salt and spices. Place the duck in a large roasting pan, breast side up, and bake for 30 minutes. Reduce the oven temperature to 350°F and bake for another 20 minutes, or until the duck is golden and cooked through. To test if the duck is cooked, pierce through the lower part of a thigh with a skewer — it is cooked if the juices run clear. Remove from the oven and let cool.

Meanwhile, to make the pasta: put the flour, semolina, eggs and sea salt in a food processor and pulse for 3 minutes, or until the dough comes together. Shape into a ball, then divide into three portions. Cover with plastic wrap and let stand at room temperature for at least 30 minutes — do not refrigerate.

To make the béchamel sauce: melt the butter in a small heavy-bottomed saucepan over low heat. Add the flour and stir for 2 to 3 minutes, or until the mixture is sandy colored. Increase the heat to medium-high. Stirring constantly, gradually add the milk. Stir until smooth and bring to a boil, then reduce the heat to low. Add the studded onion and cook, stirring regularly, for 45 minutes. Remove from the heat, discard the studded onion, season with salt to taste and let cool.

To make the ragù: heat the olive oil in a heavy-bottomed saucepan over medium-high heat. Add the onion and sauté for 5 minutes, or until lightly browned. Add the garlic, thyme and chicken livers and cook, stirring regularly, for another 10 to 15 minutes, or until the onion is well colored. Increase the heat to high and stir in the wine using a wooden spoon, scraping up any cooked-on bits from the bottom of the pan. Bring to a boil, then add 1 3/4 cups cold water and the sea salt. Reduce the heat to medium and cook, uncovered, for 30 minutes.

Meanwhile, remove the meat from the duck, leaving the skin attached. Roughly chop the meat, then add to the ragù with the breadcrumbs and parsley. Stir for 2 to 3 minutes, then remove from the heat and blend using a food processor until a very coarse purée forms. Cover and set aside.

Using a pasta machine, roll out each portion of dough into thin sheets, starting at the highest setting on the machine, until you reach setting number 3, or until the sheets are about 1 mm thick. Cut each pasta sheet into four 8-inch lengths. (The remaining pasta can be frozen for up to 1 month.) Cook the pasta sheets in a large saucepan of boiling salted water for 2 minutes, then carefully remove and place in a single layer over clean dish towels. Pat dry.

Preheat the oven to 350°F.

Using a pastry bag fitted with a 3/4-inch tip, pipe one-quarter of the ragù lengthways along one edge of each pasta sheet. Fold the pasta over to form a long roll, then cut each roll into three pieces. Spread one-third of the béchamel sauce over the base of a 10-inch square baking dish. Lay the cannelloni pieces over the béchamel, seam side down, then cover with the remaining béchamel. Bake for 20 minutes, or until golden. Serve hot.

RAGÙ

1/3 cup extra virgin olive oil

I large yellow onion, finely chopped

3 garlic cloves, finely chopped

I tablespoon thyme leaves

1/2 lb chicken livers, cleaned

1 1/8 cups red wine

I teaspoon fine sea salt

2 3/4 cups fresh breadcrumbs

a handful of parsley, finely chopped

COCKEREL, THAT IS ROOSTER, IS STILL USED IN CATALONIA. I'D BET VERY FEW READERS OF THIS BOOK HAVE EVER EATEN COCKEREL. ALL OF OUR CHICKEN (INCLUDING FREE-RANGE CHICKEN) COMES FROM FLOCKS OF ALL-FEMALE BIRDS — MALES ARE EUTHANIZED WHEN THEY HATCH. COCKEREL HAS A MUCH STRONGER FLAVOR, FIRMER FLESH AND STRONGER BONES THAN CHICKEN DOES. IT IS AVAILABLE FROM A FEW SPECIALTY BUTCHERS IN MAJOR CITIES — AND FROM A FEW FARMER FRIENDS WHO GET TIRED OF THE EARLY MORNING CROWING. COCKEREL NEEDS A GOOD, LONG, SLOW SIMMER, AND TO KEEP IT MOIST, IT IS COOKED IN PLENTY OF RED WINE. THE PEOPLE OF THE PRIORAT PATRIOTICALLY USE THEIR LOCAL RED WINE TO MAKE THIS GREAT DISH. IF YOU CAN'T FIND COCKEREL, USE GOOD FREE-RANGE CHICKEN AND REDUCE THE WINE BY HALF AND THE COOKING TIME TO 45 MINUTES. MAKE SURE THE WINE IS GOOD.

GALL AMB VI DEL PRIORAT
COCKEREL IN RED WINE

6 RACIONES

2 cockerels, about 3½ lb each
8 garlic cloves, bruised
6 bay leaves
I large carrot, chopped
I leek, white part only, chopped
6½ cups red wine
3 cinnamon sticks
10 whole black peppercorns
1⅓ cups extra virgin olive oil
I yellow onion, chopped
crusty bread or steamed potatoes,
   to serve

Cut each bird into nine pieces, leaving the breast on the bone. Place in a large glass or stainless-steel container. Add the garlic, bay leaves, carrot, leek, wine, cinnamon sticks and peppercorns and combine well. Cover and refrigerate overnight.

The next day, pour the cockerel and marinade into a colander set over a bowl. Remove the cockerel and pat dry using a paper towel. Reserve the vegetables and wine separately.

Heat ½ cup of the olive oil in a large heavy-bottomed saucepan or heat-proof casserole dish over high heat. Add half of the cockerel, season well and cook for 2 to 3 minutes on each side, or until golden. Remove from the pan and set aside. Discard the oil in the pan, wipe clean with a paper towel and place back over high heat. Add another ½ cup olive oil to the pan and repeat with the remaining cockerel.

Add the remaining olive oil to the pan. Add the onion and sauté over high heat for 3 to 5 minutes, or until slightly golden. Add the reserved vegetables and garlic and cook for another 10 minutes, or until golden, then stir in the reserved wine using a wooden spoon, scraping up any cooked-on bits from the bottom of the pan. Bring to a boil, reduce the heat to low and simmer for 2 to 3 minutes.

Add the cockerel and 3 cups water and simmer gently, uncovered, for 2½ hours, or until tender. If using chicken, do not add the extra water, but do cover with a *cartouche* (a piece of parchment paper cut into a round the same circumference as the pan), and cook for only 45 minutes, or until tender.

Remove the cockerel and place in a deep serving dish. Strain the cooking liquid through a fine sieve into a jug, pushing a small portion of the vegetables through the sieve — just enough to thicken the sauce slightly. Spoon the fat from the surface, then place the liquid in a small saucepan and simmer over low heat for 5 minutes. Pour the sauce over the cockerel and serve with plenty of crusty bread or steamed potatoes.

IF THE CASTILIANS HAVE THEIR *COCIDO* AND THE GALICIANS HAVE THEIR *CALDO GALLEGO*, THEN THE CATALANS HAVE THEIR *ESCUDELLA*. IT'S A MIGHTY BIG SOUP FILLED WITH LOTS OF VEGETABLES, LEGUMES, PASTA, SAUSAGES, A WHOLE CHICKEN AND LOTS AND LOTS OF BONES AND OTHER MEATS TO GIVE IT LOADS OF FLAVOR AND TEXTURE. THIS IS DEFINITELY A WINTER MEAL — PROBABLY SUITABLE FOR A FAMILY THE SIZE OF THE BRADY BUNCH. GET THE FIRE GOING, OPEN A BOTTLE OF RED WINE, WARM THE CRUSTY BREAD AND SETTLE IN FOR A MEAL THAT WILL LAST THE WHOLE OF A LAZY SUNDAY AFTERNOON.

ESCUDELLA
CATALAN HOT POT

6 RACIONES

Place the trotter, veal bones, bacon, *jamón* and whole chicken in a large stockpot and cover with 5 1/2 quarts cold water. Bring to a boil over high heat, then reduce the heat to low and simmer for 1 hour, skimming the surface regularly. Remove the trotter, bones, bacon and *jamón* from the pan and set aside, then add the turnips, carrots and chickpeas and simmer gently for another 40 minutes.

Add the pork sausages and cook for another 30 minutes. Remove the turnips, carrot, sausages and chicken and set aside. Add the *morcilla* and *fideos* to the stock and simmer for 10 minutes.

To serve, cut the bacon, *jamón*, chicken, pork sausages and vegetables into small pieces and place in warm bowls. Remove the meat from the trotter, then shred and add to the bowls. Ladle in the hot broth with the chickpeas, *morcilla* and *fideos* and serve with plenty of crusty bread.

1 pig's trotter

1 lb veal bones

5- to 6-oz piece of bacon

7-oz piece of *jamón*

1 boiling chicken, about 3 1/2 lb

1 bunch of baby turnips, topped and peeled

3 carrots, cut into 3/4-inch chunks

1 1/3 cups cooked chickpeas, or a 14-oz can chickpeas, rinsed well

1 lb pork sausages

9 oz *morcilla* (see glossary), cut into 6 pieces

3 1/2 oz *fideos* (see glossary)

crusty bread, to serve

GEMMA

THE TRADITIONALIST

Gemma Peyri is one of a handful of Catalan women who are championing the food of their past. For many this is not necessarily a popular idea, as for them the past connotes poverty. Gemma, however, finds beauty in the simplicity and honesty of the traditional food of her region. She has been a pioneer in the Priorat, encouraging guests from all over Spain and around the world to try the beautiful but simple local cuisine. Her kitchen is perched on top of a bluff looking over a valley filled with hazelnut trees growing above a little stream. In her kitchen, she skillfully and caringly prepares the meals for her family and guests. As a chef, I recognize the grace and beauty with which she handles her produce, some of which she has grown, and the rest she has carefully selected from growers, farmers and fishermen from around the Tarragona region. Below she reflects on days gone by.

"I started cooking when I was two years old. Our traditional food is quite beautiful, but it comes from a tradition of subsistence cooking. That is quite normal across Spain, but even more so here. I can remember the days when chickens and livestock were kept in the house on the ground floor. Our thick-skinned tomatoes hung from the rafters. People lived upstairs.

"The Priorat is not very fertile; not everything grows effusively — but what grows, grows well. It has a certain quality that has flavor.

"The people who were not badly off had a pig. What they didn't put into sausages on the day of the kill was cut into pieces; it was cooked and stored under oil in earthenware pots. Not everything from the past is good — the pork under oil was actually rather offensive. The food we really loved was from the hunt: rabbit, quail, partridge.

"We ate beef twice a year: that's it. The townsfolk bought a vealer and it was slaughtered in the town square and the families shared the carcass. I remember watching it as a young girl. It was very bloody, but we appreciated that we would get to eat beef.

"Let me explain the poverty of the region better. My grandmother came from a big family. At the age of seven, she was sent to work with a wealthy family. (I see you're surprised.) While some children worked in the laundry, others worked in the garden; she worked in the kitchen. And this was a great benefit to me. You see, the family she worked for was rich and could afford rich food and rich desserts — food like that was never cooked in her family house. My grandmother learned to make custards and cakes. There was a clear definition between the haves and the have-nots, even at this basic level. Sugar, cream and butter were luxury items, but she learned to cook with them and passed the recipes to me.

"I am lucky to have experienced both the poverty and the luxury of the region. I still make the conserves from the "must" of wine; I collect the wild mushrooms, I fry the zucchini flowers, I make the *menjar blanc* — the milk of almonds sweetened with sugar, flavored with lemon zest and cinnamon and thickened with rice flour.

"There are so many dishes that are no longer cooked in this region as they were in the past. But my granddaughter still makes *galetes* with my mother, so there is still hope that the food of the Priorat will always be served."

JUST DOWN THE ROAD FROM THE RUINS OF THE CARTHUSIAN PRIORY AT SCALA DEI IS A LITTLE SHOP RUN BY AN IRREPRESSIBLY HAPPY LADY CALLED NEUS. SHE SELLS HER EXCELLENT OIL AND HER HUSBAND'S *VI RANCI* (SHERRY-LIKE WINE) AND *VINS DOLÇOS* (MUSCAT-LIKE WINE). "TRADITIONALLY, YOU ALWAYS HAD A BOTTLE OF THIS NEAR THE FRONT DOOR OF THE HOME," SHE SAID. "YOU'D POUR A GLASS FOR THE VISITING PRIEST OR DOCTOR AND OFFER THEM SOME NUTS OR SOME PASTRY." SHE OFFERED ME SOME OF HER PASTRIES — *ORELLETES*, WHICH MEANS "BIG EARS" IN CATALAN. THEY WERE HALF THE SIZE OF AN 8 X 10 INCH SHEET OF PAPER, COVERED IN DELICATE BUBBLES WHERE THE PASTRY HAD BLISTERED AS IT DEEP-FRIED, AND DUSTED WITH CONFECTIONERS' SUGAR. *ORELLETES* ARE REALLY SIMPLE, BUT WITH THE ADDITION OF A FEW SPLASHES OF ANISE LIQUEUR, VERY VERY ADDICTIVE, AS IS THE *VI DOLÇ!*

ORELLETES
DEEP-FRIED ANISE PASTRIES

40 PASTRIES

4 eggs

3¼ cups confectioners' sugar, plus extra, to dust

4½ cups all-purpose flour, plus extra, to dust

¼ cup anise liqueur (see glossary)

4½ tablespoons unsalted butter, softened

olive oil, for deep-frying

Whisk together the eggs and confectioners' sugar using an electric beater for 10 to 15 minutes, or until light and creamy.

Gradually sift in the flour and fold in gently, then add the liqueur and butter and stir until a sticky dough forms. Shape the dough into a ball and dust with a little extra flour. Place in a bowl, cover with a damp cloth and let stand at room temperature for 1 hour.

Cut the dough into eight equal portions. Using a pasta machine, roll out each portion of dough into thin sheets, starting at the highest setting until you reach setting number 3, or until the sheets are 1 mm thick. Cut the sheets into 2 x 4 inch strips, fold in half lengthways, then roll through the pasta machine again at setting number 3.

Fill a deep fryer or large heavy-bottomed saucepan one-third full of oil and heat to 375°F, or until a cube of bread dropped into the oil browns in 10 seconds. Deep-fry the strips in small batches for 1 to 1½ minutes, or until golden and puffed. Drain on a paper towel and dust with confectioners' sugar. The pastries will keep for up to 3 days in an airtight container.

I BOUGHT A PACKET OF THESE CASTLE-SHAPED COOKIES AS A PRETEXT TO WATCH HOW THE LOCALS IN THE TOWN OF FALSET BOUGHT THEIR WINE IN BULK. POLISHED BRASS TAPS JUTTED FROM THE TILED BACK WALL OF THE COOPERATIVE. A CUSTOMER WOULD BRING IN A PLASTIC 4-LITER BOTTLE AND THE SHOPKEEPER WOULD FILL IT WITH QUITE GOOD-QUALITY BULK WINE FOR AROUND 8 EUROS. IT WAS MORE GAS STATION THAN BOTTLESHOP, BUT WITH A WONDERFUL CONVERSATIONAL AIR. THE *CASTELLS* I NIBBLED ON WERE ALSO REMARKABLY GOOD — EXCELLENT IN FACT. THESE SHORTBREADS MAKE THE MOST OF THE WONDERFUL HAZELNUTS THAT GROW IN THE REGION. I HAVE BEEN UNABLE TO FIND A CASTLE-SHAPED COOKIE CUTTER, SO I MADE A TEMPLATE OUT OF CARDBOARD AND CUT AROUND IT.

CASTELLS DE FALSET

HAZELNUT SHORTBREAD

24 COOKIES

1/2 cup hazelnuts

7 1/2 tablespoons unsalted butter, softened

1/4 cup superfine sugar

scant 1 cup all-purpose flour, plus extra, to dust

confectioners' sugar, to dust

Preheat the oven to 350°F.

Place the hazelnuts on a baking sheet and bake for 8 to 10 minutes, or until golden. Scoop the hot hazelnuts into a dish towel and rub off the skins. Cool, then chop in a food processor until a coarse meal forms.

Using a wooden spoon, beat the butter and sugar in a bowl until well combined. Add the flour and the hazelnut meal and stir until a dough forms. Place the dough on a well-floured sheet of parchment paper and roll out until 1/16 inch thick. Allow to set a little in a cool place — but not the refrigerator — for 10 minutes.

Using a 1 1/2-inch cookie cutter, cut out shapes from the pastry and place on a greased and lightly floured baking sheet. Place in the freezer for 30 minutes.

Preheat the oven to 300°F.

Place the baking sheet on the top rack of the oven and bake for 20 minutes, or until the shortbreads are golden and a wonderful smell of baked cookies fills the air. Place on a wire rack to cool a little, then dust with confectioners' sugar. The cookies will keep for 4 to 5 days in an airtight container.

THE MARCONA ALMONDS FROM TARRAGONA ARE PERHAPS THE BEST IN THE WORLD. FLAT OVAL AT ONE END AND POINTED AT THE OTHER, THEY ARE CRUNCHY TO THE TOOTH AND MELT INTO A CREAMY PASTE IN THE MOUTH. THEY SAY YOU CAN'T IMPROVE ON PERFECTION, BUT THE DELICATE COATING OF SUGAR CRYSTALS THEY ARE GIVEN IN THIS RECIPE WOULD SURELY COME CLOSE. IT'S A FAIRLY TRICKY METHOD TO GET RIGHT — IT TOOK ME A FEW TRIES! — SO DON'T BE DISCOURAGED BY ANY EARLY DISAPPOINTMENTS.

AMETLLES GARAPINYADES
SUGARED ALMONDS

SERVES 4

I cup almonds

I cup superfine sugar

Put the almonds, sugar and 1⅛ cups water in a small heavy-bottomed frying pan and stir over medium-high heat for 5 to 8 minutes, or until the mixture begins to thicken. As the liquid becomes thicker and more viscous, the bubbles will become larger and appear more sluggish when they burst. Reduce the heat to medium-low and stir gently for I minute. The liquid will soon become white and frothy.

Remove from the heat and allow just the very edge of the frying pan to remain in contact with the heat. Crystals will appear on the side of the pan — stir these into the mixture to hasten the crystallization.

Stir the mixture continuously until it begins to thicken — you will feel more resistance and crystals will begin to form. Remove from the heat and continue mixing as it cools. Larger crystals will form around the nuts, and the bits that do not stick to the nuts will have the appearance of breadcrumbs.

Stir for another 2 minutes, then return to the stovetop over high heat. The sugar will begin to melt and part of it will start to caramelize.

When there is a fine layer of caramel over some of the crystals, remove the pan from the heat and pour the mixture over a silicon mat or a baking sheet lined with parchment paper. Do not allow more than one-fifth of the crystals to melt before removing from the heat.

Allow to cool completely before serving with tea, coffee, fortified wine or sweet sherry. The almonds will keep for up to 2 weeks in an airtight container.

I ATE THIS DESSERT IN A RESTAURANT AS PART OF ITS *MENÚ DEL DIA* (MENU OF THE DAY). IT WAS AN UPMARKET LITTLE JOINT CALLED QUINOA IN THE TOWN OF FALSET AND IT HAD THE MOST REASONABLE SET-LUNCH MENU. THE CHEF TOLD ME HIS *MENÚ DEL DIA* WAS A CHANCE FOR HIM TO PLAY AROUND WITH RECIPES. FOR THE FRUGAL LOCALS, IT WAS A SENSIBLE PRICE AT AROUND 10 EUROS; FOR ME, IT WAS A GLORIOUS CHANCE TO ENJOY THIS GREAT SPANISH TRADITION — AND EVEN WITH THE BATTERED EXCHANGE RATE, IT WAS STILL CHEAP. THIS DESSERT IS AN EASY PURÉE OF ROASTED FRUITS TOPPED WITH HAND-MADE GRANOLA. THE SUGAR USED TO COOK THE FRUIT IS NOT FOR SWEETNESS, BUT TO DRAW THE LIQUID FROM THE FRUIT.

CREMA DE FRUITES AL FORN
ROASTED FRUIT CREAM

SERVES 6

2 quinces

6 small Granny Smith apples

4 Packham, Bosc, Bartlett, or Anjou pears

2 cinnamon sticks

3/4 cup superfine sugar

2 bananas

3 tablespoons unsalted butter

3 tablespoons rolled oats

CARAMEL SAUCE

1 cup superfine sugar

1/2 cup cream

3 tablespoons unsalted butter

Preheat the oven to 350ºF.

Put the quinces, apples and pears in a large roasting pan. Add the cinnamon sticks, 1/4 cup of the sugar and 1/2 cup water. Bake, uncovered, for 30 minutes, then remove the apples. Bake for another 15 minutes, then remove the pears and cook the quinces for another 15 minutes, or until tender. Allow the fruit to cool, then discard the pan juices.

Slice the bananas thickly. Melt half of the butter in a small frying pan over medium-low heat. Add the bananas and another 1/4 cup of the sugar and cook, stirring occasionally, for 10 minutes, or until the sugar caramelizes a little. Remove from the heat and let cool.

Place the oats, the remaining butter and the remaining 1/4 cup sugar in a heavy-bottomed frying pan and stir over high heat for 3 to 4 minutes, or until the oats are golden and crisp. Set aside.

Peel and core the cooled quinces, apples and pears. Place in a blender with the banana mixture and process until smooth.

To make the caramel sauce: heat the sugar in a small heavy-bottomed saucepan over medium heat for 7 to 8 minutes, stirring occasionally, until the sugar melts and begins to caramelize. Stir gently to ensure all the sugar has dissolved, then stir in the cream and simmer for 5 minutes, or until slightly thickened and reduced. Add the butter, combine well and remove from the heat.

Spoon the roasted fruit cream into small bowls, sprinkle with the crisp oat topping and drizzle with the hot caramel sauce. Serve immediately.

IN A SMALL CORNER RESTAURANT, AFTER A MEAL OF PORK AND VEGETABLES COOKED OVER A WOOD-FIRED GRILL, I ESCHEWED THE *CREME CATALAN* AND JUST HAD COFFEE AND A LITTLE ALMOND MERINGUE. MADE WITH THE STUNNING MARCONA ALMONDS — FOR WHICH THERE IS A *DENOMINACIÓN DE ORIGEN* — THESE BEAUTIFUL, CRISP MERINGUES ARE SO RICH, SO NUTTY, SO DAMN SIMPLE AND GOOD!

MERENGUE D'AMETLLES
ALMOND MERINGUES

20 MERINGUES

²/₃ cup blanched almonds, toasted
6 egg whites
I cup superfine sugar
3 teaspoons freshly ground coffee

Preheat the oven to 225°F.

Grind the almonds in a food processor into a medium-coarse meal.

Whisk the egg whites, using a whisk or electric beaters, until soft peaks form, then gradually add the sugar and whisk until stiff peaks form. Add the ground coffee and whisk for another 5 minutes, or until thick and glossy, then gently fold in ²/₃ cup of the almond meal.

Spoon tablespoons of the meringue onto two baking sheets lined with parchment paper. Sprinkle with the remaining almond meal and transfer to the oven. Bake with the door slightly ajar for I hour and 20 minutes. Turn the oven off and leave the meringues in the oven, with the door slightly ajar, for 40 minutes, or until cool and crisp. The meringues will keep for 4 to 5 days in an airtight container.

MUSICIANS, LIKE WRITERS, ARE RENOWNED FOR BEARING THE
CROSS OF POVERTY FOR THEIR CRAFT. TRADITIONALLY, BEING
UNABLE TO AFFORD RICH DESSERTS FILLED WITH COSTLY CREAM,
BUTTER AND SUGAR, THEY HAD TO SETTLE FOR A HANDFUL OF
NUTS AND FRUIT SERVED WITH A LITTLE ALCOHOL. THIS DISH IS
LITERALLY CALLED "DESSERT OF THE MUSICIAN." TELL YOU WHAT
THOUGH, IT'S SENSATIONAL! THERE'S THE CRUNCH OF NUTS . . . THE
HIT OF SWEETNESS FROM THE FRUIT . . . AND A NICE LITTLE PUNCH
FROM THE SHERRY. USE ONLY THE BEST DRIED FRUIT AND NUTS.

POSTRE DE MÚSIC
DRIED FRUIT AND NUTS WITH OLOROSO

SERVES 6

Combine all the ingredients except the sherry in a bowl. Divide among six warm serving bowls, sprinkle with the sherry and serve immediately.

scant I cup toasted hazelnuts

I cup raw almonds

heaped $1/3$ cup pine nuts

I $1/4$ cups shelled walnuts

30 dried Iranian or other
  very small figs, halved

$1/2$ cup good-quality raisins or
  golden raisins

$1/2$ cup oloroso sherry or cream sherry

LA COSTA VERDE

THE GREEN COAST

⭐ ⭐ ⭐

"HERE, YOU ASK SO MANY QUESTIONS ABOUT MY *ALMEJAS*," SAID CARMEN THE CLAM-DIGGER, "JUST TASTE THIS." SHE WAS JUST ONE OF A SMALL ARMY OF FEMALE CLAM-DIGGERS WORKING THE SHALLOWS AT LOW TIDE IN O GROVE — A FISHING PORT ON A SMALL PENINSULA IN GALICIA. THEY WERE PART OF AN ASSOCIATION OF 700 LOCALS WHO HARVEST CLAMS AND COCKLES FROM THE SANDY BEDS OF THE MANY BAYS AND INLETS THAT EAT INTO THE WESTERN ATLANTIC COAST OF SPAIN.

The clam was small, meaty and slightly chewy, but with a richness and a wonderfully sweet, mouth-filling experience. Carmen was watching me eating it and when I turned to acknowledge her, she was smiling. "They're good, eh?" she said. "So good."

It was the festival of the scallop. O Grove was festooned with banners, and a band was playing in the car park near the harbor by the scallop boats. Scallops are big business in Galicia, providing an aquaculture industry worth millions of euros to the locals. The scallop is virtually sacred in Galicia. It is the sign of Saint James the apostle who, legend has it, once saved a knight covered in scallop shells. I thought this story absurd until I realized that the pinkish-blue cladding on some Galician houses wasn't some high-tech material but thousands of scallop shells embedded into wet render. And in pre-literate Spain, pilgrims making their way to the cathedral at Santiago de Compostela wore a scallop shell to show their intent.

Whenever I visit Galicia, I get homesick. Any Australian would. The granite hills could be the Sterling Ranges of Western Australia, the populated shoreline like midcoast New South Wales and the stands of blue gums like the Otway Ranges near my hometown in Victoria. Even the little painted houses remind me of my holidays driving through the hydroelectricity towns of Tasmania. Facing the Atlantic, showered by generous rains, Galicia is so different from the rest of Spain.

The region is full of granite, and, not surprisingly, this was the building material for generations. Old corn houses dot the landscape like small mausoleums; in them, corn could winter, sheltered from the rain and out of reach of rats. The grapevines, to avoid mildew in such a damp climate, are still grown on granite trellises, about the height of the average Galician vineyard worker, to let the breeze through.

In Andalusia, I was born into a sense of the here and now, of living in the moment. In Galicia, however, this attitude gives way to a more languid acknowledgment of the past. With their Celtic heritage, the people here have a longing for times already gone, a lament perhaps more familiar to the Scots than the Spanish. Like the Catalans and the Basques, the Galicians are a different people with a different tongue. That is not to say that we don't understand each other: as food is a "universal" language, there is so much common ground.

At the heart of the region is the Cathedral of Santiago de Compostela. "Santiago" means "Saint James," and apparently the body of James the Apostle was exhumed from the Holy Land and reinterred in Santiago. In the 10th century, an elaborate cathedral was built above the site. The wet weather has encouraged a patina of lichen that gives the monument an aura not dissimilar to the ruins of Angkor Wat in tropical Cambodia. Every year, thousands of pilgrims come to worship at the site, as they have done since the Middle Ages.

May I suggest that pilgrims are not necessarily great payers, so the restaurants around the cathedral are not the best indication of the quality of food available. I suggest you go "off-piste" to enjoy the best Galician food. Yep, get out of town.

What strikes me as a lesson to the world is how these people balance population, environment and aquaculture. The Galicians appreciate their waterways, and the seafood industry here helps protect the ecology. I watched men harvest cockles from their boats just 50 yards from the shores of Carril. The coast here is almost completely developed, yet there is still wild harvesting taking place just yards offshore and a thriving wholesale shellfish market exists in the park by the little protected harbor.

The little towns along the bays of the Rías Baixas have some outstanding cafes, bars and restaurants that deal in the local seafood. From these and the fish markets, food markets and some of the local cooks, I have found recipes that typify Galician fare. It is a cuisine based on perfect raw ingredients — a cuisine that has not changed much over the years, and reflects a people who are not distracted by the fashions of food.

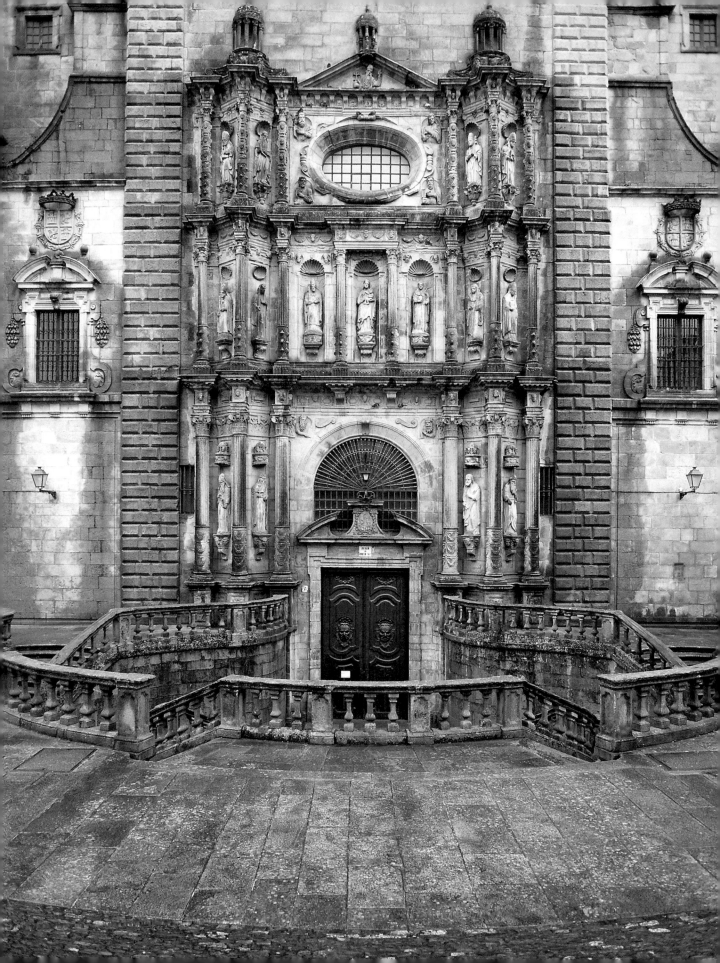

PADRÓN PEPPERS LOOK LIKE BABY GREEN BELL PEPPERS — BUT ONE IN TEN HAVE A KICK LIKE AN ANGRY MULE. IN THE PAST 20 YEARS, THEY HAVE BECOME INCREASINGLY POPULAR IN BARS, WHERE THEY ARE SERVED FRIED OR GRILLED WITH PLENTY OF SALT. THE OCCASIONAL HOT ONE IS THE THRILL OF THE CHASE, AND IT'S ALWAYS FUN IN PADRÓN SEASON WATCHING YOUNG MEN THROW BACK BEER TO QUENCH THE FLAMES AND YOUNG LADIES FAN THEIR OPEN MOUTHS TO COOL THEM DOWN. THIS IS A DISH I NICKNAMED *FUEGO Y SANGRE* ("FIRE AND BLOOD") — A LITTLE PADRÓN STUFFED WITH *MORCILLA* (BLOOD SAUSAGE), THEN DEEP-FRIED AND SPRINKLED WITH SEA SALT. IF YOU CHOOSE TO USE ZUCCHINI FLOWERS INSTEAD OF THE PADRÓNS, INCREASE THE AMOUNT OF *MORCILLA* SAUSAGE TO 2 POUNDS.

PIMIENTOS DEL PADRÓN RELLENOS

PADRÓNS STUFFED WITH BLACK SAUSAGE

12 TAPAS

1 tablespoon extra virgin olive oil

1 lb *morcilla* (see glossary), peeled and crumbled

12 padróns, small peppers or zucchini flowers, rinsed and patted dry

seasoned all-purpose flour, to coat

olive oil, for deep-frying

coarse sea salt, to sprinkle

Heat the extra virgin olive oil in a large heavy-bottomed frying pan over medium heat. Add the crumbled *morcilla* and cook, stirring continuously, for 5 minutes, or until a smooth paste forms. Remove from the heat and let cool for 5 minutes.

Cut the tops off the padróns and reserve the tops. Using the end of a teaspoon or a skewer, scrape out and discard the seeds. Stuff the padróns with the *morcilla* mixture, then replace the tops and secure with a toothpick. Dust with the seasoned flour.

Fill a deep fryer or large heavy-bottomed saucepan one-third full of oil and heat to 375ºF, or until a cube of bread dropped into the oil browns in 10 seconds.

Deep-fry the padróns in batches for 2 to 3 minutes, or until the skin blisters. Drain on a paper towel and sprinkle with sea salt flakes. Serve hot, with cold beer or a Spanish wine such as *mencia*, a light red wine from the Bierzo region.

THERE IS A BAR IN THE BACKSTREETS OF SANTIAGO DE COMPOSTELA RUN BY A ONE-ARMED MAN. THE FIRST TIME I WENT THERE I WAS GREETED WITH THE WELCOMING SMELL OF *CALDO GALLEGO*, THE GALICIAN VERSION OF *COCIDO*. I WAS TOLD THE SOUP WOULDN'T BE READY UNTIL THE NEXT DAY, A THURSDAY — THE DAY FARMERS TRADITIONALLY CAME TO TOWN TO SELL THEIR PRODUCE. IT TOOK ME OVER A YEAR TO GET BACK TO SANTIAGO AND AFTER A DAY TRAVELING THROUGH THE RAIN AND FOG, I ARRIVED EARLY ONE THURSDAY EVENING. I WAS AGAIN GREETED BY THE WELCOMING SMELL OF THE SOUP. I ASKED FOR A BOWL. "HAVE YOU RESERVED?" WAS THE REPLY. "BECAUSE WE CAN ONLY SERVE YOU IF YOU HAVE MADE A RESERVATION." I SAT AT THE BAR AND FOUND SOLACE IN THE GREAT PLATE OF MARINATED MUSSELS THEY SERVED AS TAPAS. THEY WERE BIG, MEATY, SWEET AND SITTING IN A WONDERFULLY SHARP AND FRAGRANT SAUCE MADE WITH SPICED WINE AND VINEGAR. WHEN PREPARING THE FOLLOWING RECIPE (PICTURED ON PAGE 9), USE ONLY THE BEST CHARDONNAY VINEGAR; IF YOU CAN'T FIND THIS, THEN USE A LITTLE LESS OF THE NEXT BEST. THESE MUSSELS ARE PERFECT WITH BEER AND CRUSTY BREAD.

MEJILLONES EN ESCABECHE

MARINATED MUSSELS

6 MEDIAS RACIONES

7 lb mussels

1 3/4 cups dry white wine

4 bay leaves

1/3 cup extra virgin olive oil

1 yellow onion, finely sliced

4 garlic cloves, finely sliced

sea salt

2/3 cup best-quality chardonnay vinegar

1 teaspoon sweet smoked paprika

6 whole black peppercorns

Scrub the mussels and pull out the hairy beards. Rinse well and drain.

Place the mussels, 1 cup of the wine and the bay leaves in a wide heavy-bottomed saucepan. Cover and cook over medium heat, shaking the pan occasionally, for 5 minutes, or just until the mussels begin to open. As soon as the mussels open, remove them from the pan and place in a colander set over a bowl. (Discard any mussels that didn't open.) Allow to cool, then remove the mussels from their shells.

Heat the olive oil in a heavy-bottomed saucepan over medium-high heat. Add the onion, garlic and a pinch of salt and sauté for 5 minutes, or until the onion is lightly colored. Add the vinegar, paprika, peppercorns and the remaining wine, then bring to a boil over high heat. Reduce the heat and simmer for 8 minutes, then remove from the heat and let cool for 10 minutes.

Stir the mussels into the *escabeche* and pour into a shallow dish. Let cool, then cover and refrigerate overnight. Serve chilled, with crusty bread and beer, or a glass of dry Spanish white wine such as *albariño*.

I ONCE SPENT A MORNING ON THE GALICIAN COAST SPEAKING WITH FISHERMEN AND WATCHING THE WOMEN ON THE WHARVES MENDING THEIR NETS BY HAND. THE WOMEN KEPT THE NETS TAUT BETWEEN ONE STRONG ARM AND THE TOES OF AN OUTSTRETCHED FOOT. MY CONCENTRATION WAS DISTURBED BY A MAN DRIVING UP TO A FISHING BOAT AND, ALMOST CLANDESTINELY, PACKING A WOODEN CRATE OF SMALL SARDINES INTO THE TRUNK OF HIS LATE-MODEL MERCEDES. "I AM GOING TO EAT THESE WITH PLENTY OF *VINO TINTO*," HE SAID IN A GRAVELLY VOICE. SUDDENLY I HAD A CRAVING FOR SARDINES. NICE SMALL, MEATY ONES WITH PLENTY OF OILY FLAVOR. LATER THAT DAY, I WAS LUNCHING WITH GALICIAN FRIENDS. THEY TOOK ME TO THEIR LOCAL RUSTIC RESTAURANT, TIO BENITO, AND AFTER PLATES OF CLAMS, MUSSELS, RAZOR CLAMS AND SEVERAL BOTTLES OF *ALBARIÑO*, OUT CAME A WONDERFULLY HOT PLATE OF MEATY LITTLE SARDINES BRAISED WITH GREEN BELL PEPPER, ENLIVENED WITH LEMON ZEST. I WORKED UP ENOUGH DUTCH COURAGE BY THE END OF THE MEAL TO GO WHERE NO MAN DARES TO TREAD — A KITCHEN RUN BY A WOMAN. THIS PARTICULAR KITCHEN WAS WORKING UNDER THE WATCHFUL EYE OF A WONDERFUL WOMAN CALLED SALADINA. THIS IS HER RECIPE AS BEST AS I CAN REMEMBER. IT IS WONDERFUL.

SARDINAS CON PIMIENTOS
BABY SARDINES BRAISED WITH PEPPERS

6 RACIONES

- 1/3 cup extra virgin olive oil
- 3 yellow onions, roughly chopped
- 4 bay leaves
- 8 garlic cloves
- fine sea salt
- 7 green bell peppers, seeded and ribs removed, roughly chopped
- 1 1/3 cups *albariño* or other dry white wine
- a handful of chopped parsley
- I cup pitted green olives
- zest of 2 lemons
- 24 fresh sardines
- 2/3 cup olive oil, plus extra, to drizzle
- seasoned all-purpose flour, to coat

Heat the extra virgin olive oil in a large heavy-bottomed saucepan over very low heat. Add the onions, bay leaves, garlic and a pinch of salt and cook, stirring occasionally, for 15 minutes, or until soft. Add the peppers, then cover and cook, stirring occasionally, for 45 to 50 minutes, or until the peppers are very soft. If the peppers appear to be browning or scorching, reduce the heat as low as possible and add a little water.

Increase the heat to high, then stir in the wine, parsley, olives and lemon zest and simmer for 5 minutes. Remove from the heat and spread the mixture over a large baking sheet.

Remove the spines from the sardines by removing the head, then laying the fish stomach side down. Hold the tail and run your thumb down the spine, breaking the little internal bones. Starting from the head end, gently pull out the spine from the inside of the fish, then cut off or break away the spine and discard.

Preheat the oven to 350°F.

Heat the olive oil in a large frying pan over medium-high heat. Dust the sardine fillets in the seasoned flour and fry for just over 30 seconds on each side, seasoning each side with sea salt as you go.

Place the sardine fillets, skin side up, over the pepper mixture on the baking sheet. Drizzle with a little more olive oil and bake for 5 minutes, or until the sardines are just cooked through. Serve immediately with plenty of chilled *albariño* wine.

THE PEOPLE YOU BUMP INTO! I MET A FISHMONGER IN THE CAMBADOS FISH MARKET, JOSEF REI, WHO USED TO WORK AS A CANE-CUTTER IN NORTHERN QUEENSLAND. HE MISSED THE GALICIAN WINTER AND WENT BACK TO LIVE IN SPAIN BUT WAS STILL THRILLED TO SEE AN AUSTRALIAN. HE WANTED TO GIVE ME SOME AMAZINGLY BEAUTIFUL BABY MACKEREL. I SAID I HAD NOWHERE TO COOK THEM, SO INSTEAD HE GAVE ME THIS RECIPE FOR COOKING OCTOPUS, WHICH HE REFERRED TO AS "GALICIA'S NATIONAL FISH." ITS SIMPLICITY PRODUCES ONE OF THE MOST FLAVORFUL DISHES. YOU LAY THE THICK LEGS OF THE OCTOPUS ON THE HOTTEST GRILL YOU CAN MUSTER, THEN, COOKED RAPIDLY IN ITS OWN JUICES UNDER A HEAVY WEIGHT, IT BECOMES TENDER AND SUPER-INTENSELY FLAVORED. THE JUICES FROM THE GRILLED OCTOPUS ARE USED TO DRESS THE SALAD.

PULPO A LA PLANCHA

OCTOPUS ON THE GRILL

8 MEDIAS RACIONES

6 RACIONES

3½ lb octopus, frozen overnight, then thawed

½ lb red radishes, trimmed

3 small cucumbers

I tablespoon chopped parsley

⅓ cup extra virgin olive oil

juice of I lemon

bread, to serve

Remove the head from the octopus and discard.

Heat a flat, lightly oiled grill grate as hot as it will go. Place the octopus on the grill, then cover with a heavy baking sheet and place a heavy weight — such as a cast-iron saucepan — on top. Cook the octopus for 7 to IO minutes on each side, then remove from the heat, place in a bowl and allow to cool. Slice the octopus into I-inch chunks and return to the bowl with any juices.

Peel the radishes and cucumbers, leaving on a little skin to add a flash of color to the plate. Cut the cucumbers in half lengthways, remove the seeds using a small spoon, then thinly slice the flesh. Cut the radishes in half lengthways, then thinly slice and add to the octopus chunks with the cucumber, parsley, olive oil and lemon juice.

Toss gently and check the seasoning. For the best flavor, serve the octopus while it is still warm, with plenty of bread to sop up the juices.

EL MERCADO DE SANTIAGO

SANTIAGO MARKET

There's an old woman sitting on a wooden box with a basket of the first of the season's padrón peppers on a low wooden table in front of her. She sits in the pale light of a spring morning. Behind her grows lichen on the roughly hewn granite wall, nourished by Santiago's frequent rain and damp air. Like most towns across Spain, Santiago's *mercado* is the town's center of shopping, as opposed to a shopping center. Some markets, like Barcelona's Boqueria, have become famous and are now packed with tourists by mid-morning. Madrid has its ageing municipal markets — concrete buildings from the late 1960s that have a brutal charm of their own.

Spanish markets are places where people congregate, sometimes daily, to perform the basic ritual of buying food. It's different from shopping. You never see a housewife in Spain with a shopping list. People don't decide what to cook, then buy the ingredients. Here, buying food is an assessment of what is in season, of what is worth buying, and what can be afforded — and only after consultation with the produce sellers is a menu decided upon.

The Santiago market in the Plaza de Abastos is a modern Franco-era building. It's made from concrete with vaulted ceilings and finished in local granite, which makes it feel like a cathedral to food. This is no coincidence: the architect understood the Galician's relationship with produce and made a monumental — no, almost mausoleum-like — edifice in which the people of Santiago could shop daily. It sits well with the Galician sentimental demeanor.

Despite this, it is a lively place. Outside, under cover, there are women who sell great slabs of their rich cakes; despite years of access to Asturian butter, they still make them with lard. In season, some women sell *grelos* — turnip greens, which are used to make the local specialty *lacón con grelos*, or salted ham with turnip greens.

The fresh cheeses, the Galician veal, the piles of shellfish, cakes and fruit are all truly wonderful and delicious. This market, like those across Spain, are part of a family's everyday life. So well worn are the paths between the front door of the family home to the gates of the market that it is almost part of the home. Mostly women, but some men, congregate not just to shop but to talk, drink coffee and assess the state of the world in the seas, fields and orchards outside the city by casting their eyes across the daily produce.

VISITING A SPANISH FISH MARKET CAN BE LIKE VISITING A PARALLEL UNIVERSE. THE FISH AND SEA CREATURES ALL LOOK STRANGELY FAMILIAR BUT ALL SLIGHTLY DIFFERENT. THERE ARE *DORADA*, WHICH ARE SIMILAR TO OUR BREAM, AND *PARGO*, WHICH AS FAR AS I CAN WORK OUT ARE SNAPPER. THERE ARE THE WILDLY SOUGHT-AFTER *MERLUZA* (HAKE). THEN THERE'S *BACALAO FRESCO*, OR FRESH COD: SWEET, FIRM-FLESHED WHITE FISH. WE'RE USING BLACK COD OR HALIBUT HERE TO MAKE THIS SIMPLE BUT LIVELY ROASTED FISH DISH. IT'S STARTED OFF IN AN EXTREMELY HOT PAN OR FLAT GRILL, FINISHED IN A MODERATE OVEN AND DRESSED WITH *AJADA* — A HOT OIL FLAVORED WITH GARLIC AND CHILE.

BACALAO FRESCO EN REFRITO

ROAST COD WITH A HOT GARLIC AND CHILE DRESSING

4 RACIONES

2 tablespoons extra virgin olive oil

2 2/3 lb skinless black cod or halibut fillets, each cut into 2 pieces

AJADA

2/3 cup extra virgin olive oil

6 garlic cloves, sliced

2 medium-size semi-hot red chiles, halved, seeded and thinly sliced

2 tablespoons finely chopped parsley

Preheat the oven to 350°F.

Heat the olive oil in a large, heavy-bottomed ovenproof frying pan over high heat. Add the fish pieces, season well and cook for 6 minutes on each side. Transfer to the oven, then bake for 6 to 8 minutes, or until just cooked through.

Meanwhile, to make the *ajada*: heat the olive oil in a small heavy-bottomed frying pan over medium-low heat. Add the garlic and shake the pan for I minute, or until the garlic is golden but not burnt. Add the chiles and stir for 30 seconds, then stir in the parsley and remove from the heat.

Place the cooked fish fillets on warm plates, spoon the *ajada* over and serve immediately.

THE SPANISH DO EAT PASTA — A LITTLE-KNOWN FACT, BUT TRUE NONETHELESS. INDEED THE SPANISH EAT VERY GOOD PASTA DISHES, WHICH GENERALLY FEATURE SHORT LENGTHS OF PASTA CALLED *FIDEOS* AND WHICH ARE USUALLY USED IN A SOUP, STEW, OR A PASTA DISH COOKED LIKE A PAELLA. THE SPANISH ALSO EAT SOME APPALLING PASTA DISHES — I KNOW BECAUSE I HAVE COOKED THEM! WHEN I WAS WORKING IN BIESCA ONE SUMMER, THERE WERE A FEW ITALIAN PASTA DISHES ON THE MENU, AND I SENT THEM OUT FOR STAFF MEALS DONE *AL DENTE*. I WAS TOLD NEVER TO UNDERCOOK PASTA AGAIN AND TO ENSURE THE PASTA WAS ALWAYS NICE AND SOFT. SO DON'T ORDER ITALIAN PASTA IN SPAIN; ORDER INSTEAD THE *FIDEOS*. THIS GALICIAN VERSION HAS A BASE OF WELL-COOKED BELL PEPPER TO WHICH FISH STOCK IS ADDED. THE PASTA SOAKS UP THE RICH FLAVOR OF THE FISH WITH WHICH IT IS COOKED.

FIDEOS

PASTA WITH FISH AND PEPPERS

6 RACIONES

3 tablespoons extra virgin olive oil

1 small yellow onion, finely diced

a pinch of saffron threads

3 bay leaves

4 garlic cloves, finely chopped

½ small green bell pepper, seeded and ribs removed, finely diced

½ small red bell pepper, seeded and ribs removed, finely diced

3 tomatoes, peeled, seeded (see glossary) and finely chopped

1⅓ cups dry white wine

10½ oz *fideos* (see glossary)

6 cups fish stock

1 teaspoon fine sea salt

12 oz Spanish mackerel fillets

1 lb clams, rinsed

Heat the olive oil in a large heavy-bottomed saucepan over high heat until very hot. Add the onion and sauté for 2 to 3 minutes, or until it begins to brown. Stir in a pinch of salt and reduce the heat to medium. Add the saffron and bay leaves and sauté for 5 minutes, then add the garlic and cook for another 5 minutes.

Add all the bell peppers and sauté for 10 minutes, then add the tomatoes and cook for another 20 minutes, or until reduced and thickened.

Increase the heat to high, stir in the wine and simmer for 2 to 3 minutes. Reduce the heat to medium, then stir in the *fideos*, stock and sea salt and bring to a simmer. Add the mackerel fillets and return to a simmer again.

Add the clams, then cover and cook for 10 to 12 minutes, or until the pasta is *al dente*. Serve immediately.

I ONCE MET A GALICIAN LADY WHO SHARED WITH ME HER RECIPE FOR LAMB. HER *OWN* LAMB — LAMBS SHE RAISED WITH OTHER ANIMALS ON HER FARM IN THE HILLS ABOVE THE COAST. HER ANIMALS WERE A COMFORT AS HER FAMILY HAD LEFT THE VILLAGE TO WORK IN OTHER CITIES AROUND SPAIN. WHEN THEY RETURNED AT EASTER, SHE WOULD ROAST A LAMB FOR THEM. I COULD TELL IT WAS A LITTLE TRAUMATIC FOR HER TO DISPATCH HER BABY LAMBS TO CELEBRATE THE RETURN OF HER PRODIGAL FAMILY. NONETHELESS, SHE NEVER BALKED FROM THE TASK. SHE ONLY SPOKE GALICIAN AND FOR ME IT WAS A BIT LIKE A LONDONER TRYING TO UNDERSTAND AN OLD PERSON FROM ABERDEEN WHO ONLY SPOKE DORIC SCOTS. "EXCUSE MY BRUTAL TONGUE," IS THE DIRECT TRANSLATION. "I COOK MY LAMB WITH COGNAC, AND A FEW HERBS, AND THAT'S ABOUT IT." HER RECIPE PROVED VERY GOOD.

CORDERO CON COGNAC
ROAST LAMB WITH COGNAC

6 RACIONES

9 lb lamb forequarter
1 garlic bulb
2 yellow onions, thickly sliced
2 tablespoons thyme
$1/3$ cup white wine
10 fl oz Cognac
$1/3$ cup olive oil
1 teaspoon fine sea salt
$1/2$ teaspoon freshly ground
   black pepper

Using a sharp pointed knife, separate the lamb leg from the shoulder, dividing the lamb into two pieces. Place them both in a large bowl. Break the garlic bulb into cloves and bruise the cloves with the flat side of a large knife. Add to the lamb with the onions, thyme, wine and Cognac and combine well. Cover and refrigerate overnight.

Preheat the oven to 425°F.

Remove the onion slices and garlic cloves from the marinade, spread them over the base of a large roasting pan and pour in the marinating liquid. Place the lamb portions over the onion slices, then drizzle with the olive oil and sprinkle with the salt and black pepper.

Place the roasting pan on the middle rack of the oven and roast for 30 minutes, without opening the oven door. Reduce the oven temperature to 300°F, baste the lamb well with the pan juices and roast for another 3 hours, basting every 30 minutes or so, and adding a little water as needed to stop the base of the roasting pan from drying out. The lamb should be done (the meat will come away from the bone when pressed), but depending on the age and breed, it may require extra cooking.

Remove from the oven and allow to rest for 15 minutes. Serve with seasonal vegetables and perhaps a glass of *mencia*, a light Spanish red wine popular in Galicia.

LA MATRIARCA

THE MATRIARCH – HERMINDA

Herminda Buezas Oubiña doesn't have delicate hands to say the least. They are strong and skilled from years of hard work. She is also one of the best home cooks I have ever met. Her tortilla is stunning. It is made with eggs from the chickens that scratch about her garden in which she grows her onions and potatoes. With their eggs, she cooks her tortilla until it is just set, with a dark golden liquid custard of egg yolks.

Her recipes are no more elaborate than "take your potatoes and onion, cook them in oil until soft, add salt, then mix them with eggs and fry the tortilla on one side and then the other." She offers no times, no weights or measures, no temperatures. She has never used these: everything she makes she measures in her hands.

Herminda is an instinctive cook. She learned by standing next to her grandmother and mother. The muscles in her arms have memorized the moves to clean mussels, to find the bones with her knife when preparing fish and to make dough from home-grown corn. Her nose can detect when the fruit in her orchard is ripe and when the pastries in her oven are ready. She knows when the potatoes and onions for her tortilla are cooked by the feel of the knife going in. She knows the bread dough is worked enough by its touch, whether there is enough salt in her sausages by the feel of the meat and when everyone has had enough to eat by the tone of the conversation.

Herminda is typical of the women in Spain who cook their traditional foods. You couldn't call her passionate about preserving the culture, nor stubbornly resistant to change. She simply knows that to make food with the flavor she recognizes, she has to use the ingredients and methods she was brought up with, and this means growing everything herself and making recipes in the way she was taught.

Across the nation, there are thousands of women like Herminda. Combined, they are a national treasure. Thankfully, they are respected by their families and countrymen for the quality of food they make. They're also respected by professional chefs, who make what some would call pilgrimages to the countryside to learn more from these women. They work together to not only collate recipes but to invigorate lively national debate about what Spanish cuisine is and what it should be.

Herminda lost her husband some years back. She takes great care and pride in feeding the vineyard workers during vintage. She will sit among the young men and take immense pleasure in watching them eat her food. I watched her grab them by the thighs and say, "Eat, eat, this is good food." This wasn't an invitation, it was an instruction. The workers have deep respect, not just for her food but for the amount of effort and love this now ageing woman has given to them. She expresses her affection through her food, and for this she is deeply loved.

IT WAS VINTAGE TIME IN THE O SALNÉS VALLEY AND I WAS VISITING A FRIEND WHO MAKES *ALBARIÑO* IN THE LITTLE TOWN OF RIBADUMIA. THE HARVEST WAS WELL UNDERWAY AND HE WAS HIGH-SPEED ORGANIZING THE COLLECTION OF GRAPES FROM SCORES OF TINY VINEYARDS ACROSS THE VILLAGE, SOME NO BIGGER THAN A BACKYARD. I WAS INVITED FOR LUNCH WITH THE GRAPE PICKERS. THEY WERE ALREADY EATING FROM A RICKETY CARD TABLE SET UP UNDER THE VINES. THE YOUNG MEN WERE DRINKING *VINO TINTO* FROM CERAMIC BOWLS — HOME-MADE RED WINE THAT WAS THICK AND TANNIC. UNDER A CLOTH WAS WHAT THEY CALLED AN *EMPANADA*, BUT YOU AND I MIGHT CALL A SLICE OF PIE. IT WAS MADE WITH POLENTA AND STUFFED WITH TINY SCALLOPS AND A *SOFRITO* OF ONIONS AND GREEN BELL PEPPERS. IT WAS AMAZING. I ASKED HERMINDA, THE ELDERLY LADY WHO MADE THE CORN *EMPANADA*, FOR HER RECIPE. SHE LOOKED AT ME QUIZZICALLY, THEN REPLIED: "IT IS EASY. FIRST YOU PLANT YOUR CORN, THEN YOU HARVEST IT, THEN YOU GRIND IT, MAKE A DOUGH, PUT IN THE FILLING, ADD SOME MORE WOOD TO THE OVEN AND COOK IT. SIMPLE." HERE IS A MODERN VERSION OF HER RECIPE. IN TRUE GALICIAN STYLE, YOU COULD ALSO USE MARKET-FRESH CLAMS, SARDINES OR SHRIMP.

EMPANADA DE VIEIRAS

HERMINDA'S CORN PIE WITH BABY SCALLOPS

10 MEDIAS RACIONES

1/3 cup extra virgin olive oil

2 leeks, white part only, trimmed and halved lengthways, then thinly sliced

6 garlic cloves, thinly sliced

3 bay leaves

1 green bell pepper, seeded and ribs removed, finely diced

sea salt

1 lb scallops, diced

1 1/2 tablespoons cornstarch (see glossary)

1 1/3 cups *alboriño* or other aromatic white wine

a small handful of chopped parsley

1 egg, lightly beaten

Heat the olive oil in a large heavy-bottomed saucepan over medium-high heat. Add the leeks and sauté for 5 minutes, or until they begin to brown. Add the garlic, bay leaves, bell pepper and a pinch of salt, then reduce the heat to medium-low and cook, stirring regularly, for 15 minutes, or until the pepper is soft.

Stir in the scallops and cook for 5 minutes. Sprinkle with the cornstarch, stir together well and cook for 2 to 3 minutes. Increase the heat to high, pour in the wine and let it bubble for a few minutes, then add 1 1/4 cups water and bring to a simmer. Reduce the heat to medium and cook for another 40 minutes, or until you have a rich, thick ragù. Stir in the parsley, check the seasoning, then remove from the heat and let cool.

Meanwhile, make the pastry. Bring 2 cups water just to a boil. Place all of the dry ingredients in a large bowl, then add the olive oil and the just-boiled water and, using a wooden spoon, stir until a rough dough forms. The dough should be very dry and feel like it isn't coming together, and some flour may remain unincorporated. Place the dough in a lightly oiled bowl, then cover and let stand in a warm place for 30 minutes.

Preheat the oven to 350°F. Lightly brush a 7 x 10 inch earthenware dish or baking sheet with olive oil. Roll out half the pastry on a well-floured surface into a rectangle $^1/_{16}$ inch thick, roughly the same size as the baking sheet. The dough will break up as you roll it out, but don't worry — it's meant to be a rustic dough.

Lift up the dough, one piece at a time, and place on the baking sheet, pressing together any holes to cover the base.

Spread the cooled filling over the pastry. Roll out the remaining pastry to $^1/_{16}$ inch thick, then place it, one piece at a time, over the filling, in slightly overlapping layers. Press down gently with your fingers to press the dough onto the filling. Brush the top with the beaten egg and drizzle with a little more olive oil. Bake for 30 minutes, or until the crust is golden and cracked like a parched riverbed. Serve warm or at room temperature.

PASTRY

I cup all-purpose flour

I $^7/_8$ cups extra-fine instant yellow polenta

$^2/_3$ cup coarse polenta

$^1/_4$ oz dried yeast

pinch of sea salt

$^1/_3$ cup extra virgin olive oil, plus extra, for brushing

IT WAS OFF-SEASON IN THE LITTLE FISHING TOWN OF CAMBADOS AND EVERY RESTAURANT MY CHEF PALS HAD RECOMMENDED WAS CLOSED. I WAS AFTER *ARROZ CON BOGAVANTE* — A MOIST RICE DISH WITH LOBSTER. THE GALICIANS, LIKE OTHER SPANIARDS, ALWAYS MAKE THE MOST OF AN EXPENSIVE INGREDIENT SUCH AS LOBSTER, AND IN THIS DISH, THEY USE EVERY SINGLE PART AND INTENSIFY THE FLAVOR BY FRYING THE SHELL WITH HERBS AND GARLIC TO MAKE A RICH STOCK. THE ONLY PLACE DOING ANYTHING MORE THAN BAR FOOD WAS THE PARADOR, THE LOCAL ARM OF THE STATE-OWNED LUXURY HOTEL CHAIN. I WAS THE ONLY PERSON IN THE DINING ROOM. WHEN THE WAITER, DRESSED IN WHITE SHIRT, TIE AND WAISTCOAT, DELIVERED THE GREAT PAN IN FRONT OF ME AND STARTED THE SILVER-SERVICE TREATMENTS, I FELT A MOMENT OF ABSURDITY. BUT THE *ARROZ CON BOGAVANTE* WAS GOOD. THE RICE HAD TAKEN ON THE FLAVOR OF THE SEAFOOD WITHOUT LOSING ITS OWN EARTHY IDENTITY, WHILE THE VEGETABLES AND HERBS SAT IN THE BACKGROUND. TWO LOBSTER TAILS HAD BEEN FINISHED IN THE OVEN AND WERE PERFECTLY DONE.

ARROZ CON BOGAVANTE

RICE WITH LOBSTER

4 RACIONES

I lobster (about I lb)
1/2 cup olive oil
I garlic bulb, halved, plus 3 cloves, roughly chopped
a few thyme sprigs
4 ripe tomatoes, peeled (see glossary) and puréed
2 cups white wine
sea salt
I yellow onion, diced
1 1/3 cups *bomba* or short-grain rice (see glossary)

Put the lobster to sleep by freezing for 30 minutes. Using a large sharp knife or cleaver, split the lobster in half lengthways. Reserve the coral. Remove the head and small legs, and keep the tail and large claws separate.

Heat 3 tablespoons of the olive oil in a large heavy-bottomed stockpot over high heat. Add the lobster heads and small legs, the halved garlic head and the thyme sprigs. Cook, stirring often, for 15 minutes. Add 1/2 cup of the tomato purée, half of the wine and 4 cups cold water. Bring to a boil, reduce the heat to low and simmer for 2 hours.

Meanwhile, cut the lobster tail in half lengthways and, using the back of a cleaver, lightly crack the claws. Heat the remaining olive oil in a *perol* (see glossary) or large ovenproof frying pan over high heat and cook the tail pieces and claws for 2 to 3 minutes, or until the shells change color, stirring frequently. Season to taste, then remove from the pan and set aside.

Reduce the heat to medium, add the onion and a pinch of salt to the pan and sauté for 5 to 6 minutes, or until soft. Add the chopped garlic cloves and sauté for another 2 minutes, then stir in the remaining tomato purée and simmer for 30 minutes. Add the remaining wine, bring to a boil, then reduce the heat and simmer for another 20 to 30 minutes, or until the sauce is thick and dark. Remove from the heat.

Preheat the oven to 350°F.

Strain the hot lobster stock through a fine sieve; add 4 cups to the tomato purée mixture (add some hot water if necessary to make up the amount). Bring to a boil over high heat, scatter with the rice and a good pinch of salt and stir. Reduce the heat to low and simmer for 10 minutes.

Add the tail and claws to the pan, transfer to the oven and bake for 10 to 15 minutes, or until the rice is *al dente*. Remove from the heat and allow to stand for a few minutes before serving.

WHEN I FIRST STARTED COOKING, I TOOK GREAT PRIDE IN MAKING CREPES: A SIMPLE WAY OF TURNING FLOUR, EGGS AND MILK INTO SOMETHING REALLY SPECIAL. IT'S A SIGN OF A GOOD COOK TO TURN OUT A GOOD CREPE EVERY TIME. WHEN I WAS COOKING IN BIESCAS IN THE PYRENEES, I WAS MAKING HUNDREDS A DAY, WITH FOUR OR FIVE PANS GOING AT ONCE. MY VERSION CALLED FOR 11 POUNDS OF FLOUR AND DIDN'T WORK OUT WELL WHEN MADE FOR SMALLER BATCHES. THIS CREPE RECIPE (SEE PHOTO ON PAGE 180) IS BASED ON A VERSION BY ONE OF AUSTRALIA'S GREAT CHEFS, STEPHANIE ALEXANDER, WHO GLADLY ALLOWED US TO SHARE HER RECIPE.

I HAD SOME CREPES SERVED LIKE THIS IN A ROADSIDE TRUCK-STOP CAFE ON THE MAIN HIGHWAY BETWEEN GALICIA AND PORTUGAL. IMAGINE EATING THESE LIGHT CREPES FILLED WITH SOFT APPLE ON A COLD GALICIAN NIGHT WHEN THE RAIN IS POUNDING DOWN, THE FIRE IS SLOWLY BURNING AND THERE'S A LITTLE GLASS OF *ORUJO* — DISTILLED SPIRITS MADE FROM *ALBARIÑO* — WAITING WHEN YOU'RE FINISHED.

FILLOAS
CREPES WITH APPLE COMPOTE

SERVES 6

2 cups all-purpose flour

sea salt

4 1/2 tablespoons unsalted butter,
   plus extra, for frying

3 eggs

1 1/2 cups milk

1 quantity of warm apple compote
   (see recipe on page 104)

confectioners' sugar, to dust

14 oz chestnuts in syrup
   (see recipe on page 181)

Sift the flour and a pinch of salt into a bowl. Melt the butter in a small frying pan over medium heat. Allow it to froth up and just as it starts to brown, remove the pan from the heat. Pour the butter over the flour and mix well using a wooden spoon.

Beat the eggs and milk together, then add to the flour and whisk until a smooth batter forms. It should have the consistency of whipping cream. If the batter is a bit too thick, add a little more milk. Strain the batter through a fine sieve, then cover and refrigerate for 2 hours.

Heat a 10-inch nonstick frying pan over medium heat. Add 1 teaspoon of extra butter and tilt the pan to coat the base. As soon as the butter begins to bubble, pour in just under 1/3 cup of the batter and tilt the pan to cover the base evenly. Cook for 1 to 2 minutes, or until the crepe is lightly browned underneath and the edges have begun to curl up. Flip the crepe and cook for another minute or until lightly browned, then stack on a warm plate and cover while you repeat with the remaining batter.

To serve, place two tablespoons of the warm apple compote on one quarter of each crepe. Fold in half to make a semicircle, then fold in half again. Dust the crepes with confectioners' sugar, then finish with the chestnuts and a little of the syrup. Serve warm.

HOW DO YOU MAKE A GREAT DESSERT WHEN YOU HAVE VIRTUALLY NOTHING? YOU LOOK AROUND AND DEEP-FRY THE ONLY INGREDIENTS YOU HAVE AND THEN COAT THEM IN SUGAR. YOUNG LEMON LEAVES — LARGE AND JUST BEGINNING TO FILL WITH THE ESSENTIAL CITRUS OILS — ARE PERFECT FOR THIS DISH. GO TO YOUR NEAREST LEMON TREE, CUT OFF A DOZEN OF THE FINEST LEAVES — INCLUDING A LITTLE OF THE LEAF STEM — THEN DIP THEM IN SOME BATTER AND DEEP-FRY. AS THE LEAF HEATS UP, IT IMPARTS ITS OILS INTO THE BATTER. YOU REMOVE THE LEAF AND EAT THE TWO GOLDEN SHELLS LEFT ON EITHER SIDE. FUNNILY ENOUGH, THESE LEAVES ARE COOKED IN OLIVE OIL, DESPITE THE ALMOST COMPLETE LACK OF OLIVE TREES IN GALICIA. NEVERTHELESS, THIS DISH IS SOMEHOW STILL A LOCAL FAVORITE.

PAPARAJOTES
LEMON LEAVES IN BATTER

SERVES 12

- 1 cup all-purpose flour
- sea salt
- zest of 2 lemons
- 1 cup soda water
- olive oil, for deep-frying
- 12 large young lemon leaves
- superfine sugar, to dust

Sift the flour and a pinch of salt into a bowl. Add the lemon zest and whisk in the soda water until a smooth batter forms.

Fill a deep fryer or large heavy-bottomed saucepan one-third full of oil and heat to 350°F, or until a cube of bread dropped into the oil browns in 15 seconds.

Take each lemon leaf and gently rub it between your hands to start releasing the oil. Working in batches, dip the leaves into the soda batter, allowing the excess to drain off. Deep-fry the leaves for 1 ½ minutes, or until golden. Drain on a paper towel, dust with sugar and serve immediately.

CANUTILLOS

GALICIAN PASTRIES FILLED WITH ORUJO CREAM

12 PASTRIES

2 eggs

2 egg yolks

1/2 cup Pedro Ximénez sherry

2 1/4 cups all-purpose flour, sifted

5 tablespoons unsalted butter,
  softened

Using an electric mixer, whisk one egg, both egg yolks and the sherry for 15 minutes, or until the mixture is frothy and doubled in volume. Add the flour and butter and mix until a sticky dough forms. Turn out onto a lightly floured surface and shape into a ball, then place in a bowl, cover with plastic wrap and refrigerate for 1 hour.

Meanwhile, to make the custard filling: place the milk and cinnamon sticks in a heavy-bottomed saucepan and bring to just below a boil. Reduce the heat to low and simmer for 5 minutes, then remove from the heat and discard the cinnamon sticks.

Whisk the sugar and egg yolks in a heatproof bowl until thick and pale. Add the cornstarch and combine well. When the milk has cooled down enough that it won't curdle the eggs, gradually whisk it into the egg mixture, then add the *orujo* and combine well.

Return the mixture to the saucepan and, whisking constantly, cook over medium heat for 10 to 12 minutes, or until thickened. Remove from the heat, pour into a bowl and cover closely with a round of parchment paper to prevent a skin forming. Allow to cool, then refrigerate for 3 hours.

Roll out the pastry on a lightly floured surface into a log about 2 inches in diameter. Slice off discs 1/2 inch thick, then roll each disc on a well-floured surface into rounds 1/16 inch thick and cover with a clean cloth. Lightly beat the remaining egg.

Fill a deep fryer or large heavy-bottomed saucepan one-third full of oil and heat to 350ºF, or until a cube of bread dropped into the oil browns in 15 seconds. Working with one at a time and leaving the other pastry rounds covered while you work, wrap one pastry circle around a lightly greased metal cannoli tube, brush the edges lightly with the beaten egg, then press the edges together to seal well.

Deep-fry the pastry for 1½ minutes, or until golden. Remove from the oil, slide the pastry off the tube into the oil and deep-fry for another 30 seconds, or until the inside is dry and crisp. Using tongs, remove from the oil and drain on a paper towel. Repeat with the remaining pastry rounds and let stand until cool.

Spoon the cooled custard into a pastry bag fitted with a ⅝-inch tip and fill the cooled pastry shells. Dust with confectioners' sugar and serve immediately.

CUSTARD FILLING

4 cups milk

2 cinnamon sticks

⅞ cup superfine sugar

6 egg yolks

½ cup cornstarch (see glossary)

2½ tablespoons *orujo* or grappa

olive oil, for deep-frying

confectioners' sugar, to dust

EUSKAL SUKALDARITZA

THE BASQUE KITCHEN

★ ★ ★

IT WAS WINTER A FEW YEARS AGO WHEN I STEPPED OFF THE TRAIN INTO THE TOWN SQUARE OF SAN SEBASTIÁN, WHICH WAS VIBRANT AND RAUCOUS WITH THE SOMEWHAT BIZARRE *LA TAMBORRADA* FESTIVAL. THE SQUARE WAS FILLED WITH MEN AND CHILDREN DRESSED AS BAKERS DRUMMING OUT A CACOPHONY ON HUNDREDS OF DISCORDANT DRUMS. THE DRUMMING WENT ON DAY AND NIGHT AND THE NEXT DAY. THE ADDITION OF MEN DRESSED AS FRENCH SOLDIERS REALLY CONFUSED ME. BUT I WAS TOLD THAT IF I FOUND *LA TAMBORRADA* BEWILDERING, THEN I'D BE BLOWN AWAY BY *EL ENTIERRO DE LA SARDINA* — A FESTIVAL WHERE MEN DRESSED AS 19TH-CENTURY WIDOWS CELEBRATE THE BEGINNING OF LENT BY PARADING AROUND TOWN WITH AN ANCHOVY IN A COFFIN.

San Sebastián is perhaps one of the most beautiful cities on Earth. It is quite small as far as cities go and looks as if the grand apartments of Paris had been built on Bondi Beach. To the locals, San Sebastián is known as *Donostia* — the Basques speak a language called Euskera that predates the Romans, has little in common with any other tongue spoken anywhere else in the world, and sets the Basques apart from the rest of Europe. I have used Basque for the recipe titles.

The three million or so people in this little region live around the Bay of Biscay and the hills and valleys of the hinterland and Navarra in the Ebro Valley. Many Basques feel fiercely independent and still resent the special treatment they received under dictator Francisco Franco, who violently oppressed their distinct culture, including some of their festivals based around food and drink. The Basques, however, are irrepressible. Instead of turning their backs on Spain and the rest of the world, Basque chefs have embraced techniques and ingredients from around Spain and across the border from France, and have used these to enhance their unique local cuisine.

They appear to me to be like the Asterix of Spain, an amazing little part of Europe that has somehow survived the Romans, the Moors, the Visigoths, Fascism and now fast food.

Today, the Basque Country is one of the culinary hot spots of Europe. The Basque Country — both in Spain and across the border into Basque-speaking France — has a disproportionate number of Michelin-starred restaurants for the size of its population. Many of its restaurants are recognized around the world, and any self-respecting food-obsessed tourist cannot consider a journey to Spain complete without having made the pilgrimage to the Basque Country restaurants.

And this is why we came. Not to have linen napkins laid across our laps and to drink from fine glassware — which we did a fair bit of — but to tease out from some of their best restaurants the underlying principles of Basque food.

More than anybody else in Spain, the Basques obsess with the provenance of food. From the top chefs to the engaged home cook, the people have a knowledge of their country and what it can grow that is probably comparable only to the indigenous peoples of Earth. I once visited a market gardener who had a small, flat patch of soil in the hills above the coast. "Being so close to the sea, our food has *yodo*," he said. "I am sorry, I don't know this word in English," he added. For a few days, I thought there was a strange unseen force called *yodo* that drew the best chefs in the Basque Country to buy his amazingly good leafy greens and herbs. *Yodo, yodo*.

It wasn't until I looked up *yodo* in a dictionary that I finally discovered *yodo* is in fact Spanish for iodine. This iodine blows in on the sea mist and settles on the leaves and soil. It was not a word bandied about in my home as I was growing up, yet a term familiar to the Basques who appreciate the minutiae of where their food comes from and how it is grown.

Picasso's *Guernica* is a painting of rage against the violence meted out to the civilians of the Basque town of the same name. Franco called in Hitler's Luftwaffe to crush the spirit of the people. He forbade them to speak Basque in public, to give their children Basque names and to practice their festivals. But food, unlike language or literature, could not be banned, and through the Franco era, Basque cooking not only sustained the bodies and souls of the Basques but also became a tacit form of defiance and a source of stability. Within their homes, in their kitchens and around their dining tables, the Basques could be themselves and celebrate who they were. With Franco's death and the global recognition of Basque cuisine, their food has become a source of immense pride.

"Basques don't like mixing things up on their plates," observed a New Yorker who had moved to San Sebastián to marry a local man. She described how although a dish may be constituted of many ingredients, it would still be the one dish and be presented on the plate by itself. "They hate having sauces mingle with things that don't normally go with it," she said. So true.

Perhaps the underlying theme in Basque food is the technique of layering. Basques view cooking as a series of time-honored techniques and stages that must be mastered and perfected at each point for the dish to work. For the *txangurro* — baked stuffed crab — for example, the carrot and the leek must be sliced in such a way that when they are cooked, they complement the texture of the crabmeat. The shell is baked to make a bisque, which is then used to make a sauce americaine; the coral is blended back in to enrich the sauce.

Despite the air of European chic in its big cities, the Basques are a nation of fishermen and farmers at heart who appreciate simple food — *excellent* simple food. Here are the dishes that lie at the foundations of their cooking.

THEY SAY ONE MAN'S TRASH IS ANOTHER MAN'S TREASURE. EVEN THOUGH THERE ARE REGULAR FERRIES BETWEEN THE SOUTH OF ENGLAND AND BILBAO, IT WAS FUNNY SEEING CRABS IN THE SAN SEBASTIÁN MARKET THAT WERE CAUGHT IN ENGLAND. WHILE THE ENGLISH ADORE DOVER SOLE, COD AND SCAMPI, THEY DON'T SEEM TO SHARE THE BASQUES' LOVE OF CRABS. THIS IS A CLASSIC DISH — A WHOLE CRAB STUFFED WITH ITS OWN FLESH, ENRICHED IN A SAUCE AMERICAINE, COVERED WITH BREADCRUMBS AND GRATINÉED. SOUNDS FRENCH, BUT THIS IS A TRUE BASQUE CLASSIC.

TXANGURROA LABEAN
BAKED STUFFED CRAB

6 MEDIAS RACIONES

$2/3$ cup extra virgin olive oil, plus extra, to drizzle

I carrot, cut into fine julienne strips

I leek, white part only, cut into fine julienne strips

4 garlic cloves, finely chopped, plus I garlic bulb, halved

8 bay leaves

sea salt

6 tomatoes, peeled, seeded (see glossary) and chopped

6 live blue Dungeness crabs

one 14-oz can chopped tomatoes

$1^{1/3}$ cups brandy

a handful of parsley, stalks reserved and leaves finely chopped

3 cups fine breadcrumbs

Heat $1/3$ cup of the olive oil in a heavy-bottomed saucepan over medium-low heat. Add the carrot, leek, chopped garlic cloves and half of the bay leaves and sauté for 15 minutes, or until the vegetables are lightly browned. Season with a pinch of salt, then add the fresh tomatoes and cook for another 30 minutes, or until they have reduced down to a thick pulp. Remove from the heat and set aside.

Meanwhile, place the crabs in the freezer for 30 minutes to send them to sleep, then drop them into a large saucepan of boiling salted water and cook for 5 minutes. Drain and allow to cool. Pick out the meat from the legs, then carefully lift off the top shells in one piece and scoop out and reserve the brown coral. Pick out any meat from the head, then place all the meat, coral and any juices in a bowl, cover and refrigerate. Rinse the top shells well and set aside.

Place the bottom shells in a large saucepan with the remaining olive oil, the halved garlic head and a pinch of salt. Stir over very high heat, crushing the shells as you go, for 15 minutes. Add the canned tomatoes and cook for another 5 minutes, then stir in the brandy and bring to a boil. Add $1^{1/4}$ cups water, the remaining bay leaves and the parsley stalks. Season to taste, reduce the heat to low and simmer for 30 minutes, or until the liquid has reduced by half.

Strain the crab stock through a fine sieve, then add the stock to the carrot and leek mixture along with the crab meat, juices and coral. Combine well and cook over high heat for 15 minutes, or until the mixture is quite thick. Stir in the chopped parsley and check the seasoning.

Preheat the oven to 350°F.

Place the cleaned dried crab shells on a baking sheet and divide the crab mixture among the shells. Sprinkle with the breadcrumbs, drizzle with a little olive oil, then bake for 6 to 8 minutes, or until the crumbs are golden. Serve immediately.

THE THINGS YOU DO FOR RESEARCH . . . A CHEF TOLD ME ABOUT ONE OF HIS FAVORITE BARS IN A FISHING TOWN WHERE THE CHEF MAKES AN ASTOUNDING FISH SOUP. IT WAS IN AN AREA WHERE BASQUE SEPARATIST FLAGS FLY AND THE BARS FILL WITH SMOKE AND MEN. MY BUSINESS PARTNER AND I FOUND THE PLACE AND ORDERED A BOWL OF SOUP BETWEEN US. MAY I JUST SAY THAT "REAL" BASQUE MEN DON'T SHARE SOUP. MAY I ALSO ADD THAT DISPARAGEMENT HAS A TONE THAT CAN BE UNDERSTOOD NO MATTER WHAT THE LANGUAGE. STILL, IT WAS WORTH IT. THIS IS A RICH SOUP WITH A DEEP OCHRE HUE AND SMOOTH TEXTURE, WITH A FEW CLAMS ADDED AT THE LAST MINUTE. THIS COULD BE A SILVER-SERVICE DINNER PARTY STARTER OR JUST THE TICKET POURED INTO A TIN MUG FROM A THERMOS BY THE PIER ON A COLD DAY.

ARRAI SOPA
RICH FISH SOUP

SERVES 6

Preheat the oven to 350°F.

Place the fish heads and bones in a large roasting pan and the shrimp heads and shells in another. Season and drizzle 3 tablespoons olive oil into each pan. Bake for 15 to 20 minutes, or until the fish bones are lightly browned and the shrimp shells are pink. Place the heads, bones and shells in a large heavy-bottomed saucepan.

Pour 1/2 cup water into each roasting pan, scrape the base to remove any cooked-on bits, then pour the liquid from each pan into the saucepan. Add the halved garlic head, bay leaves, parsley stems, peppercorns, fresh tomatoes, a pinch of salt and another 3 tablespoons of the olive oil. Add enough cold water to cover, then bring to a boil over high heat. Reduce the heat to low and simmer for 1 hour, skimming the surface regularly. Strain through a fine sieve and discard the solids.

Meanwhile, heat the remaining olive oil in a large heavy-bottomed stockpot over high heat, then add the onion and sauté for 5 to 6 minutes, or until golden. Reduce the heat to medium-high, season to taste, then add the carrots, leeks, sliced garlic cloves and the chopped parsley. Season again and cook for 15 minutes, or until the onion and leeks are tender.

Increase the heat to high, stir in the wine and brandy and cook for 2 to 3 minutes to evaporate the alcohol. Reduce the heat to medium again, simmer for 5 minutes, then add the puréed canned tomatoes and simmer for 30 minutes, or until the tomatoes have cooked down to a pulp.

Add the fish fillets and shrimp to the tomato mixture and simmer for 30 minutes. Add 8 cups of the hot fish stock and simmer for another 15 minutes. Remove from the heat, allow to cool a little, then process the soup in a blender or food processor until a smooth purée forms. Check the seasoning and keep warm.

Put the clams and 2 tablespoons water in a small heavy-bottomed pan. Cover and cook over high heat, shaking the pan, for 3 to 4 minutes, or just until the shells open. Drain the clams and remove the meat from the shells.

Pour the soup into warmed bowls, scatter with the clams and drizzle with a little olive oil. Serve immediately.

Ingredients

4 lb heads and bones of white fish such as snapper or whiting

2 lb raw shrimp, peeled and deveined, leaving the tails intact and reserving the heads and shells

1 cup extra virgin olive oil, plus extra, to drizzle

1 garlic head, halved, plus 5 garlic cloves, thinly sliced

4 bay leaves

a handful of parsley, stems reserved and leaves roughly chopped

10 black peppercorns

4 tomatoes, roughly chopped

sea salt

1 yellow onion, finely sliced

3 carrots, diced

2 leeks, white part only, finely sliced

1 cup white wine

1/2 cup brandy

two 14-oz cans chopped tomatoes, puréed

2 lb fillet of skinless black cod or halibut, cut into large chunks

1 lb clams, rinsed

THE CHEF MADE HIS INDEX FINGERS INTO LITTLE HOOK SHAPES AND JERKED ONE UP AND DOWN, THEN THE OTHER. "THIS IS HOW THE OLD MEN CATCH THE BABY SQUID," HE SAID. "THEY TEASE THEM TO THEIR BAIT. THEY BRING ME PERHAPS HALF A DOZEN. BUT THEY ARE ALWAYS SO SMALL AND BEAUTIFUL." THE OLD MEN WHO BROUGHT HIM THEIR CATCH WERE TRULY OLD — RETIRED FISHERMEN TOO FRAIL TO GO TO SEA AND TOO WEDDED TO THE WATER TO LEAVE IT. THEY SPENT THEIR DAYS SITTING ON THE WHARVES AND BREAKWATERS WATCHING THE FISHING FLEET COME AND GO. CATCHING FISH WASN'T A RETIREMENT HOBBY, IT WAS THEIR LIFE. IN THE HANDS OF A BASQUE CHEF, THEIR LITTLE SQUID ARE LIFTED TO ANOTHER LEVEL — VERY QUICKLY SIZZLED AND SERVED ALONGSIDE A SLOW-COOKED ONION CONFIT.

PELAIO TXIPIROIAK
BABY SQUID IN ONION CONFIT

6 RACIONES

2 1/2 lb white onions, sliced

10 black peppercorns

4 bay leaves

3/4 cup extra virgin olive oil, plus extra, to drizzle

2 teaspoons sea salt, plus extra if needed

4 1/2 lb baby squid

5 garlic cloves

a handful of chopped parsley

2 1/2 tablespoons olive oil

Put the onions in a large heavy-bottomed saucepan. Add the peppercorns, bay leaves, 1/3 cup of the extra virgin olive oil and 1 teaspoon of the sea salt. Cover and cook over low heat, stirring regularly, for 2 hours, or until the onion confit has a jam-like consistency.

Meanwhile, to clean the squid, pull the tentacles out of the hoods and pull out the clear cartilage from the hoods. Peel off and discard the skin. Cut the tentacles off just below the eyes, then rinse the hoods and tentacles. Drain well and place in a bowl.

Place the garlic cloves on a cutting board, sprinkle with the remaining sea salt and finely chop. Add to the squid with most of the parsley (reserve some for serving) and the remaining extra virgin olive oil. Mix well, then cover and refrigerate for at least 1 hour.

When the onion confit is ready, heat the olive oil in a large heavy-bottomed frying pan over high heat until the oil is nearly smoking. Add the squid hoods and cook for 1 minute, then season to taste, turn and cook for another minute. Add the tentacles and cook for 30 seconds. Season to taste, turn the tentacles and hoods and cook for another 30 seconds, then remove from the pan.

Spoon the onion confit over warm serving plates. Stuff the squid tentacles back into the hoods and arrange them over the onion. Drizzle with extra virgin olive oil, sprinkle with the remaining parsley and serve hot.

IT HAD BEEN A COLD DAY IN BILBAO AND WE HAD DONE OUR BEST TO KEEP WARM BY WALKING THROUGH THE MARKETS. THE RIVERSIDE MARKET IS A MULTI-FLOORED AFFAIR AND REMINDED ME OF A SHOPPING CENTER THAT ONLY SELLS FOOD. FOR ME, THIS WAS HEAVEN. I WAS STRUCK BY THE QUALITY OF BOTH THE FISH — PARTICULARLY THE SHELLFISH AND SCAMPI, A TYPE OF VERY SMALL LOBSTER — AND THE CURED HAMS, WITH A FEW BAYONNE HAMS FROM ACROSS THE FRENCH BORDER. IMAGINE MY JOY WHEN WE FOUND A BAR THAT HAD SCAMPI TAILS THAT HAD BEEN WRAPPED IN HAM AND COOKED SLOWLY IN OIL. THEY WERE SERVED STILL WARM WITH A NICE LITTLE GUERNICA PEPPER AND A SLICE OF PRESERVED WHITE ASPARAGUS. ALTHOUGH YOU MIGHT NOT FIND GUERNICA PEPPERS, *GUINDILLAS* ARE NOW MORE WIDELY AVAILABLE. AND IF YOU CAN'T FIND SCAMPI, USE LARGE SHRIMP TAILS. I'VE ALSO USED PALM HEARTS, AVAILABLE FROM SPECIALTY FOOD SHOPS, BUT IF YOU CAN'T GET THEM, JUST USE ASPARAGUS.

ZIGALA

SCAMPI CONFIT

6 TAPAS / PINTXOS

6 raw scampi

sea salt

6 slices of *jamón*

2 cups olive oil

2 garlic cloves

2 palm hearts, cut into thirds

18 *guindillas* (see glossary)

½ teaspoon sweet smoked paprika

Peel the scampi and remove the alimentary canal (black vein). Season to taste, then wrap each scampi in a slice of *jamón* and secure with a toothpick.

Place the scampi, olive oil and garlic cloves in a heavy-bottomed saucepan that is small enough that the oil covers the scampi. Cook over medium heat until the temperature reaches 175ºF. Reduce the heat to low to maintain the heat at 175ºF and cook for 25 minutes. Remove the scampi, drain on a paper towel, then remove the toothpicks.

Thread a piece of palm heart, three *guindillas* and a warm scampi onto six new toothpicks. Sprinkle with the paprika and serve warm.

THERE'S A FASHION IN THE BASQUE COUNTRY THAT IS JUST CATCHING ON IN THE REST OF SPAIN, AND THAT IS THE UP-MARKET *PINTXOS* OR TAPAS BAR. SOMETIMES THESE PLACES ARE SECLUDED AND COOL WITH STAINLESS STEEL AND DIMLY LIT SPACES IN WHICH CHEFS SERVE UP DECONSTRUCTED CLASSICS AND A FEW INVENTIONS OF THEIR OWN. SOME ARE WONDERFULLY GOOD, OTHERS CAN BE A TOUCH "TRY-HARD" FOR MY TASTE. THIS RECIPE IS THE CLASSIC CHICKEN LIVER PÂTÉ PIPED INTO A MALSOUQUA PASTRY CONE AND DRIZZLED WITH A PEDRO XIMÉNEZ REDUCTION. SOME MAY FIND IT A LITTLE FUSSY TO PREPARE, BUT IT TASTES FABULOUS. THIS RECIPE CALLS FOR A GARNISH OF *KIKOS*, OR TOASTED CORN — A SNACK SOLD IN SPANISH FOOD STORES — BUT IT IS NOT ESSENTIAL TO THE DISH. YOU'LL FIND THE METAL CONES THAT ARE USED TO WRAP THE PASTRY AROUND FROM GOOD KITCHENWARE SHOPS.

KUKURUTXOA
CORNETS WITH CHICKEN LIVER PÂTÉ

12 TAPAS / PINTXOS

$^1/_3$ lb chicken livers, cleaned

$^1/_2$ small yellow onion, finely sliced

I teaspoon extra virgin olive oil

a pinch of thyme leaves

sea salt

I$^1/_2$ cups Pedro Ximénez sherry

$^1/_2$ cup superfine sugar

$^1/_4$ cup whipping cream

3 tablespoons butter, softened

I large sheet of *malsouqua* pastry (also called brik pastry), available from Middle Eastern delicatessens, or phyllo (see glossary)

I egg, lightly beaten

I cup toasted corn (*kikos*), finely ground

Preheat the oven to 300°F.

Place the chicken livers in a small baking dish with the onion, olive oil, thyme leaves and a pinch of salt. Mix together and bake, stirring occasionally, for 20 minutes, or until the chicken livers are cooked through but still a little pink in the middle. Remove from the oven and allow to cool slightly.

Meanwhile, place I$^1/_3$ cups of the sherry and all of the sugar in a small heavy-bottomed saucepan and stir over low heat until the sugar has dissolved. Bring to a boil, then reduce the heat to low and simmer for 20 to 30 minutes, or until reduced by one-third. Remove from the heat and let cool.

Place the cooled chicken liver mixture in a food processor. Add the cream, butter and the remaining sherry, season to taste and process until smooth. Push the mixture through a very fine sieve into a small bowl. Cover closely with plastic wrap and refrigerate for I hour, or until the mixture is cool but still soft enough to pipe.

Increase the oven temperature to 400°F.

Lay the pastry sheet on a work surface and cut into 12 even rectangles. Roll one pastry piece around a lightly oiled metal cone that is about 4 inches long and $^3/_4$ inch in diameter. Brush the edges with the beaten egg and place on a baking sheet lined with parchment paper. Repeat with the remaining pastry to make 12 cornets. Bake for 3 to 5 minutes, or until golden, then remove from the oven and leave to cool on wire racks.

To serve, carefully spoon or pipe the chicken liver mixture into the cones, sprinkle with the ground corn and drizzle with a little sherry syrup. Serve immediately.

THE WORD *PINTXOS* FILLS ME WITH BOTH DREAD AND JOY. *PINTXOS* ARE BASQUE TAPAS. IN THE BASQUE CITIES, THERE ARE BARS WHERE GREAT PLATES STACKED WITH SLICES OF BREAD TOPPED WITH BOILED FISH IN MAYONNAISE WAIT UNDER LIGHTS FOR TOURISTS TO EAT THEIR WAY THROUGH. THERE IS ONE WORD FOR THESE PARTICULAR *PINTXOS*, AND THAT IS "AVOID." INSTEAD, THE GREAT FOOD OF BASQUE BAR CULTURE NEEDS TO BE ORDERED OFF THE LITTLE CHALKBOARDS BEHIND THE BAR. THESE *PINTXOS* ARE GREAT LITTLE DISHES — SOMETIMES INCORPORATING A LITTLE BIT OF FRESHLY COOKED FISH, BUT ALWAYS FRESHLY MADE. IT WAS THIS TRADITION THAT INSPIRED THE BEST-SELLING TAPAS AT OUR MELBOURNE RESTAURANT. ANCHOVIES ARE BIG BUSINESS ON THE NORTHERN COASTLINE OF SPAIN AND THIS RECIPE COMBINES THEIR SALTINESS WITH A HIT OF TANGY, SMOKY TOMATO. ADMITTEDLY, SOME OF THE INGREDIENTS MAY BE HARD TO GET — BUT I PROMISED TO PUBLISH THE RECIPE!

ANTXOA TOMATE KETUA SORBETEAREKIN
ANCHOVIES WITH SMOKED TOMATO SORBET

12 TAPAS / PINTXOS

¼ loaf of two-day-old heavy
  sourdough bread
2 tablespoons fruity extra virgin olive
  oil, such as Arbequina or Hojiblanca,
  plus extra, to drizzle
sea salt
9 oz smoked tomatoes
⅓ cup corn syrup
12 perfect canned anchovies
3 teaspoons tiny Spanish capers
1 tablespoon finely chopped parsley

Preheat the oven to 350°F.

Using a very sharp bread knife, trim the crusts off the bread, then cut into a block 1 inch wide and 4 inches long. Cut the bread into the finest slices you can. This will make far too many, so choose the 12 best slices and place them flat on a baking sheet, brush generously with the olive oil and season to taste. Bake for 10 minutes, or until golden and crisp, then place on a wire rack to cool completely.

Purée the smoked tomatoes in a blender until completely smooth. Strain through a fine sieve into a bowl and measure how much liquid you have. Add this back to the blender with exactly half the amount in corn syrup, then process until smooth.

Place the mixture in an ice-cream maker and churn according to the manufacturer's instructions, then freeze for 3 to 4 hours.

To serve, place an anchovy on each crouton. Using two teaspoons, shape a little of the frozen tomato sorbet into quenelles (or small oval dumplings), place one on top of each anchovy and sprinkle with the capers. Drizzle with a little more oil, sprinkle with the parsley and some sea salt and serve immediately.

FERDINAND MAGELLAN'S NAVIGATOR WAS A BASQUE CALLED JUAN SEBASTIÁN ELKANO, WHO FINISHED MAGELLAN'S VOYAGE AROUND THE WORLD AFTER MAGELLAN WAS KILLED IN THE PHILIPPINES. THERE'S A STATUE OF ELKANO IN GETARIA, OVERLOOKING BOTH THE *PELOTA* (BASQUE HANDBALL) COURT AND THE SEAFOOD RESTAURANT NAMED AFTER HIM. IT'S NOT SURPRISING THAT THE BASQUES COULD SAIL AROUND THE WORLD: THEY HAD ALREADY BEEN FISHING FOR COD IN THE ATLANTIC OCEAN SINCE BEFORE THE NORMAN INVASION OF ENGLAND AND HAD DEVELOPED A CURING INDUSTRY AND TRADE ROUTES AROUND THE MEDITERRANEAN BY THE 12TH CENTURY. AND PERHAPS FOR THIS REASON ALONE, I CAN THANK THEM, BECAUSE DEEP-FRIED SALT COD IS AMAZING. THE SUCCULENT, TRANSLUCENT FLAKES OF FLESH ARE EMBRACED BY A THIN BATTER OF FLOUR, AND A SPRINKLING OF SALT ENHANCES THE JUICY SWEETNESS. THIS IS A RECIPE THAT EXTENDS THE FRIED SALT COD INTO A MEAL. AS SOON AS YOU HAVE A SAUCE, YOU HAVE A MEAL BECAUSE BREAD WILL BE USED TO MOP UP THE JUICES, MAKING IT AN INEXPENSIVE WAY OF FEEDING A FAMILY.

BAKAILAO FRIJITUA TOMATEAREKIN

FRIED SALT COD WITH TOMATO

6 RACIONES

1/3 cup olive oil, plus extra for
   deep-frying
I large yellow onion, sliced
3 garlic cloves, finely sliced
3 bay leaves
sea salt
three 14-oz cans chopped tomatoes
2 1/4 lb salt cod, soaked in cold water
   for 48 hours, changing the
   water four times
seasoned all-purpose flour, to coat
2 tablespoons chopped parsley

Heat the olive oil in a large heavy-bottomed saucepan over high heat. Add the onion and sauté for 5 minutes, or until browned. Reduce the heat to medium-high, then add the garlic, bay leaves and a pinch of salt and cook for 5 minutes.

Add the tomatoes, reduce the heat to medium-low, then cover and cook for 20 minutes. Add 7/8 cup water and cook for another 30 minutes, or until the raw tomato flavor has cooked out of the mixture. Remove from the heat and discard the bay leaves. Blend in a food processor until very smooth, then return to the pan.

Drain the salt cod, then trim off the fins, skin, brown patches and bones. Cut the flesh into strips measuring about 3/4 x 3 1/4 inches and pat dry with a paper towel.

Fill a deep fryer or large heavy-bottomed saucepan one-third full of oil and heat to 375°F, or until a cube of bread dropped in the oil browns in 10 seconds. Dust the cod pieces in the flour and deep-fry in small batches for 2 minutes, or until golden and crisp.

Warm the tomato purée over medium heat until heated through. Arrange the fried cod over the tomato purée, spoon a little of the sauce over the top, then scatter with the parsley and serve immediately.

IT WAS A SPRING AFTERNOON AND WE HEADED TO A RESTAURANT JUST OUT OF SAN SEBASTIÁN LOOKING OUT OVER THE BEACH. WE WERE AMONG WELL-DRESSED FAMILIES IN A ROOM FILLED WITH SOFT LIGHT. CHILDREN WITH WET COMBED HAIR SAT WITH THEIR PARENTS AND GRANDPARENTS. IT WAS VERY POLITE AND QUITE BEAUTIFUL. I WAS BROUGHT BACK TO MY SENSES, LITERALLY, BY THE SMELL OF A PLATE OF WHITE SQUID IN BLACK SAUCE PLACED IN FRONT OF ME. I COULD SMELL THE SEA, SWEET ONIONS, BAY LEAVES, GARLIC, COOKED WINE — SENSATIONAL. SOFT PIECES OF BRAISED SQUID SAT IN A RICH SAUCE OF ONIONS, WINE AND TOMATOES, TINTED BLACK WITH ITS INK. NOT AN UNUSUAL COMBINATION, BUT IT'S THE WAY THE SAUCE IS COOKED THAT REALLY SETS THIS DISH APART.

TXIPIROI BARRUBETEAK BERE TINTAN

SQUID IN RICH INK SAUCE

6 RACIONES

4 1/2 lb squid

1/2 cup extra virgin olive oil

2 yellow onions, finely chopped

2 garlic cloves, finely chopped

3 bay leaves

sea salt

2 teaspoons squid ink (available from good delicatessens)

7 ripe tomatoes, peeled, seeded (see glossary) and chopped

7/8 cup dry white wine

To clean the squid, pull the tentacles out of the hood, cut off the tentacles just below the beaks and discard the top half. Remove the "wings" and the skin from the hood, then cut the hoods in half lengthways.

Heat 1/3 cup of the olive oil in a large heavy-bottomed saucepan over high heat. Add the onions and cook, stirring constantly, for 5 minutes, or until they begin to brown. Add the garlic, bay leaves and a pinch of salt and cook for 2 minutes, then reduce the heat to medium.

Add the squid ink and stir for 2 minutes, then add the tomatoes and cook for 5 minutes. Reduce the heat to medium-low, stir in the wine, then cover and cook for 30 minutes, or until the wine has cooked out and the sauce has thickened slightly.

Meanwhile, heat the remaining olive oil in a large heavy-bottomed frying pan over high heat until the oil is nearly smoking. Add half of the squid hoods and tentacles, season to taste and cook for I minute, or until light golden. Turn, season again and cook for another minute, then remove from the pan. Reheat the pan over high heat and repeat with the remaining squid.

Add the squid to the ink sauce and bring to a simmer. Add 2 cups water, then cover and simmer for 45 to 60 minutes, or until the sauce has thickened and the squid is very tender.

Spoon the squid onto warm plates and spoon over a little sauce. Serve hot.

WHERE DOES FACT END AND MYTH BEGIN? EVERYWHERE I WENT IN THE BASQUE COUNTRY, CHEFS WERE TELLING ME OF THE INCREDIBLE BEEF GROWN THERE. THAT IT WAS RARE, EXPENSIVE AND CAME FROM ANIMALS THAT WERE UP TO 12 YEARS OLD AND HAD BEEN FED ON GRASS ALL THEIR LIVES. THAT PRICKED UP MY EARS! I LOOKED FOR THIS BEEF IN THE MARKETS AND FOUND A LOT OF YEARLING AND VEAL FROM GALICIA. I WENT TO FARMS AND THE FARMERS TOLD ME THEIR BEEF WAS AROUND 2 YEARS OLD, BUT HAD BEEN FED A LOT OF GRAIN. I WENT TO A BUTCHER AND HE SHOWED ME HIS CARCASSES HANGING IN HIS TILED COOL ROOM. THOSE ANIMALS, HE SAID, JUDGING BY THE BONES, WERE NO MORE THAN 3 YEARS OLD. IN A GRILL HOUSE ON A HILL, I HAD THE MOST WONDERFUL CHARGRILLED SIRLOIN, BUT THE CHEF THERE SAID THE ANIMAL WAS NO MORE THAN 4 YEARS OLD. SOMEWHERE IN THE BASQUE COUNTRY, SOMEONE ONCE ATE A STEAK FROM AN OLD OX, BUT I CAN'T SAY I HAVE EVER TRIED IT. THIS RECIPE MAKES A LOVELY SLOW-COOKED DARK BEEF-CHEEK BRAISE. DON'T BE AFRAID OF COOKING THE BEJESUS OUT OF THE VEGETABLES.

IDIKIREN MASAILAK PXREKIN

BEEF CHEEKS WITH PEDRO XIMÉNEZ SAUCE

6 RACIONES

3 ¹/₃ lb beef cheeks

fine sea salt

¹/₂ cup olive oil

3 carrots, roughly chopped

1 garlic head, halved

1 yellow onion, sliced

2 cups Pedro Ximénez sherry

2 cups red wine

3 bay leaves

3 tablespoons thyme leaves

1 head of cauliflower, broken into florets

³/₄ cup whipping cream

3 tablespoons butter

Trim the beef cheeks to neaten them up and remove any sinew and silver skin. Season well.

Heat half of the olive oil in a large heavy-bottomed saucepan over high heat. Brown the beef cheeks for 2 minutes on each side, or until golden, then remove from the pan.

Add the remaining olive oil, then add the carrots, garlic and onion and sauté over high heat for 12 to 15 minutes, or until well browned. Stir in the sherry, wine, bay leaves, thyme, 1 teaspoon sea salt and 2 cups water. Reduce the heat as low as possible, add the beef cheeks, then cover and cook for 3 to 4 hours, or until the cheeks are beginning to fall apart.

Meanwhile, put the cauliflower, cream and butter in a saucepan, season to taste with salt, then cover and cook over low heat for 35 minutes, or until very tender. Place the cauliflower mixture in a blender and process until smooth. Keep the purée warm.

The sauce from the beef cheeks should by now be reduced and glaze-like. If it needs further reducing, remove the cheeks from the pan, cover with foil to keep them warm and simmer the sauce over high heat until nicely reduced. Strain the sauce through a fine sieve and return to the pan; gently reheat the cheeks in the sauce if necessary.

Serve the cheeks and their sauce on warm plates with the cauliflower purée to the side.

EUSKAL TXOKOAK

SECRET MEN'S BUSINESS

A man called Jesús opened the door and welcomed us in. He closed the door behind us and turned the big key to lock it. We were in, finally: a men's-only cooking society. No women allowed. It was a big space with a kitchen at one end and well-worn wooden tables and stools at the other. With my bag of groceries under my arm, Jesús ushered me into the kitchen where two men were cooking the first of the season's boletus mushrooms on a flat grill. Other men had already cooked and were sitting down to a plate of hake and a bottle of *txacoli,* the local tart white wine.

Since the 1870s, Basque men have been gathering in small groups and cooking together. Not necessarily cooking to feed each other, but cooking to impress each other — to compete, to work together in a team . . . things blokes like to do. It's a bit like being at a pub, but with something to keep both hands occupied. That is not to say drinking doesn't go on; it does. Not at the ludicrous pace of drinking in British pubs, but still a reasonable effort put in by all.

I put together a good feed of pork stuffed with cheese and slow-cooked Swiss chard. The thrill of being in one of the world's most exclusive culinary sects was muted a little by the reality. It was a bit like being in a youth hostel kitchen on your first night. The men around me were mostly a little older and came from all walks of life, but mostly middle class. A lawyer and a friend were cooking some tuna belly. "Are women allowed?" I asked them. "Yes, of course!" one said. "She comes in the morning to clean our pots and pans!" (In truth, the men's cooking societies have opened their doors to women and families in recent years. "Why bother?" was the response of one local woman I spoke to about it one day. "It's boring. All they do is sit around and play cards and smoke and drink. It's good the men go, it gets my husband out of my kitchen.")

As the night wore on, smoke from the grill replaced smoke from cigars and the two old gentlemen playing cards were berating each other louder and louder. We said our goodnights and stepped out into the harborside promenade, where a group of teenagers was sitting by the boats, passing around bottles of cola and packets of chips.

IT WAS LATE ON A RAINY SUNDAY MORNING AND SAN SEBASTIÁN'S BEST-DRESSED WERE WANDERING THE STREETS OF THE OLD QUARTER. PASTELERIA OTAEGUI WAS A DESTINATION FOR MANY. THE FRONT WINDOW OF THIS ELEGANT PASTRY SHOP WAS FILLED WITH ORDERED ROWS OF CAKES, TARTS AND LITTLE PIES. THERE WERE LITTLE FRUIT CAKES COOKED IN CYLINDERS AND WRAPPED IN PRINTED BAKING PAPER, SO EASILY FINISHED IN A FEW BITES; THERE WERE DELICIOUS TARTS WITH PASTRY THAT WAS SHORT ON THE CRUST, BUT WET AND FLAKY NEAR THE FILLING. HERE ARE SOME WONDERFUL LITTLE PIES WITH A VERY EASY-TO-MAKE PASTRY. THE DRIED CHERRIES FOR THE FILLING ARE NOW AVAILABLE IN THE CITY MARKETS, BUT PLEASE FEEL FREE TO USE SOME FRUIT CONSERVE AS AN ALTERNATIVE TO MAKING THE FILLING IN THIS RECIPE.

EUSKAL PASTELAS

BASQUE CHERRY PIES

SERVES 6

- 1 1/2 cups dried cherries
- 1 1/3 cups superfine sugar
- 1 tablespoon brandy
- grated zest of 1/2 lemon
- 3 eggs
- 2 3/4 cups all-purpose flour, sifted, plus extra, to dust
- 14 tablespoons unsalted butter, softened and chopped
- 2 1/2 tablespoons dark rum

Place the cherries in a small saucepan with 1/4 cup of the sugar, the brandy, lemon zest and 1 cup plus 2 tablespoons water. Stir well to dissolve the sugar and cook slowly over medium-low heat for 45 minutes, or until a loose "jam" forms. Remove from the heat and let cool.

Meanwhile, lightly beat two of the eggs in a bowl. Add the flour, butter, rum and remaining sugar and stir until the dough comes together. Shape the dough into a ball, dust with a little extra flour, then wrap in plastic wrap and refrigerate for 30 minutes.

Preheat the oven to 350°F.

Roll the pastry into a large log on a well-floured surface. Slice into twelve rounds about 1/2 inch thick, then roll each round out until about 1/4 inch thick.

Grease and flour six 4-inch heavy-bottomed pie pans. Use half of the pastry rounds to line the pans, then spoon the cherry jam into the pastry shells. Cover with another round of pastry and press the sides to seal well.

Lightly beat the remaining egg and brush it over the pie tops. Using a small sharp knife, score the tops for decoration. Set the pie pans on a baking sheet and bake for 30 minutes, or until golden. Serve warm.

I DON'T HAVE MUCH OF A SWEET TOOTH, SO IT TOOK A FRIEND OF MINE I JUST HAPPENED TO BUMP INTO IN SAN SEBASTIÁN ONE NIGHT TO PUT ME ON TO THE LOCAL CHEESECAKE. IT IS COOKED IN A HOT OVEN, SO THE OUTSIDE HAS A WELL-DEVELOPED CARAMELIZED SKIN THAT GOES FROM GOLDEN TO BROWN TO BLACK — DON'T BE ALARMED, AS IT'S ALL PART OF THE ACT. IT IS SO LOVELY THAT WHEN I FINISHED TESTING THIS VERSION, I ENDED UP EATING NEARLY HALF OF IT. AND YES, SPANISH CHEFS DO USE PHILADELPHIA CREAM CHEESE!

GAZTA TARTA
CHEESECAKE

SERVES 8

butter, for greasing
all-purpose flour, to dust
2 cups whipping cream
$3/4$ cup superfine sugar
$1 1/4$ cups soft cream cheese
5 eggs
6 oz goat's curd
$1/2$ cup thick plain yogurt
grated zest of 2 lemons
juice of 1 lemon
$2 1/4$ tablespoons brandy
2 tablespoons confectioners' sugar

Preheat the oven to 350°F.

Lightly grease a 10-inch springform pan with butter, then dust with flour, shaking out the excess.

Place all of the ingredients except the confectioners' sugar in a food processor and blend until smooth. Pour into the prepared pan and bake for 30 minutes, or until just set.

Carefully remove the cheesecake from the oven, sprinkle the confectioners' sugar over the top and bake for another 10 minutes. Remove the cheesecake from the oven and, using a kitchen blowtorch, brown the top until it is very dark. Alternatively, brown the cheesecake under a very hot broiler.

Allow to cool before serving.

I ONCE MET A BASQUE FARMER WHO NOT ONLY MADE HIS OWN CHEESE BUT ALSO HIS OWN RENNET — AN ENZYME FROM THE STOMACH OF LAMBS. HE HELD AN ORANGE-SIZE BALL OF THE STUFF, PRESERVED WITH SALT, IN THE PALM OF HIS HAND. HE AND I SOON FOUND WE SHARED A LOVE OF *MAMIA* AS HE CALLED IT — OR *CUAJADA* AS IT WAS KNOWN IN MY HOUSEHOLD, AND MOST LIKELY AS *JUNKET* IN YOURS. HE STILL DID THE TRADITIONAL BASQUE THING AND WARMED HIS MILK — RAW SHEEP'S MILK — WITH A STONE HEATED IN THE FIRE AND THEN DROPPED IT INTO THE JUG, SIZZLING AND BUBBLING AS IT SANK TO THE BOTTOM. SADLY, MOST SUPERMARKETS HAVE REMOVED JUNKET FROM THEIR SHELVES, BUT YOU CAN STILL BUY IT IN SOME FOOD STORES AND ONLINE.

MAMIA
BURNT JUNKET WITH HONEY

6 RACIONES

4 cups milk

about ⅓ teaspoon rennet
  (see glossary)

½ cup light honey, such as clover
  honey

Pour the milk into a heavy-bottomed saucepan. Heat a solid metal object such as a carefully cleaned meat mallet or fire poker over the flame of the stove until hot, then place into the milk. Check the temperature of the milk — it should reach 98°F. (If you don't have a thermometer, the milk should feel just warm — at body temperature.) Alternatively, place the milk over low heat and heat briefly.

Stir the rennet into the milk, then divide the mixture among six 7- to 8-oz glasses. Cover each glass with a small cloth and secure with a rubber band, then let stand in a warm place for 10 minutes. Refrigerate for 4 hours, or until set.

Drizzle with the honey just before serving.

MORE CAKE THAN TART, THIS IS AN ASTONISHINGLY SIMPLE CROWD-PLEASER. THE PASTRY IS LIKE SOFT CRUMBLY CAKE AND THE FILLING IS PLEASANTLY TART. THIS IS ONE OF MY OWN INVENTIONS THAT I THOUGHT UP WHILE WAITING FOR A PLANE IN THE HONDARRIBIA AIRPORT. I WAS LOOKING OUT THROUGH THE LOUNGE WINDOW TO THE HILLS ALONG THE COAST. A FEW DAYS BEFORE, A FRIEND HAD BEEN DRIVING ME ALONG ONE OF THE WINDING BACK ROADS AND WAS PEERING ABOVE THE STEERING WHEEL LOOKING UP AT THE APPLE TREES GROWING OVER THE TRACK. "SOMEWHERE ALONG THIS ROAD IS A PARTICULARLY GOOD TREE," HE SAID. "THE SHEEP SLEEP UNDER IT AND I THINK THEIR MANURE FERTILIZES THE TREE VERY WELL," HE SAID HALF JOKING, HALF POSTULATING. "I PICK THOSE APPLES FOR MY WIFE AND SHE MAKES A WONDERFUL TART." I NEVER GOT A CHANCE TO ASK HIM FOR THE RECIPE, SO HERE'S ONE FROM ME.

SAGAR TARTA

APPLE TART

SERVES 8

6 Granny Smith apples
1/2 cup superfine sugar
I cinnamon stick
grated zest and juice of I lemon
I tablespoon Calvados (apple brandy)

PASTRY
butter, for greasing
all-purpose flour, to dust
2 cups self-rising flour
I cup superfine sugar
1/2 cup unsalted butter, melted
2 eggs
grated zest of I lemon

CIDER SAUCE
1 1/4 cups dry apple cider
1/2 cup superfine sugar

confectioners' sugar, to dust

Peel, core and cut each apple into eight wedges, then place in a saucepan with the superfine sugar, cinnamon stick, lemon zest, lemon juice and Calvados. Cover and cook over low heat for 25 minutes, or until the apples are soft. Remove from the heat and let cool.

Preheat the oven to 400°F.

To make the pastry: Lightly grease an 8-inch pie pan with butter, then dust with flour, shaking out the excess. Place the flour, superfine sugar, melted butter, eggs and lemon zest in a food processor and blend for I minute, or just until a rough, crumbly dough forms. Press half of the dough into the base of the pan.

Remove the cinnamon stick from the apple mixture and evenly spoon the mixture over the dough in the pan. Using your fingers, coarsely crumble the rest of the dough over the top and gently press to roughly cover the apples. Loosely cover the pan with a sheet of parchment paper and bake for 30 minutes, or until golden. Remove from the oven, let stand in the pan for 5 minutes, then turn out onto a rack to cool slightly.

To make the cider sauce: put the cider and sugar in a small saucepan and stir to dissolve the sugar. Bring to a boil over high heat, reduce the heat to medium-low and simmer for 30 minutes, or until reduced by two-thirds.

Serve the warm tart dusted with confectioners' sugar and drizzled with the sauce.

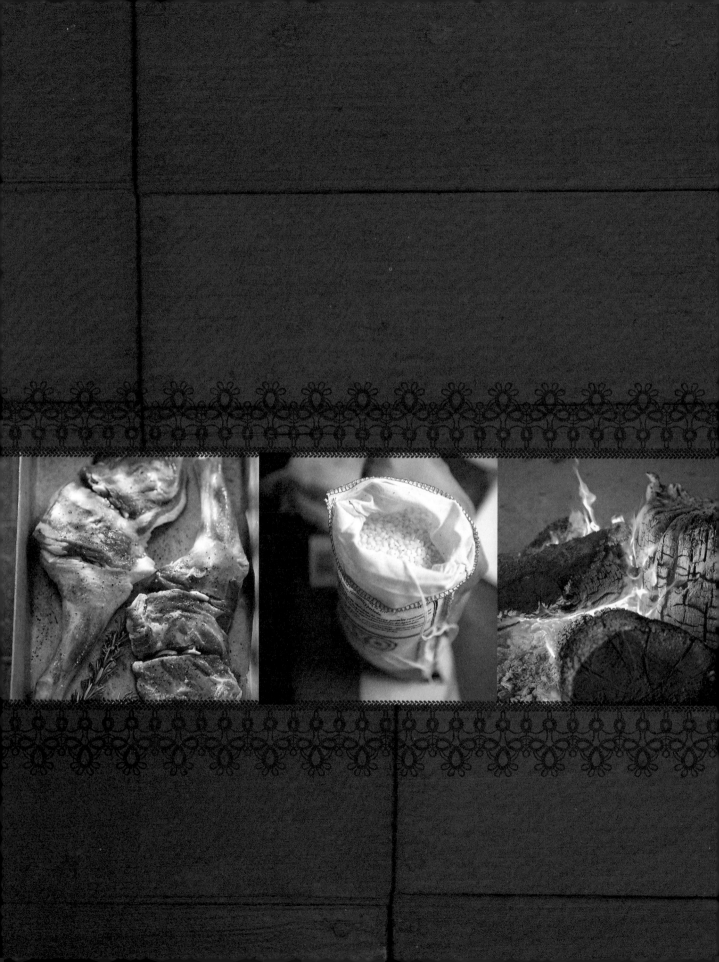

COCINAR CON FUEGO

COOKING WITH FIRE

★ ★ ★

FIRE IS ELEMENTAL TO SPANISH COOKING. REAL FIRE — WOOD AND COALS AND STICKS AND SMOKE. THE SPANISH, MORE SO THAN ANY OTHER PEOPLE IN EUROPE, HAVE NEVER TURNED THEIR BACKS ON THE POWER OF FIRE. THEY UNDERSTAND HOW IT NOT ONLY DRAWS PEOPLE TO THE HEARTH, BUT HOW THE DELICATE AROMA OF SMOKE IS IMPARTED TO FLESH AND HOW HEAT MAKES ITS INDELIBLE MARK ON MEAT.

I grew up with food cooked over fire, or to be more correct, food cooked over coals. I can remember Mum always berating Dad to hurry up and get the meat on the grill and he was always saying, *paciencia, paciencia*: Dad was waiting for the fire to die down. He would have built up a hardwood fire, probably from eucalyptus trees, and was waiting for the hot flames to burn themselves out and give way to the long-lasting embers. These embers cook without burning, release juices without drying out the flesh, and impart a flavor to the meat without overpowering it. His outdoor brick grill takes up a good part of the backyard and I'm still not quite sure if it doesn't require a building permit.

Fire, coals, smoke and flames lie at the heart of Etxebarri, a restaurant in the hills above Bilbao in the Basque Country. It is noted as being one of the best restaurants in the world — and is ostensibly a grill. The chef, Victor Arguinzoniz, uses different woods to impart different flavors to different foods, as well as different distances between the food and the coals.

In Spain, cooking with fire is special but nothing novel, so do not be misled into thinking that every meal is roasted over a pile of oak embers. It is, however, far more common than in the rest of Europe and the developed world. There are *hornos de legna* (wood-fired ovens) and *asadores* (roast houses) across Spain, and every region has its speciality, from cooking sardines on the beach to hilltop grills where people go for what they say is the best steak in the world.

The Spanish also have a very deep understanding and love of the *parrilla* — a flat grill made from a great block of steel that generates so much heat it cooks food very quickly without losing heat. Almost anything can be thrown on the *parrilla*; my favorite is seafood. A *parrilla* can be heated by wood, but these days they are more often than not powered by gas.

If you have the opportunity to cook over coals, please make the most of it, although it does take a little preparation. Hardwoods are excellent and the harder and drier the wood, the slower burning it is. I won't tell you how to make a fire as this is a skill that can only be learned by watching other people do it. One word of advice, though — you don't need a huge fire, and rarely do you cook over live flames.

THE SPANISH LOVE THEIR MUSHROOMS. IN BOLETUS SEASON, THERE IS NOTHING BETTER THAN SOME GRILLED BOLETUS AND A GLASS OF *RIOJA*. ALTHOUGH SPAIN IS SUCH AN INDUSTRIALIZED NATION, IT HOLDS A COMMUNAL BELIEF THAT SOME PARTS OF THE COUNTRY ARE STILL SUFFICIENTLY UNTOUCHED TO BRING FORTH A WILD CROP OF CHANTERELLES OR BOLETUS EVERY YEAR. IN TRUTH, MUCH OF THE AUTUMN CROP IS NOW TRUCKED IN FROM EASTERN EUROPE! THAT SAID, THERE ARE STILL SOME AMAZING QUANTITIES OF WILD MUSHROOMS HARVESTED ACROSS SPAIN. THERE IS EVEN A BAR IN SAN SEBASTIÁN WHOSE SPECIALITY IS FUNGI AND WHERE THEY COOK THEIR MUSHROOMS ON A GREAT FLAT GRILL.

SETAS A LA PLANCHA
GRILLED MUSHROOMS

6 MEDIAS RACIONES

9 oyster or other wild mushrooms
6 garlic cloves, thinly sliced
2 tablespoons thyme leaves
extra virgin olive oil, to drizzle
sea salt
fino sherry, to drizzle
2 tablespoons finely chopped parsley

Slice the mushrooms in half, then make three incisions in the stalks. Push a slice of garlic and some of the thyme leaves into each incision.

Heat a flat griddle to very high. Place the mushrooms on the griddle, cap side down. Drizzle with a little olive oil, season to taste and splash with a little sherry. Cover with a lid or foil and cook for 2 minutes, then turn, season again and cook for another 1½ minutes.

Drizzle with a little more olive oil and another splash of sherry and cook for a final 30 seconds. Place on a warm plate, scatter with the parsley and serve warm.

ANYONE WHO HAS BEEN TO THE SOUTH OF SPAIN IN SUMMER WOULD HAVE SEEN THE *CHIRINGUITOS* — THE SEASONAL BEACH BARS THAT SERVE BEER, SANGRIA AND SEAFOOD. SOME ALSO SERVE SARDINES IN THE TRADITIONAL MANNER. IT'S SIMPLE: YOU GET FRESH SARDINES, YOU SEASON THEM, YOU IMPALE THEM ON TWO STICKS AND YOU GRILL THEM OVER COALS. THE RESULT IS SENSATIONAL. THE MEATY SARDINES DRIP THEIR JUICE ONTO THE HOT COALS; THE JUICE VAPORIZES, RISES UP AND BATHES THE FISH IN THEIR OWN FUMES. YOU CAN CLEAN THE SARDINES IF YOU LIKE, OR DO AS THE ANDALUSIANS DO AND GRILL THEM WITH THE GUTS INTACT TO INCREASE THE FLAVOR.

SARDINAS A LA PARRILLA
GRILLED FRESH SARDINES

12 TAPAS

12 fresh sardines, scaled
sea salt
olive oil, for greasing
lemon wedges, to serve

Using a pair of kitchen scissors, cut away all the fins and tails from the sardines. Use a small sharp knife to cut down the belly, then remove and discard the innards. Rinse the sardines and pat dry with a paper towel, then season inside and out with sea salt.

Heat your coals to a temperature where you can only hold your hand 6 inches above them for no more than 3 seconds. Alternatively, heat a gas grill to high. Lightly grease a fish rack with olive oil. Place the sardines inside the grill or rack with a little space between each fish. Place over the hot coals and cook for 3 minutes on each side, or until just cooked through.

Season with a little more sea salt and serve immediately with lemon wedges. To eat the sardines, grasp the fish at both ends and sink your teeth to the spine.

WHEN I OPENED OUR NEW BAR NEXT DOOR TO OUR RESTAURANT, I WAS SCRATCHING MY HEAD OVER HOW TO SHARE MY LOVE OF FOOD COOKED OVER COALS IN A BAR ENVIRONMENT. I WAS LOOKING FOR A LITTLE CHARCOAL BOX AND COULDN'T FIND ONE TO SUIT. MY DAD, A RETIRED BOILERMAKER WHO HAS NEVER REALLY PUT DOWN HIS TOOLBOX, CAME INTO THE BAR AND QUIETLY MEASURED UP THE STOVE. HE RETURNED A FEW DAYS LATER WITH A GREAT LITTLE STEEL FIRE-BOX HE'D WELDED IN HIS SHED. I PUT THE STEEL BOX, FULL OF CHARCOAL, OVER A GAS BURNER, AND ONCE IT'S ALIGHT, IT GOES ALL NIGHT. ONE OF THE FIRST DISHES WE COOKED OVER IT WAS THESE TASTY LITTLE GRILLED CHICKEN LIVERS, MARINATED IN OIL AND SEASONED WITH CUMIN AND JUNIPER.

BROCHETAS DE HÍGADO DE POLLO
GRILLED CHICKEN LIVER SKEWERS

6 MEDIAS RACIONES

¾ lb cleaned chicken livers
I teaspoon ground toasted cumin
I teaspoon ground toasted juniper
¼ cup extra virgin olive oil
coarse sea salt

Put the chicken livers, cumin, juniper and olive oil in a bowl and mix together well. Cover and refrigerate overnight.

Heat your coals to a temperature where you can only hold your hand 6 inches above them for no more than 3 seconds. Alternatively, heat a gas grill to high. Thread each chicken liver onto two parallel metal skewers. Seasoning them with plenty of sea salt flakes as you go, cook the chicken livers for 2 to 3 minutes on each side, or until just cooked through but still pink in the middle.

Dress with a good sprinkle of sea salt and leave until the skewers have cooled enough to touch. Enjoy with a glass of fino sherry.

LA PAELLA

FOOD FOR FAMILY AND FRIENDS

Roger Felip Ibars is owner of Mas Trucafort, a restaurant in the wine-producing region of Montsant, a few hours southwest of Barcelona. His is a restaurant known for regionally inspired recipes. He researches local dishes and brings them to the table in a way that is most agreeable with the wines of Montsant and nearby Priorat. Although he doesn't serve paella in his restaurant, he makes this particular paella for family and friends.

To watch him make and tend the fire is to watch a craftsman at work. Although he casually chats as he pokes more dried grapevines into the fire, he is actually concentrating on the flames and coals. He is not mesmerized like one would watch a log fire in winter, but engaged like an engineer standing over his lathe. Here, Roger describes how he makes a paella over a fire. He uses some Catalan words, but I'm sure you can work out his meaning.

"People think about paella and they think about seafood. They think paella is a coastal food. What a lot of people don't understand is that paella is made everywhere rice is grown. In the country, people will use the animals they hunt, like rabbit, hare, wild boar. From the land, we sometimes use lamb and vegetables. We also use dried cod — traditionally, we didn't have contact with the coast, so we went to the market and bought salt cod once a year. It is typical in Catalonia for people in villages to have some land. On a Sunday, they go to their land with their family and friends and make a fire and cook in this way.

"I start the fire with chopped almond wood. This is a hardwood and has much energy. I add larger and larger pieces to build a bigger fire. I then let it burn down for an hour to make the coals. I put on the *paellera* [paella pan] and pour in some oil, and add two whole heads of garlic and a bunch of thyme. It is important to cook the thyme into the oil as it is the oil that communicates the flavor of the ingredients into the rice.

"Then I add a handful of dried grapevines to the fire. They burn quickly and this is like a shock of heat. This we call *flamejar*. The vines give me instant control; I can increase the heat immediately. Then I *marcar*, or brown, two rabbits that have been cut up. I then put some salt on the rabbit.

"For me, it is very important, as the *paellera* is very thin, that the flames *envoltar* or envelop the paella. I cook the rabbit, then put the rabbit in a pot over coals with some water and fresh parsley to make a stock.

"The fire under the *paellera* has now died a little and I begin to make the *sofregit* or *sofrito* with one red and one green bell pepper, a small bunch of thyme and three finely chopped onions. I throw another handful of sticks onto the fire and brown the onions. You can smell the almonds in the smoke. I also add some pinecones to the fire — it adds a Mediterranean aroma to the *sofregit*.

"Now I let the flames die away and make a reduction of the onions and bell peppers. I add a little of the stock every now and then. When the onions are golden, I add four chopped and peeled tomatoes. Over the next 20 minutes, I add some more vines every few minutes to increase the flames.

"When the *sofregit* has cooked down, I add peeled and boiled artichokes and cook for another 10 minutes. I then add the cooked rabbit back into the pan, increase the flame, then sprinkle in the rice. The rice I use is the *bomba* variety from the Ebro Delta. *Bomba* rice just takes 17 to 18 minutes to cook in total. I cook the rice for a few minutes over a high flame, then I pour in the stock; the stock has to be double the amount of the rice.

"I put more vines on the fire and season the rice with salt — rice needs a lot of salt. I add some parsley and fresh thyme and let it cook, bubbling . . . if it cooks too fast, I add some more water, perhaps the juice from the artichokes. It should bubble for 10 minutes on a high flame. I always taste the stock as it cooks. The stock needs to taste saltier than you expect the paella to taste.

"In the last 5 minutes, I add the desalted *bacalao* (cod). I then let the fire die down and let the paella *covar* — this means to rest covered; sometimes you put newspaper on top to keep the humidity. On the edges and on the bottom, there is a little *sucarrat* — this is the crust on the bottom of the paella. This is a much-desired feature of the paella. Now everyone must take a spoon and take what they want. *Bon profit!*"

AS NOT EVERYONE HAS A PLACE WHERE THEY CAN LIGHT A FIRE, I HAVE ADAPTED MY FRIEND ROGER'S PAELLA SO YOU CAN COOK IT ON A BARBECUE GRILL, GAS GRILL OR ONE OF THOSE LARGE GAS BURNERS YOU CAN BUY AT THE HARDWARE STORE OR ASIAN GROCERS. PREPARING PAELLA OVER A FIRE IS DIFFERENT FROM ANY OTHER COOKING TECHNIQUE. HAVING A LEVEL COOKING SURFACE IS IMPORTANT BECAUSE IF THE *PAELLERA* IS ON AN ANGLE, THE LIQUID WILL GO TO ONE END AND THE RICE AT THE OTHER END WILL NOT COOK. SOME PEOPLE HAVE BEEN KNOWN TO GET OUT THE SPIRIT LEVEL — NOT A SILLY IDEA IF YOU HAVE ONE! REMEMBER, YOU NEED TO CONCENTRATE ON THE COOKING AND NOT BE DISTRACTED.

PAELLA DE CATALAÑA
ROGER'S CATALAN PAELLA

SERVES 6

1 lb salt cod, soaked in cold water for 48 hours, changing the water four times

2/3 cup extra virgin olive oil

1 garlic head

1 bunch of thyme

3 1/4 lb farmed white rabbit, cut into 12 pieces

1 large yellow onion, finely chopped

1 red bell pepper, seeded and ribs removed, cut into 1/2-inch chunks

1 green bell pepper, seeded and ribs removed, cut into 1/2-inch chunks

sea salt

4 ripe tomatoes, peeled and chopped

1-lb can of artichokes preserved in brine, drained and quartered

1 3/4 cups *bomba* (short-grain) rice (see glossary)

Drain the salt cod, then trim off any fins and dark or brown flesh. Run your hands along the flesh and cut out the bones as you find them. Cut the flesh into six equal portions. Cover and refrigerate until required.

Place a 16 1/2- to 17 1/2-inch *paellera* or paella pan over very high heat. This heat source could be some coals on a wood barbecue or a very hot gas burner. Add 1/3 cup of the olive oil and cook the whole garlic head in the oil until the skin begins to blacken, turning frequently. Remove the garlic from the pan and reserve. Add half of the thyme sprigs to the oil, being careful as the oil will spit. Cook for 1 minute, then remove and discard the thyme. Add the rabbit pieces, season well and cook on each side for 5 minutes, or until well browned.

Transfer the rabbit to a heavy-bottomed saucepan, reserving the oil in the paella pan. Add enough water to the saucepan to just cover the rabbit and season with salt. Bring to a boil over high heat, then reduce the heat to medium and simmer for 30 minutes. Remove from the heat, then remove the rabbit pieces from the pan. Strain the stock, reserving 3 1/2 cups, and keep it hot.

Meanwhile, to make the *sofrito*, heat the remaining olive oil in the paella pan over medium-high heat. Add the onion and sauté for 5 minutes, or until lightly browned. Add all of the bell peppers and cook, stirring regularly, for 12 to 15 minutes, or until soft. Season to taste, then add the chopped tomatoes and cook, stirring regularly, for another 15 to 20 minutes, or until the *sofrito* has a jam-like consistency.

Add the artichokes and reserved garlic head to the paella pan, then pour in the rice and stir for 2 minutes, or until well coated. Pour in the reserved hot stock, then place the rabbit pieces, cod and the remaining thyme sprigs evenly over the rice. Bring to a boil over high heat, then reduce the heat to medium-high and simmer, uncovered, for 18 minutes — do not stir.

Remove from the heat, cover with a clean cloth and allow to stand for 10 minutes, or as long as it takes everyone to get to the table and be seated. Serve with a glass of a Spanish red such as *maius* or *tempranillo*.

PERHAPS ONE OF THE MOST MEMORABLE EATING EXPERIENCES I HAVE EVER HAD IN SPAIN WAS IN THE BASQUE COASTAL VILLAGE OF GETARIA. IT'S A SMALL TOWN WHERE LOCALS DESCEND TO EAT CHARGRILLED FISH BY THE SEA. RESTAURANTS LINE THE COURSE OF A LONG-BURIED STREAM THAT FLOWS UNDER THE ARCH OF THE CHURCH BY THE HARBOR. BY NOON EVERY DAY, THE CHARCOAL IN THE OUTSIDE GRILLS IS BLAZING; BY LUNCHTIME AT 2 PM, THEIR FIERCE HEAT HAS DIED DOWN AND FLAT FISH ARE BEING COOKED IN BLACKENED FISH BASKETS OVER COALS. I ORDERED THE TURBOT, WHICH LOOKS LIKE A GIANT FLOUNDER. I WATCHED THE OWNER OF ELKANO, PEDRO ARREGUI, SALT THE TURBOT INSIDE AND OUT, SQUIRTING IT WITH A SALTY MARINADE FROM A SQUEEZE BOTTLE. WHEN IT WAS COOKED, HIS SON AITOR GAVE US A GUSTATORY TOUR AROUND THE FISH, ENCOURAGING US TO COMPARE THE TASTE OF THE DIFFERENT PARTS. THE FLESH NEAR THE DORSAL SPINES WAS SWEET AND GELATINOUS, THE MEAT FROM THE BELLY MOIST AND SWEET. I HAVE TESTED THEIR SQUEEZE-BOTTLE MARINADE TECHNIQUE WITH SNAPPER — AND BELIEVE ME, YOU WILL APPRECIATE FISH DIFFERENTLY AFTER EATING THIS.

PARGO A LA PARRILLA
GRILLED SNAPPER

6 RACIONES

6 snapper or other sea fish, about
  I lb each, scaled and cleaned
fine sea salt
olive oil, for greasing
3 tablespoons lemon juice
2 garlic cloves
I½ oz *jamón* off-cuts, chopped

Using a pair of kitchen scissors, cut all the fins off each fish. Pat dry with a paper towel, then season inside and out with plenty of sea salt. Oil a fish rack or other heatproof cooking rack with olive oil.

Put the lemon juice, garlic cloves, *jamón* and I tablespoon fine sea salt in a squeeze bottle, add ⅓ cup water and shake well until the salt has dissolved.

Heat your coals to a temperature where you can only hold your hand 6 inches above them for no more than 3 seconds. Alternatively, heat a gas grill to high. Place the fish in the rack above the coals and after a few minutes, give them a quick squirt from the bottle. Cook the fish for another 5 minutes, then turn and give another quick squirt with the marinade. Cook for a further 7 minutes, or until the flesh is opaque.

Place the fish on a large serving plate and dress again with a few squirts of the marinade. Serve immediately, with a little of the cooking juices spooned over the fish just before eating. Enjoy with a crisp acidic white wine such a new riesling or a Spanish *txacoli*. Any leftover marinade will keep in the fridge for a few weeks.

IN THE FOLDS OF THE GREEN HILLS OF THE BASQUE COUNTRY, THE STREAMS ARE LINED WITH OLD APPLE TREES, LICHEN WRAPPED AROUND THEIR GNARLED BRANCHES. THESE TREES WITNESSED SPAIN'S GOLDEN AGE OF CIDER IN THE EARLY 20TH CENTURY WHEN APPLE TREES COVERED THE COUNTRYSIDE AND THE SHARP, SLIGHTLY YEASTY AND OXIDIZED CIDER FLOWED OUT FROM THE HILLTOP VILLAGES WHERE IT WAS MADE, ACROSS THE BASQUE COUNTRY, INTO THE SURROUNDING REGIONS AND ACROSS SPAIN. THE SPANISH CIVIL WAR AND THE HARD YEARS UNDER FRANCO SAW THE ORCHARDS RIPPED UP AND CIDER PRODUCTION PLUMMET. A MODERN RESURGENCE IN CIDER-MAKING NOW SEES *SAGARDOTEGI* (CIDER HOUSES) BECOMING POPULAR AGAIN ACROSS THE BASQUE COUNTRY. MANY OF THEM DOUBLE AS GRILLS. THESE LITTLE LAMB CUTLETS ARE A FAVORITE DISH IN THE *SAGARDOTEGI*.

CHULETAS DE CORDERO A LA PARRILLA

GRILLED LAMB CUTLETS

12 TAPAS
....
4 RACIONES
....

12 lamb cutlets
....
sea salt
....
olive oil, for greasing
....

Season the cutlets on both sides with sea salt, then place in a well-oiled grilling rack.

Heat your coals to a temperature where you can only hold your hand 6 inches above them for no more than 3 seconds. Alternatively, heat a gas grill to high.

Grill the cutlets on each side for 5 to 7 minutes, or until cooked to your liking. Season again and allow to rest for a few minutes before serving.

THE BEST LAMB I HAVE EVER EATEN WAS IN A RESTAURANT IN AN OLD FARMHOUSE IN THE HILLS ABOVE SAN SEBASTIÁN. IT WAS SUCKLING LAMB, AND A WHOLE SHOULDER BARELY FED ONE PERSON. IT WAS COOKED OVER A LITTLE POOL OF AROMATIC LIQUID THAT STEAMED THE FLESH FROM BELOW. THE SKIN WAS LIKE A DELICIOUS PARCHMENT COVERING SWEET SHREDS OF SOFT FLESH. IT WAS SUPERB.

CORDERO ASADO

AROMATIC ROAST BABY LAMB

4-6 RACIONES

6 lb baby lamb forequarter, including the rib (or one larger lamb forequarter)

2 cups white wine

1/3 cup olive oil

sea salt

Preheat the oven to 425°F.

To cut the lamb into four pieces (two legs and two ribs), run the tip of a sharp knife through the "armpit" of the lamb and pull the leg away from the ribs to make it easier to remove the leg.

Place the lamb pieces on a wire rack in a large roasting pan. Pour the wine, 2 tablespoons of the olive oil and 2 cups water into the pan. Drizzle the remaining olive oil over the lamb, then sprinkle generously with sea salt and rub in well.

Roast the lamb for 40 minutes, then reduce the oven temperature to 300°F and roast for another 60 to 70 minutes, or until the lamb is well done. You may need to add some more hot water to the roasting pan during cooking. Remove from the oven and allow the lamb to rest for 10 minutes before carving.

Alternatively, you can cook the meat in a wood-fired oven. Wait until the heat has died down to under 425°F, or the intense heat will burn the skin before it cooks. Roast the lamb for 20 minutes, or until the skin is brown and crisp, turning regularly. Remove from the oven and cover loosely with foil to keep the meat warm, and allow the oven temperature to drop to moderate (around 350°F). Then remove the foil and roast the lamb for another 30 minutes, or until cooked and tender. Remove from the oven and allow to rest for 10 minutes before carving.

IT'S HARD TO FIND CHICKEN IN A SPANISH RESTAURANT, AS RESTAURANTS ARE PLACES WHERE PEOPLE GO TO ESCAPE THE ORDINARINESS OF HOME. THEY WANT A TOUCH OF LUXURY, WITH WAITERS AND DISHWASHERS. CHICKEN IS SO CLOSELY ASSOCIATED WITH HOME, HOME COOKING AND EVEN POVERTY THAT IT DOESN'T OFTEN MAKE IT ONTO THE RESTAURANT MENU: THE SPANISH ARE MORE LIKELY TO EAT QUAIL, PARTRIDGE OR PHEASANT. POUSSIN IS JUST A NAME FOR LITTLE CHICKENS, AND THIS IS A QUICK DISH TO DO OVER THE COALS OR A GAS GRILL. THEY'RE AVAILABLE FROM GOOD POULTRY SUPPLIERS. YOU CAN ALSO MAKE THIS DISH WITH QUAIL — SIMPLY REDUCE THE COOKING TIME.

CAPÓN A LA PARRILLA
GRILLED POUSSINS

8 MEDIAS RACIONES
4 RACIONES

4 poussins
8 garlic cloves, crushed
4 bay leaves
I bunch of thyme, roughly chopped
$1/3$ cup extra virgin olive oil
I teaspoon fine sea salt
$1/2$ teaspoon freshly ground black
   pepper

Rinse the birds and pat dry with a paper towel. Using a pair of kitchen scissors, remove the spine by cutting along both sides of it from the tail to the neck. Discard or keep for stock. Trim away the first two joints of the wings. Spread the legs and remove the thigh bone, then place the poussins on a work surface, skin side up. Press down to flatten.

Combine the remaining ingredients in a shallow dish or container. Add the birds and massage the marinade all over, then lay the birds flat and cover with more marinade. Cover with plastic wrap and refrigerate overnight, or for at least 2 hours.

Heat your coals to a temperature where you can only hold your hand 6 inches above them for no more than 3 seconds. Alternatively, heat a gas grill to high. Place the poussins in two lightly oiled grilling racks and cook, skin side down, for 6 minutes, seasoning as you go. Turn and cook the other side for 6 minutes, seasoning again.

Turn the poussins again and grill, skin side down, for a final 4 minutes. Remove from the heat and let rest in a warm place for 8 minutes before serving.

CASA BOTIN

THE WARM HEART OF SPAIN

In the heart of Madrid lies what is considered the world's oldest restaurant. It is called Casa Botin and it centers around an old wood-fired oven that has not gone cold since it was first lit in 1725. In it are cooked the house specialties: suckling pig and milk-fed lamb. The floor of the kitchen is lined with worn blocks of granite, kept hygienic by a layer of coarse salt that the brigade of chefs grind underfoot as they march between wood-fired burners and the oven, which is warm, round and covered in ornate hand-painted tiles. Its raised hearth has been worn down with nearly 300 years of meals passed over it to be cooked and eaten. The old oven has seen so much human activity that it seems to have gained a life of its own.

IN CENTRAL SPAIN, SUCKLING PIG IS KING. PEOPLE WILL DRIVE SEVERAL HOURS FROM THEIR TOWN OR CITY INTO THE COUNTRY TO THEIR FAVORITE *ASADOR* OR ROAST HOUSE. SOME ARE INTIMATE LITTLE ROOMS; OTHERS LOOK LIKE TRUCK-STOP DINERS WITH A CHIMNEY; SOME ARE GREAT 300-SEATER RESTAURANTS. SOME DINERS COME FOR THE STEAK, OTHERS THE LAMB, BUT MOST COME FOR THE PIG. LITTLE PIGLETS ONLY A FEW POUNDS IN WEIGHT ARE SPLAYED WITH THEIR LEGS OUT AND COOKED WHOLE IN LARGE TERRACOTTA *CAZUELAS*. NOTHING IS ADDED EXCEPT SALT. THE SKIN IS PAPER THIN AND TOFFEE BRITTLE. THE FLESH IS SO MOIST, AND PEELS OFF AT THE TOUCH OF A FORK. IT CAN BE NEARLY IMPOSSIBLE TO GET PIGS SO SMALL OUTSIDE SPAIN, BUT YOU CAN GET SLIGHTLY LARGER AND OLDER PIGLETS FROM BUTCHERS AT THE MARKETS.

COCHINILLO ASADO
ROAST PIGLET

18 RACIONES

I suckling pig, about 20 lb
2 cups white wine vinegar
4 bay leaves
6 garlic cloves, plus I garlic head, halved
I bunch of thyme
3 carrots, roughly chopped
2 yellow onions, roughly chopped
fine sea salt
extra virgin olive oil, to drizzle

Using a hacksaw or cleaver, cut the head off the pig, then cut the pig in half lengthways by cutting down the spine. Cut the pig into hindquarter, forequarter, rump and rib portions. Using a sharp knife, carefully remove the thigh bone from the hindquarter and the shoulder bone from the shoulder by running the tip of the knife along the bone and cutting it away from the flesh. You may need to twist the thigh bone away from the leg bone to remove it. This takes some work and some time, and some may find it easier to ask their butcher to do this.

The next step helps ensure that the skin becomes crisp during cooking. Pour the vinegar into a large roasting pan, add the bay leaves, garlic cloves, half of the thyme and 4 cups water, then cook over high heat until it comes to a boil. Place the pieces of meat in the hot marinade, skin side down first. Cook for 90 seconds on each side, then remove from the roasting pan and discard the vinegar mixture.

Scatter the carrots, onions, halved garlic head and the remaining thyme in the large roasting pan. Spread the meat pieces evenly across the pan. Sprinkle both sides with sea salt, then turn the pieces skin side up and let stand for 30 minutes to allow the skin to dry.

Preheat the oven to 425°F. Drizzle all the meat with olive oil and rub the oil into the skin. Season again with a generous amount of sea salt and thoroughly rub it into the meat. Roast for 45 to 50 minutes, or until the skin is golden and crisp. Reduce the oven temperature to 300°F and roast for another 20 to 30 minutes, or until the meat is cooked and tender.

Alternatively, you can cook the meat in a wood-fired oven. Wait until the heat has died down to under 425°F, or the intense heat will burn the skin before it cooks. Roast the meat for 30 minutes, or until the skin is brown and crisp, turning regularly. Remove from the oven and cover loosely with foil to keep the meat warm, and allow the oven temperature to drop to moderate (around 350°F). Then remove the foil and roast the meat for another 30 minutes, or until cooked and tender.

Remove the meat from the oven and allow to rest for a few minutes. Discard the vegetable base, then carve the meat into serving portions using a very sharp knife.

AL ANDALUS

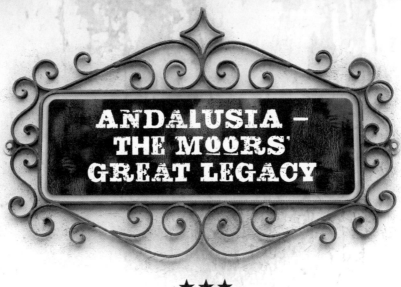

ANDALUSIA – THE MOORS' GREAT LEGACY

★ ★ ★

WHEN I WAS GROWING UP, DAD USED TO SAY TO ME, "YOU'RE SPANISH, BUT YOU ARE PART MOOR. IT'S EVEN IN YOUR NAME," REFERRING TO THE "MOOR" SOUND IN CAMORRA. RETURNING AGAIN TO CÓRDOBA, THE CITY WHERE I GREW UP AND WHERE MUCH OF MY FAMILY STILL LIVE, I CAN SEE THAT THE MOORS NEVER REALLY LEFT SPAIN. DURING THE TIME OF THE MOORS' INVASION FROM NORTHERN AFRICA IN THE 8TH CENTURY TO THE FALL OF THEIR IBERIAN COLONY IN THE 15TH CENTURY, THERE WERE GREAT PERIODS OF COEXISTENCE WHEN CHRISTIANS, MUSLIMS AND JEWS LIVED AND TRADED TOGETHER SIDE BY SIDE. DESPITE THE EPIC BATTLES, BLOODSHED AND PERSECUTION, THE MOORISH RETREAT FROM SPAIN WAS SLOW. WHO COULD BLAME THEM WANTING TO STAY IN THE COUNTRY IN WHICH THEY WERE BORN — ONE OF THE MOST BEAUTIFUL AND BOUNTIFUL PLACES ON EARTH.

During the Moorish occupation, Middle Eastern foods such as eggplant, palm dates, rice and pomegranates were introduced to the Iberian Peninsula. The Moors brought with them their irrigation skills and opened up new areas of Spain to agriculture, and left Spain with both a love of spices and a tooth-numbingly sweet taste for sugar.

So many foods, ingredients, techniques and practices from that period have remained part of everyday life in Spain. Like the Moors, the Spanish — particularly in Andalusia, the modern Spanish version of the Arabic *Al Andalus* — still make big dishes to share, they thicken sauces with bread, and readily use spices such as saffron and cumin.

Walking through Córdoba, I see this Moorish heritage, not just in the arched doorways or carved decorations of the Mezquita — the 8th century mosque that dominates the old quarter — but in the faces of the people. The strong, dark looks of many Spaniards show me that the Moorish influence is alive in the blood of the people.

Although the Moors invaded almost all of the Iberian Peninsula, their stronghold was in the south and their base was Córdoba. These are the recipes from the city where I spent the first years of my life. I have also included some dishes from the small country towns nearby where many of my family still live. While many of these recipes reflect the Moorish influence, they just as much reflect the food that has developed since, for Andalusia is a land that can be both scorchingly hot and amazingly fertile. Robust, full flavored and lively, these dishes are energetic, entertaining and close to my heart.

IN CÓRDOBA IN SUMMER, AT ABOUT 11 AM, A HIGH-PITCHED DRONE SEEMS TO EMANATE FROM THE VERY WALLS OF EVERY HOUSE. THIS IS THE SOUND OF THE BLENDERS WORKING AWAY MAKING GAZPACHO FOR LUNCH. GAZPACHO IS A COLD SOUP THAT CAME TO SPAIN WITH THE ARABS. IT WAS ORIGINALLY MADE WITH BREAD, WATER, GARLIC AND SALT. OVER THE CENTURIES, THIS BASIC SOUP HAS EVOLVED INTO MANY VARIATIONS. THE BEST KNOWN IS *GAZPACHO ANDALUZ*: A COLD SOUP MADE FROM BREAD, WATER, GARLIC AND SUMMER VEGETABLES. ANOTHER VARIATION IS *SALMOREJOS* — A COLD TOMATO SOUP. THE NEED FOR A LIGHT, COLD SOUP CAN BE EXPLAINED BY THE MOORISH ARCHITECTURAL LEGACY. THERE ARE COUNTLESS TOWNS AND CITIES IN THE SOUTH WHERE THE OLD CENTER IS MADE UP OF A LABYRINTH OF NARROW STREETS HEDGED IN BY SOLID BRICK AND STONE WALLS. IN THE SUMMER, THESE BECOME A STIFLINGLY HOT ENVIRONMENT WHERE COMFORT IS SOUGHT IN EVERY BREATH OF WIND, EVERY SIP OF WATER — AND EVERY SPOONFUL OF COLD GAZPACHO.

GAZPACHO DE HABAS

COLD FAVA BEAN SOUP

4 MEDIAS RACIONES

2 slices of *jamón*

2 slices two-day-old bread

4½ lb unshelled fava beans, or about 1¼ lb shelled fava beans

1 garlic clove

3 tablespoons fruity extra virgin olive oil

1 tablespoon fine sea salt

1 tablespoon finely shredded mint

Preheat the oven to 325°F.

Place the *jamón* slices on a baking sheet in a single layer and bake for 8 to 10 minutes, or until brown and crisp. Drain on a paper towel and set aside.

Put the bread in a large bowl, pour in just enough water to cover, then let soak for 1 hour.

Shell the fava beans from their pods — at this stage, do not remove the smooth outer skin, also known as double shelling or double podding. Reserve two small handfuls of the beans and keep them separate.

Scoop the bread and soaking water into a food processor. Add the fava beans, garlic and olive oil and purée until smooth. Strain the mixture through a fine sieve, pressing well to extract as much liquid as possible. Stir in the sea salt, then refrigerate until chilled.

Double shell the reserved fava beans. Drop the beans into a saucepan of boiling salted water and cook for 2 minutes, then drain and refresh in iced water.

Pour the soup into chilled bowls, then scatter with the reserved fava beans and mint. Crumble the *jamón* over the soup and serve with a lightly chilled amontillado sherry.

A SPANISH CHEF RECOMMENDED A RESTAURANT JUST OUTSIDE CÓRDOBA'S OLD TOWN. HE TOLD ME TO TRY THE EGGPLANT AND *SALMOREJO* — NORMALLY A COLD VEGETABLE SOUP, BUT HERE SERVED MORE LIKE PURÉE TO GO WITH ASTONISHINGLY GOOD FRIED EGGPLANT. THE RESTAURANT WASN'T OPEN WHEN I ARRIVED, SO I WAITED IN THE SHADE OUTSIDE A BAR ACROSS THE STREET. SEVERAL HOURS LATER, THE DOORS OPENED AND I HALF STUMBLED IN. THE RESTAURANT WAS UNASSUMING, WITH SOME ANTIQUE TOOLS AND BULLFIGHTING MEMORABILIA TO SOFTEN THE HARD TILED ROOM, WHICH WAS TO BECOME THE SET IN WHICH THE WAITERS WOULD PERFORM THEIR SCHTICK. THE CHEF WAS TURNING OUT SOME GREAT STANDARDS — *CROQUETAS DE BACALAO* AND LESS COMMON SUPER-SAVORY DEEP-FRIED SEA ANEMONES. BUT WHAT REALLY MADE ME SIT UP AND TAKE NOTICE WERE THE CRUNCHY EGGPLANT STICKS WITH THEIR SUCCULENT SOFT, SWEET INTERIORS, AND A RANGE OF *SALMOREJOS* THAT HE WAS SERVING LIKE DIPS. AFTER A LITTLE PLEADING, THE CHEF CAME OUT TO SPEAK TO ME. "THESE *BERENJENAS FRITAS* WERE AN ACCIDENT," HE SAID. "ONE DAY WE WERE VERY BUSY AND I KNOCKED A CAN OF LEMONADE INTO THE EGGPLANT AND FORGOT ABOUT IT. LATER I FRIED THEM AND THEY WERE WONDERFUL. THEY HAVE BEEN ON THE MENU EVER SINCE."

TRES SALMOREJOS Y BERENJENAS FRITAS
DEEP-FRIED EGGPLANT STICKS WITH THREE FRESH PURÉES

6 MEDIAS RACIONES

3 eggplants
sea salt
4 cups lemon-lime soda

CAULIFLOWER SALMOREJO

3 slices two-day-old bread, crusts removed
4 tablespoons butter
3 cups cauliflower florets
⅓ cup extra virgin olive oil
very small garlic clove, finely chopped
sea salt

Cut the eggplants into long strips about ½ inch wide and place them on a wire rack over a baking sheet. Sprinkle generously with sea salt and let stand for I hour.

Meanwhile, to make the cauliflower *salmorejo*: put the bread in a shallow bowl and cover with water. Melt the butter in a heavy-bottomed saucepan over low heat, add the cauliflower, then cover and cook, stirring occasionally, for 20 minutes, or until the cauliflower has cooked down and browned slightly. Place the cauliflower in a blender with the olive oil, garlic, 1⅓ cups water and a good pinch of sea salt. Squeeze the water from the bread, add the bread to the blender and process for 5 minutes, or until smooth. Pour into a bowl, cover and refrigerate until chilled.

To make the hazelnut *salmorejo*: put the bread in a shallow bowl, cover with water and let stand for 10 minutes. Squeeze the water from the bread, then place the bread in a blender with the hazelnuts, olive oil, garlic, 1½ cups water and a good pinch of sea salt. Process for 5 minutes, or until smooth. Pour into a bowl, cover and refrigerate until chilled.

To make the tomato *salmorejo*: purée the tomatoes and garlic in a food processor for I minute, or until smooth. Strain through a sieve, pressing on the solids to extract as much juice as possible. Discard the solids. Break the bread into golf ball–size pieces and place in a large stainless-steel bowl. Pour the strained tomato mixture and olive oil over the bread and sprinkle with the sea salt. Using very clean hands, squish the tomato mixture into the bread, really working the liquid through. Let stand for 15 minutes, then purée the mixture again until smooth and velvety, adding a little chilled water if necessary. Pour into a bowl, cover and refrigerate until chilled.

Rinse the salt from the eggplants and pat dry on a clean cloth. Soak the eggplants in the lemon-lime soda for 5 minutes, then drain, shaking off the excess.

Meanwhile, fill a deep fryer or large heavy-bottomed saucepan one-third full of oil and heat to 375ºF, or until a cube of bread dropped into the oil browns in 10 seconds.

Dust the eggplant in the flour and deep-fry for 5 minutes, or until golden and crisp. Drain on a paper towel and sprinkle with sea salt. Serve hot, with the chilled *salmorejos*.

HAZELNUT SALMOREJO

3 slices two-day-old bread, crusts removed

2 cups hazelnuts, roasted and peeled

1/3 cup extra virgin olive oil

very small garlic clove, finely chopped

sea salt

TOMATO SALMOREJO

2 to 3 vine-ripened, soft tomatoes (10 to 11 oz), roughly chopped

small garlic clove, finely chopped

3 slices two-day-old bread, crusts removed

2 tablespoons extra virgin olive oil

1/2 teaspoon fine sea salt

olive oil, for deep-frying

seasoned all-purpose flour, to dust

THE CHEF AT THE CÓRDOBA PARADOR, TIMOTEO GUTIÉRREZ RODRÍGUEZ, IS A BREED OF SPANISH CHEF WHOSE CALLING IN LIFE IS TO SOURCE AND PRESERVE TRADITIONAL REGIONAL RECIPES. HE, LIKE MANY OF HIS LIKE-MINDED COLLEAGUES, WORKS AT A PARADOR, AN UPMARKET STATE-OWNED HOTEL CHAIN SET UP IN THE MID-20TH CENTURY TO PRESERVE OLD BUILDINGS AND REGIONAL CUISINE. AT ANY PARADOR, YOU WILL BE GUARANTEED GOOD TRADITIONAL REGIONAL FOOD. IT MAY NOT BE CUTTING-EDGE AND YOUR DINING PARTNERS MAY ALL BE AGEING AMERICANS, BUT THE FOOD WILL BE GOOD QUALITY AND BASED ON TRADITIONAL RECIPES. TIMOTEO'S MENU IS BASED ON RECIPES HE RESEARCHED AFTER YEARS SPENT VISITING THE HOMES OF HOUSEWIVES WELL KNOWN IN THEIR TOWNS AS BEING EXCELLENT CHEFS. SHRIMP HAVE ALWAYS BEEN POPULAR IN CÓRDOBA, TRADITIONALLY SHIPPED IN ON THE INCOMING TIDE OF THE GUADALQUIVIR RIVER. THIS IS A QUICK, LIGHT AND SUCCULENTLY SALTY TORTILLA. IF YOU CAN'T FIND NETTLES, USE SPINACH INSTEAD.

TORTILLA DE ORTIGAS Y GAMBAS
SHRIMP AND NETTLE TORTILLA

12 TAPAS
6 MEDIAS RACIONES

fine sea salt

1/2 yellow onion

1 garlic clove

3 bay leaves

1 lb raw shrimp, peeled and deveined

10 to 11 oz nettles (available from produce markets and select grocers)

12 eggs

1/4 cup olive oil

Pour 8 cups water into a saucepan. Add some sea salt, the onion, garlic clove and bay leaves and bring to a boil. Add the shrimp and cook for 1 minute, then drain.

Wearing rubber gloves, pick the nettle leaves from the stems, then rinse. Bring a large saucepan of water to a boil, add the nettle leaves and blanch for 1 minute. Drain, refresh in cold water and squeeze dry. Don't worry about the stings on the nettles — they dissolve when cooked.

Place the nettles in a food processor with the eggs and 1 teaspoon of fine sea salt. Process until blended, then transfer to a bowl. Break the shrimp in half with your fingers and mix through the egg and nettle mixture by hand.

Heat the olive oil in a large nonstick frying pan over high heat. Pour the shrimp mixture into the pan and swirl to cover the base. Using a wooden spoon, draw the outside mixture into the middle for 1 1/2 minutes to start to bring the cooked mixture into the center of the tortilla, then reduce the heat to medium and form nice rounded edges with the spoon. Cook for another minute, then cover the pan with a large plate and invert the tortilla onto the plate. Carefully slide the tortilla back into the pan, uncooked side down. Cover and cook for another 2 minutes, then remove from the heat and place on a warmed dish. Cover tightly with plastic wrap and allow to stand for 20 minutes.

Serve the tortilla at room temperature with a cold beer, a lightly chilled *godello* or even a white *rioja*.

THE SPANISH SO LOVE THEIR *COGOLLOS*, OR BABY LETTUCES, THAT THEY LOBBIED FOR THEIR OWN *DENOMINACIÓN DE ORIGEN*. A LETTUCE WITH A D.O. MUST BE SPECIAL — AND INDEED, THE *COGOLLOS DE TUDELA* ARE REMARKABLY SMALL AND COMPACT, WITH A SHARP, MILKY FLAVOR. ALTHOUGH THE LETTUCE COMES FROM NAVARRA, THIS RECIPE COMES FROM A MATE IN CÓRDOBA. IN THIS DISH, A WARM VINAIGRETTE, INFUSED WITH GARLIC AND ANCHOVIES, IS DRIZZLED OVER THE OPEN HEART OF THE LETTUCE, MAKING ITS WAY THROUGH EVERY FOLD. LETTUCES LIKE THESE ARE HARD TO COME BY OUTSIDE SPAIN, SO FIND THE SMALLEST, TIGHTEST ROMAINE LETTUCE YOU CAN GET YOUR HANDS ON AND PEEL AWAY THE OUTER LEAVES TO REVEAL THE DELICATE HEART WITHIN.

COGOLLOS A LA VINAGRETA

BABY LETTUCE HEARTS WITH GARLIC VINAIGRETTE AND ANCHOVIES

24 TAPAS

6 MEDIAS RACIONES

6 baby romaine lettuces
14 anchovy fillets
1/3 cup extra virgin olive oil
5 garlic cloves, finely sliced
1/3 cup sherry vinegar

Wash the lettuces and peel off the outer leaves to reveal the hearts. Slice the lettuce hearts lengthways into quarters, discard the stalks, then pat dry and place on a serving platter.

Using a fork, crush two of the anchovy fillets until well mashed. Cut the remaining anchovy fillets in half lengthways.

Heat the olive oil in a heavy-bottomed frying pan over medium-high heat. Add the mashed anchovies and cook for 1 to 2 minutes, or until they have "melted" into the oil. Add the garlic and cook for 3 to 4 minutes, or until light golden but not brown. Remove from the heat and stir in the vinegar.

Pour the oil mixture over the lettuce hearts. Top each lettuce quarter with a slice of anchovy and serve immediately.

A DARKLY GOLDEN DISH WHOSE RICH, DEEP FLAVORS AND REFRESHING SPICY AROMA GIVE ITS NORTH AFRICAN ORIGINS AWAY. LIKE SO MANY FOODS WITH MOORISH ROOTS, *ALBORONÍA* HAS BECOME PART OF THE ANDALUSIAN CULINARY VERNACULAR. THE INGREDIENTS ARE ALL COOKED SEPARATELY AND BROUGHT TOGETHER AT THE END, LEAVING THE TASTY CHUNKS OF FRUIT AND VEGETABLES INTACT. THE SLIGHT SHARPNESS OF THE QUINCE AND THE SWEETNESS OF THE PUMPKIN MAKE *ALBORONÍA* A GOOD EXAMPLE OF MOORISH *AGRIDULCE*, OR MIX OF SWEET AND SOUR. IT CAN BE SERVED WITH GAME OR LAMB, BUT I THINK THE BEST WAY TO UNDERSTAND THIS DISH IS TO DESCRIBE IT AS A SPICY AUTUMN SALAD THAT CAN BE ENJOYED JUST AS WELL ON ITS OWN.

ALBORONÍA

RICH QUINCE AND PUMPKIN RATATOUILLE

6 MEDIAS RACIONES

5 quinces

1 lb pumpkin or kabocha squash, peeled and cut into 1-inch dice

sea salt

2/3 cup olive oil

3 eggplants, cut into 1/2-inch dice

3 tablespoons extra virgin olive oil

1 large yellow onion, diced

2 green bell peppers, seeded and ribs removed, then diced

5 bay leaves

1 tablespoon cumin seeds, roasted and ground

2 1/4 lb tomatoes, peeled, seeded (see glossary) and puréed

a handful of parsley, chopped

Preheat the oven to 350°F.

Wash the quinces and wipe dry, then place on a large baking sheet. Roast for 1 hour, or until soft and pinkish/golden.

Meanwhile, spread the pumpkin on another baking sheet, sprinkle with 1 teaspoon sea salt and drizzle with 1/4 cup of the olive oil. Shake the baking sheet to coat the pumpkin with the oil and bake for 20 to 30 minutes, or until tender.

Heat the remaining 6 tablespoons olive oil in a large heavy-bottomed frying pan over high heat until almost smoking. Add the eggplant, season to taste and toss for 7 to 8 minutes, or until golden and tender. Drain on a paper towel.

Heat the extra virgin olive oil in a large heavy-bottomed saucepan over medium-high heat. Add the onion and a pinch of salt and sauté for 5 minutes, or until soft but not colored. Stir in the bell peppers, bay leaves and cumin, reduce the heat to medium-low, then cover and cook for 30 minutes, or until the mixture is soft and has a jam-like consistency.

Meanwhile, peel and quarter the roasted quinces and cut into 1-inch dice.

Add the puréed tomatoes to the bell pepper mixture and cook for 2 to 3 minutes, or until warm. Add the roasted pumpkin, quince, eggplant and parsley, then gently mix together. Season to taste and serve warm.

YOU DON'T SEE MANY RABBITS IN SPAIN — THEY'VE ALL BEEN
EATEN! AS SOON AS ONE POPS HIS LITTLE HEAD ABOVE HIS WARREN,
THERE'RE A DOZEN HUNTERS WAITING TO TURN HIM INTO DINNER.
AND THIS DISH MAKES SUCH A WONDERFUL DINNER. IT HAS THE
EARTHY FLAVORS OF BROWNED RABBIT FLESH; THE AROMA OF
ROSEMARY; THE SWEETNESS OF ONION, GOLDEN RAISINS AND
CARROT; THE FLAVOR OF CITRUS; THE SHARPNESS OF WINE
AND A FINISHING OF SUGAR, VINEGAR AND BITTERSWEET SPANISH
PAPRIKA. IT JUST SINGS OF THE INFLUENCE OF MUSLIM COOKS.
EVERYWHERE THEY WENT — SPAIN, SOUTHERN ITALY AND INDIA —
YOU'LL FIND THIS LEGACY OF SWEET AND SOUR FOOD.

CONEJO AGRIDULCE
SWEET AND SOUR RABBIT

8 MEDIAS RACIONES
6 RACIONES

2 farmed rabbits, about 3½ lb each
⅓ cup olive oil
sea salt
I lb baby onions, peeled and left whole
I lb shallots, peeled and left whole
I½ cups white wine
I tablespoon chopped thyme leaves
I tablespoon chopped rosemary
2 large carrots, peeled and sliced
   into ½-inch rounds
rind of 2 lemons, cut off in large
   strips, white pith removed
scant ¼ cup pine nuts
scant ⅔ cup golden raisins
3 tablespoons sherry vinegar
2 tablespoons superfine sugar
I teaspoon agridulce smoked paprika
crusty bread, to serve

Time to practice your knife skills — or smile sweetly and ask your butcher to do the following for you! Using a heavy knife or cleaver, cut off the hind and fore legs of each rabbit and trim off the knuckles. Cut the back legs into three pieces (the lower leg, the thigh with bone, and the thigh without the bone). Trim away the stomach flaps from the saddle and the lower part of the rib cage. The part of the body nearest the head makes very bony eating, so trim off about an inch, including the neck, and discard or reserve for making stock or sauces. Cut the saddle into five equal portions across the spine.

Heat the olive oil in a very large heavy-bottomed saucepan over high heat. Brown the rabbit in batches for 3 to 5 minutes on each side, seasoning to taste as you go. Remove from the pan and set aside, then reduce the heat to medium-high. Add the onions and shallots and cook, shaking the pan frequently, for 10 minutes, or until deep golden.

Stir in the wine using a wooden spoon, scraping up any cooked-on bits from the bottom of the pan. Simmer for 2 minutes, then add the herbs, carrots, lemon rind strips and rabbit and enough water to nearly cover the rabbit. Cover with a *cartouche* (a piece of parchment paper cut into a round the same circumference as the pan), then reduce the heat to low and simmer very gently for I hour.

Remove the *cartouche*, then sprinkle the pine nuts, golden raisins, vinegar, sugar and paprika over the rabbit and shake them into the juices. Put the *cartouche* back on and simmer for another 15 minutes. Serve the rabbit in shallow bowls, with plenty of crusty bread to soak up the juices.

ACEITE DE OLIVA

OLIVE OIL

I remember watching an old olive farmer and his son standing in their olive grove. Their young trees, only a few years old, barely came up to their chests and were probably grown from cuttings made from the gnarled trees farther up the hill. Those trees were well over a hundred years old and had trunks as thick as two soccer players. It was raining, and the two men were getting as wet as the trees. They were soaking up the rain too, quietly rejoicing that there would be enough moisture to ensure a good olive crop.

The towns where my family are from, Montilla and Aguilar de la Frontera, are in the heart of Spain's olive-producing industry. Here, every hill and river flat has been planted with olives, except a patch here and there for the odd goat dairy or *huerta*. Olive oil mills sit on the edge of towns — great modern industrial plants that use state-of-the-art technology. However, some artisan processors still prefer the old stone presses.

In Spain, more than 250 different varieties of olive are grown for oil. Three of those varieties are becoming popular in groves in the New World. Picual is a savory, slightly peppery oil, good for dressing salads. Hojiblanca can be sweet to bittersweet with a lovely nuttiness; it is good for cooking and baking and is used as a dressing in desserts. Arbequina is a very fruity and aromatic oil that adds a lovely aroma when drizzled onto a hot dish.

It would be easy to understate the importance of olive oil in the Spanish kitchen. Let's just say that it is used in almost every process from frying to shortening, to enriching, flavoring, preserving, decorating and serving!

I HAVE ALWAYS WONDERED WHY — APART FROM THE FACT THAT IT TASTES SO GOOD — THE SPANISH EAT SO MUCH PORK. PERHAPS IT ORIGINATED AS A KNEE-JERK REACTION DURING THE POST-MOOR PERIOD WHEN THE SPANISH INQUISITORS WERE ROAMING THE COUNTRY TORTURING ANYONE WHO DIDN'T CONFORM TO THEIR PARTICULAR BRAND OF MONOTHEISM. JEWS AND MUSLIMS WHO HAD ·CONVERTED TO CHRISTIANITY OFTEN LIVED IN FEAR AND PROCLAIMED THEIR NEW FAITH BY PUBLICLY EATING PORK; THE MORE ENTHUSIASTIC CONVERTS WOULD HANG A HAM OR SAUSAGES ABOVE THEIR DOOR. EVERY TIME MY DAD GOES BACK HOME, HE HEADS DOWN TO THE OLD TOWN AND SEEKS OUT HIS FAVORITE GRILL, JUST NEAR THE MEZQUITA (GREAT MOSQUE). THERE HE SITS AND ORDERS A GREAT PLATE OF SLICED GRILLED PORK LOIN SERVED WITH TWO LIVELY SAUCES: A FRESH OREGANO AND RAW GARLIC SAUCE, AND A RED SAUCE MADE FROM *PIQUILLO* PEPPERS AND CHILES. I NOW FIND MYSELF FOLLOWING IN MY FATHER'S FOOTSTEPS.

CHURRASCO
GRILLED PORK LOIN

6 RACIONES

SALSA VERDE
2 handfuls of fresh oregano leaves

4 garlic cloves, chopped

a handful of parsley

1 cup extra virgin olive oil

2 tablespoons fennel seeds, toasted and ground

juice of 1/2 lemon

SALSA DE PIQUILLO
one 9-oz jar of *piquillo* peppers, drained

2 medium-size semi-hot red chiles, seeded

2 garlic cloves

1 teaspoon smoked paprika

1 tablespoon ground cumin

1/2 cup extra virgin olive oil

3 pork loin fillets, about 12 oz each

fine sea salt

olive oil, for pan-frying (optional)

To make the salsa verde: put all of the ingredients in a food processor and blend for 1 to 2 minutes, or until smooth. Season to taste, pour into a serving bowl, then cover with plastic wrap and refrigerate.

To make the salsa de *piquillo*: put all of the ingredients in a food processor and blend for 1 to 2 minutes, or until smooth. Season to taste, pour into a serving bowl, then cover with plastic wrap and refrigerate.

The pork loins can be chargrilled or pan-fried. To chargrill the pork, heat some barbecue coals so that you can only hold your hand 4 1/2 inches above them for no longer than 3 seconds. Season the fillets well and grill each of the four sides for 3 minutes each, then turn and cook each side again for 1 minute. Remove from the heat and allow to rest in a warm place for 5 minutes.

To pan-fry the pork, preheat the oven to 400°F. Place 2 1/2 tablespoons olive oil in a large, heavy-bottomed, ovenproof frying pan over medium-high heat until very hot. Add the pork fillets and cook on all sides for 1 minute each, sprinkling each side with fine sea salt as you go. Transfer the pan to the oven and cook the pork for 5 minutes, then remove from the oven and allow to rest in a warm place for 5 minutes.

To serve, cut the fillets into slices 3/4 inch thick and enjoy with the two salsas.

IT WAS HOT AND I NEEDED A DRINK. I WAS IN THE LITTLE OLIVE OIL TOWN OF BAENA, JUST SOUTH OF CÓRDOBA. ON THE COUNTER IN A LITTLE SHOP WAS A PACKET OF *TORTAS DE ACEITE*, OR OLIVE OIL COOKIES. *TORTAS DE ACEITE* ARE FOUND THROUGHOUT ANDALUSIA. THEY ARE GENERALLY MADE WITH OLIVE OIL, WHICH MAKES FOR A VERY SHORT PASTRY. A SHOT OF ANISE AND A FEW FENNEL SEEDS GIVES A LOVELY FLAVOR AND AROMA OF ANISEED. I BOUGHT A BOTTLE OF WATER AND A PACKET OF THE *TORTAS*. THEY WERE MUCH RICHER THAN ANY I HAD EVER TASTED. I LOOKED ON THE SIDE OF THE PACKET AND THE INGREDIENTS LISTED *MANTECA DE CERDO* AND NOT *ACEITE*: THEY WERE MADE WITH LARD AND NOT OIL. THE ANDALUSIANS JUST CAN'T DO WITHOUT THEIR PIG FAT! BUT WE CAN DO WITHOUT IT HERE. SERVE WITH TEA, COFFEE, CHEESE OR ANISE.

TORTAS DE ACEITE
CRUNCHY ANISE COOKIES

24 COOKIES

scant 1 2/3 cups all-purpose flour
1/3 cup superfine sugar, plus extra,
   to sprinkle
2 teaspoons ground cinnamon
1/3 cup extra virgin olive oil
2 teaspoons fennel seeds
zest of 1 lemon
3 tablespoons anise liqueur
   (see glossary)
1 egg, lightly beaten

Preheat the oven to 350ºF.

Sift the flour, sugar and cinnamon into a bowl. Mix well.

Heat the olive oil in a frying pan over medium-high heat. Add the fennel seeds and cook for 30 seconds, then carefully pour the oil mixture over the dry ingredients and combine very well. Add the lemon zest and liqueur and bring together to form a rough dough.

Divide the dough in half, then roll out each portion on a well-floured surface into a log about 1 1/4 inches in diameter. Cut off slices about 3/4 inch thick, then roll out each slice into large rounds approximately 1/16 inch thick.

Place the rounds on a lightly greased baking sheet, brush the tops with the beaten egg and sprinkle with a little extra sugar. Bake for 12 to 15 minutes, or until golden and crisp, then remove from the oven and let cool on wire racks. As soon as the cookies are cool, store in an airtight container for up to 3 days. They should be short and slightly brittle.

SOMETIMES TRANSLATIONS FAIL. SOMETIMES FOODS FROM ONE CULTURE DON'T MOVE EASILY ACROSS INTO ANOTHER. IF I TOLD YOU THAT WHAT WE ARE ABOUT TO MAKE IS KNOWN AS "FAT FROM HEAVEN," I DON'T THINK THIS WOULD MAKE MY TASK ANY EASIER. THIS IS A SUPER-SWEET PUDDING BASED ONLY ON EGGS AND SUGAR AND COVERED IN A LAYER OF CARAMEL. THE EGGS MAKE THE SUGAR TASTE SWEETER, AND THE SUGAR MAKES THE EGGS MORE LUSCIOUS. A LITTLE SQUARE OF THIS CUSTARD IS A BEAUTIFUL GUSTATORY PUNCTUATION MARK, A REMINDER OF ONE OF THE MOORS' GIFTS TO SPAIN: THE SWEET TOOTH. ENJOY A SMALL SQUARE WITH COFFEE, OR SLICE OFF A SLIVER TO SERVE WITH SEASONAL FRUIT.

TOCINO DE CIELO
SWEET EGG CUSTARD

18 PORTIONS

2 1/2 cups superfine sugar

16 egg yolks

2 eggs

Preheat the oven to 350°F.

Place 1 cup of the sugar in a heavy-bottomed saucepan and cook over high heat, tilting the pan frequently, for 6 to 8 minutes, or until the sugar liquefies and becomes a dark but not burnt caramel. Pour into a 6 x 12 inch ovenproof dish.

Put the remaining sugar in a saucepan, add 1 1/2 cups water and stir over medium heat until the sugar has dissolved. Simmer for 15 minutes.

Whisk the egg yolks and eggs in a large bowl until well combined. Whisking continuously, gradually add the hot sugar syrup, ensuring it is well combined. Pour the egg mixture over the caramel layer and place the dish in a deep roasting pan. Place the roasting pan in the oven, then pour in enough hot water to come two-thirds up the side of the dish. Bake for 50 minutes, then carefully remove from the hot water bath. Allow to cool to room temperature, then refrigerate until chilled.

To serve, run a flat-bladed knife around the edge of the dish and invert the custard onto a serving plate. Slice thinly and serve as you would a petit four or an accompaniment to a sweet tart, cake or fruit dish.

IN AUTUMN, THE STREETS OF ANDALUSIA FILL WITH THE SCENT OF *AZAHAR*. THE MOORS LEFT TO SPAIN NOT ONLY THE CITRUS, BUT THE WHISPERINGLY POETIC WORD TO DESCRIBE BOTH THE ORANGE BLOSSOM AND ITS SEASON. *AZAHAR* IS THE TIME OF THE YEAR WHEN THE PALE WHITE WAXY FLOWERS ERUPT, FILLING TOWN SQUARES WITH A HEADY SWEET PERFUME. A STROLL ON A WARM NIGHT IN CÓRDOBA OR SEVILLE DURING *AZAHAR* IS ONE OF THE MOST INTOXICATING EXPERIENCES. FUNNILY ENOUGH, IN SPRING WHEN THE FRUIT IS RIPE, NOBODY EATS THE ORANGES! CONSIDER USING ONLY THE BEST FRUIT FOR THIS DESSERT — BLOOD AND NAVEL ORANGES IN WINTER, OR VALENCIA ORANGES IN SUMMER. MAY I SUGGEST YOU ALSO SEARCH OUT HOJIBLANCA OLIVE OIL AS IT IS FRUITY, AROMATIC AND TRADITIONALLY USED IN DESSERTS IN SPAIN.

SORBETE DE MANDARINAS Y NARANJAS CON ACEITE DE OLIVA
MANDARIN SORBET WITH ORANGES AND OLIVE OIL

SERVES 6

1/2 cup sweet extra virgin olive oil, such as Arbequina or Hojiblanca
1/2 vanilla bean, halved lengthways
3 3/4 cups superfine sugar, plus I tablespoon, extra, to sprinkle
6 3/4 lb mandarins
juice of I lemon
3 oranges, plus the juice of 1/2 orange
3 blood oranges
3 tangelos

Infuse the olive oil the day before serving. To do this, simply pour the olive oil into a glass jar, add the vanilla bean, then seal. Let stand overnight in a cool place, but not the refrigerator.

Also on the day before serving, prepare the mandarin sorbet. Place the sugar in a saucepan with 3 cups water and stir over low heat until the sugar has dissolved. Bring to a boil, then remove from the heat and allow to cool. Chill.

Slice the tops off six of the best-shaped mandarins. Carefully remove the segments from inside the cut mandarins (this takes a little skill), then put the skins on a baking sheet and place in the freezer. These will become your serving receptacles for the mandarin sorbet.

Peel the remaining mandarins and juice them in a mechanical juicer along with the segments from the six hollowed-out mandarins. Add the lemon juice, strain, then measure 5 1/4 cups juice. If there is not enough juice from the mandarins, top up with bottled orange juice if necessary. Chill.

Stir 3 cups of the chilled sugar syrup into the chilled juice, then pour into an ice-cream maker and churn according to the manufacturer's instructions. Freeze for 5 hours, or overnight.

On the day of serving, make the citrus salad. Using a very sharp knife and reserving all the juices, slice away the tops and bottoms of all the oranges and tangelos. Working from top to bottom, remove the skin and white pith. Cut all the citrus in half widthways and remove the white pith in the center, then cut the flesh into 1/2-inch chunks. Place in a bowl with any juices and the extra orange juice, then sprinkle with the extra sugar. Pour the vanilla-infused olive oil over the salad and mix together well.

Fill the frozen mandarin skins with the sorbet and place on chilled plates. Spoon a little citrus salad and juices around the sorbet and serve.

A DESSERT DURING THE HARD TIMES UNDER FRANCO WAS A SQUARE OF CHOCOLATE, SPRINKLED WITH SALT AND NIBBLED WITH A PIECE OF BREAD DRIZZLED WITH OLIVE OIL. OUT OF THE SIMPLICITY OF NECESSITY CAME A FLAVOR COMBINATION THAT IS UNDENIABLY GOOD. THE HARSHNESS OF THE SALT THROWS THE SWEETNESS AND RICHNESS OF CHOCOLATE INTO STARK RELIEF. THE BREAD GIVES BODY, AND THE OIL EXTENDS THE FLAVOR OF THE CHOCOLATE. I HAVE EATEN DIFFERENT VERSIONS OF THIS RECIPE, FROM THE POVERTY-INSPIRED ORIGINAL ON MY GRANDFATHER'S KNEE TO MODERN ADAPTATIONS IN SUPER-SWISH RESTAURANTS IN MADRID. THEY ALL HAVE FOUR THINGS IN COMMON: BREAD, SALT, CHOCOLATE AND OLIVE OIL.

PAN CON CHOCOLATE
CHOCOLATE WITH SWEET OLIVE OIL

SERVES 6

10½ oz dark chocolate
   (50% cocoa solids), chopped
4 eggs, separated
7 tablespoons unsalted butter,
   softened, plus extra, for greasing
2 tablespoons superfine sugar
6 very thin slices two-day-old
   sourdough baguette
sweet olive oil such as Arbequina
   or Hojiblanca, to drizzle
fine sea salt, to sprinkle

Grease a 4 x 10 inch loaf pan and line with parchment paper.

Put the chocolate in a heatproof bowl over a saucepan of simmering water, making sure the base of the bowl doesn't touch the water. Allow the chocolate to gently melt for about 5 minutes, stirring occasionally.

Remove from the heat, then whisk in the egg yolks. Add the butter and stir until all the butter has melted.

In another bowl, whisk the egg whites until soft peaks form. Whisking continuously, gradually add the sugar and beat until a thick and glossy meringue forms.

Gently fold one-third of the meringue into the chocolate mixture until nearly combined, then gently fold the remaining meringue through. Pour the mixture into the prepared pan, then cover with plastic wrap and refrigerate for 2 hours.

Meanwhile, preheat the oven to 350°F.

Spread the bread slices in a single layer on a large baking sheet, then cover with another baking sheet of the same size. Transfer to the oven and bake for 15 minutes, or until the bread wafers are crisp. Let cool, then place the wafers in an airtight container and refrigerate until ready to use.

To serve, invert the chocolate marquis onto a cutting board and cut into slices ½ inch thick. Divide among chilled plates, drizzle with a little olive oil, then sprinkle with a tiny pinch of salt crystals — a dozen crystals or so at most — and serve with the chilled toasts. To enjoy, simply take a small amount of the chocolate and spread it over a little of the toast.

ACROSS SPAIN, THERE IS AN EARLY MORNING RITUAL PRACTICED ALMOST EXCLUSIVELY BY HUSBANDS. THE MEN GET DRESSED, LEAVE THE HOUSE AND THE HUNGRY KIDS, AND WALK OUT INTO THE MORNING SUN. THEY WANDER TO THE *KIOSKO* OR NEWSSTAND, PICK UP A COPY OF *EL MUNDO* OR *EL PAÍS* DEPENDING ON THEIR POLITICAL LEANING, AND THEN BUY A BAG OF *MAGDALENAS* FOR BREAKFAST. THESE SWEET LITTLE YEASTY PASTRIES ARE SERVED WITH A BIG CUP OF *CAFÉ CON LECHE* INTO WHICH THEY ARE DUNKED. TO THE NORTH, THE PASTRIES ARE MADE WITH BUTTER, BUT IN THE SOUTH, THEY CAN ALSO BE MADE WITH SWEET HOJIBLANCA OLIVE OIL. MUM MAKES REALLY RICH ONES WITH OLIVE OIL AND YOGURT. I HAVE OPTED FOR A RECIPE MADE WITH BUTTER. IF YOU CAN GET YOUR HANDS ON SOME SWEET OLIVE OIL SUCH AS ARBEQUINA OR HOJIBLANCA, TRY THE OIL INSTEAD OF THE BUTTER FOR A REAL TASTE OF ANDALUSIA.

MAGDALEÑAS
MADELEINES

18 MADELEINES

5 eggs
½ cup superfine sugar
9 tablespoons unsalted butter, melted
½ cup rice flour
1 cup self-rising flour
grated zest of 1 lemon
confectioners' sugar, to dust

Preheat the oven to 350°F.

Put all of the ingredients except the confectioners' sugar in a food processor and blend until smooth. Place 18 double-layered cupcake liners on a baking sheet. Divide the mixture among the paper liners, dust with confectioners' sugar and bake for 18 minutes, or until golden and risen.

Remove from the oven and turn out onto a wire rack to cool. Best eaten on the day of making.

DOWN THE STREET FROM MY AUNTY CARMEN IS A CORNER CAFE THAT FROM THE OUTSIDE SEEMS A PRETTY PERFUNCTORY AFFAIR. THE OWNER, JAVIER, SELLS A FEW BAGS OF NUTS, SOME PACKET PASTRIES AND CANNED SOFT DRINKS. BUT HE'S PERPETUALLY BUSY BECAUSE HE MAKES GREAT COFFEE AND ALWAYS HAS A GREAT BIG *PASTEL CORDOBÉS* — A BIG PASTRY FILLED WITH *CABELLO DE ÁNGEL* OR ANGEL'S HAIR, A FANCY NAME FOR THE FLESH OF A PARTICULAR MELON THAT HAS BEEN CANDIED WITH SUGAR. (IN SPAIN IT'S CALLED *CEDRA*.) IN SOME BAKERIES IN CÓRDOBA, *JAMÓN* IS ADDED TO THE ANGEL'S HAIR, MAKING A RATHER UNUSUAL BLEND OF SWEET AND SALTY. WHATEVER THE CASE, THEY ARE ALWAYS EXCEPTIONALLY SWEET AND MAKE A GREAT LITTLE PICK-ME-UP WITH A MID-AFTERNOON COFFEE. OUTSIDE SPAIN, THESE FRUITS ARE AVAILABLE IN ASIAN GROCERY STORES AND ARE KNOWN AS SPAGHETTI SQUASH. IF THE MELONS ARE HARD TO FIND, SPANISH FOOD STORES USUALLY HAVE CANNED *CABELLO DE ÁNGEL* FILLING.

PASTEL CORDOBÉS
FLAKY PASTRY WITH CANDIED MELON

SERVES 8

8 lb fresh *cabello de ángel* melons

4 cups superfine sugar, approximately, plus extra, to sprinkle

I quantity of rough puff pastry (see recipe on page 104)

I egg, lightly beaten

Cut the skin from the melons and discard. Remove the seeds and discard; use only the fibrous part of the flesh. Coarsely chop and weigh the flesh — the melons should yield about 3½ lb. Place half the equivalent weight in sugar in a large heavy-bottomed saucepan. Add the melon flesh and cook over medium heat, stirring occasionally, until the mixture bubbles. Reduce the heat to low and simmer, stirring frequently, for 1½ hours, or until the mixture has a jam-like consistency — you now have angel hair. Remove from the heat and let cool.

Preheat the oven to 350°F.

Lightly grease two baking sheets. Bring the puff pastry to room temperature, then cut into quarters. Roll out each quarter on a well-floured surface into an 8-inch square. Place one pastry square on each baking sheet, then spread half of the cooled angel hair mixture on each square, reaching almost to the edges. Brush the edges with the beaten egg, then cover with the remaining pastry squares. Press down the edges to seal well, then crimp with a fork.

Brush the tops with the beaten egg and sprinkle with extra sugar. Bake for 20 to 25 minutes, or until the pastry is golden brown. Remove from the oven and let cool. Cut into squares to serve.

I CAN'T IMAGINE CHRISTMAS WITHOUT NOUGAT. IT WOULD BE LIKE WAKING UP ON DECEMBER 25 AND STARING AT A COLD, EMPTY LIVING ROOM. WHEN I WAS A KID, DAD WOULD GO TO GREAT TROUBLE TO OBTAIN SPANISH NOUGAT. HE KNEW A SPANISH MAN WHO WOULD IMPORT A CONTAINER LOAD FROM SPAIN FOR ALL THE SPANISH EXPATRIATES IN MELBOURNE. DAD WOULD LOAD UP HIS TRUNK AND DELIVER IT TO FRIENDS AND FAMILY IN NEARBY GEELONG. SWEET, SOFT, FLAVORED WITH HONEY AND FULL OF TOASTED ALMONDS, NOUGAT IS SURPRISINGLY EASY TO MAKE WITH THE HELP OF AN INEXPENSIVE KITCHEN THERMOMETER — BUT SURPRISINGLY, MOST SPANIARDS DON'T. WHEN I GO BACK TO SEE MY FAMILY IN CÓRDOBA AT CHRISTMAS, I VISIT MY FAVORITE PASTRY SHOP NEAR THE ROMAN RUINS AND BUY AN ARMFUL AND GIVE THEM TO MY FAMILY. I SIT DOWN WITH MY AUNTIES AND SLOWLY EAT EACH DELICIOUS MORSEL AS I HEAR HOW WELL THE COUSINS ARE DOING IN THEIR BUSINESSES AND HOW THE NIECES AND NEPHEWS ARE DOING AT SCHOOL.

TURRÓN
NOUGAT

12 PIECES

1/3 cup honey
7/8 cup corn syrup
7/8 cup superfine sugar
2 egg whites
rice paper, for lining
1 1/3 cups blanched almonds, toasted
grated zest of 1 lemon

Place the honey and three-quarters of the corn syrup in a small heavy-bottomed saucepan. Stir over low heat until well combined, then cook until the temperature reaches 250°F on a kitchen thermometer.

Meanwhile, put the sugar, remaining corn syrup and 3 tablespoons water in another small heavy-bottomed saucepan. Stir over low heat until the sugar has dissolved, then cook until the temperature reaches 325°F.

While the syrups are cooking, beat the egg whites, using an electric mixer, until stiff peaks form. As soon as the honey syrup reaches 250°F, very slowly pour it into the egg whites, beating continuously. When the sugar syrup reaches 325°F, very slowly add it to the egg whites and continue beating until the mixture has cooled enough so that it is just hot, but not hot enough to burn you.

Lightly grease a 6 x 10 inch baking dish and line with rice paper.

Stir the almonds and lemon zest into the nougat mixture, then pour it into the prepared dish. Cover the top of the nougat with more rice paper, cutting the sheets to fit. Let cool, then cut into 12 pieces. The nougat will keep in an airtight container for up to 1 month.

LA ROMERÍA

THE ROMERÍA

Last time I was in Córdoba, I went back to Aguilar de la Fronterra, where Dad was born. It's the kind of small town where not much goes on and not much has changed since I was a kid. My Aunt Pepa had arranged a lunch for the family to celebrate my return — but the day *before* I arrived: a classic family mix-up.

When I got there the following day, they had forgotten about my no-show as they were all preparing for the Romería. This is a religious procession where the statue of the Virgin Mary is carried on an ornate litter through the town, down the hill, across a stream to a grotto in the olive groves, where there was to be a night-long celebration. To call it purely religious, however, would be to say that Kentucky Derby Day is only about a horse race.

On the morning of the festival, the hilltop townsfolk were summoned to the church by a man setting off noisy skyrockets in the plaza. Thousands responded. The women were dressed in their flamenco best, colorful dresses with revealing plunging backlines. Some were practicing the alluring art of "obscure and reveal" with their fans. Men on horseback wearing flat, broad-brimmed hats, grey waist-length riding jackets and knee-high riding boots walked their animals down the cobbled streets. I have never seen a more proud, beautiful or handsome people than those in Aguilar that day.

I followed the procession out of town with my cousin and her husband Javier, but instead of walking all the way down the hill with her family, we stopped at a friend's "holiday house," about a 15-minute walk from the town square. As the Romería procession disappeared in the heat haze, we sat in the cool of Francisco's shed under his house and drank his home-made sherry while the wives were upstairs making *mejillones en escabeche* and *albóndigas de atún*. It was a festival day and although we weren't with the masses, we were still celebrating the Romería by taking the day off, eating food picked from their garden and drinking home-made wine.

As the sun set, we made our way down to the olive grove where the Romería celebration was entering its evening phase. More than **2000** people were packed into the olive grove by the banks of a small river. Tents had been pitched on the rocky ground, and strings of electric lights were festooned between the trees. By now the Virgin was well and truly safe inside the grotto. Over the years, the local holy site, built on the site of a spring, has become more of a walled pilgrim hotel-cum-church. Dotted around this are a dozen or so *casetas*. These are the Andalusian equivalent of a beach shack — a roughly built entertaining shed-cum-kitchen put together by a family team or group.

Javier and I were called into a *caseta* by an old man, who thrust glasses of red wine into our hands. His name was Paco, he knew my family and started talking town business as if I knew every detail of the past **40** years. From his place, cooking on the open grill, came another younger man who handed me a *pincho* — a skewer of lamb. I watched as Paco started berating an old friend about the quality of his olive oil. The friend retorted with a criticism of Paco's sausages. It was a conversation they probably had every year at the Romería.

I ripped a piece of lamb off the skewer; it was crisp, salty and redolent of smoke and *pimentón*. I wandered out into the makeshift party town. Music was flowing from the *casetas* — some flamenco, some pop, some electronic. Smoke from frying *churros* and dust from the stony soil caught the pale yellow light from the lightbulbs. Teenagers were beginning to break up from their groups of friends and wander into the darkness under the olive trees as couples. A young man, upright that morning, was finding it easier to lean forward and let his horse find their way home.

I propped myself at the bar on the edge of a tent. The music was so loud I couldn't hear Javier speak. I knew it was late and that it may be decades before I returned to this Romería again. Ordering my thoughts, I knew, as a chef, that I could write down the recipes of the food I was eating, such as the flavors of the *pincho* I still had in my hand. I realized, however, that no matter how hard I might try to capture Spanish food in words and images, it is just one element to the everyday intensity of the human experience in Spain.

Spanish food is the Spanish way of life and must be lived to be truly understood.

★ ★ ★

GRACIAS

THANK YOU
★★★

THE AUTHORS WOULD LIKE TO ACKNOWLEDGE IN SPAIN

Andrés Madrigal, Ricardo García, Elías Juanas, Adam Melonas, Fernando Córdoba, Juan Peña Aguilar, Tomás Ruiz Fabrellas, Timoteo Gutiérrez, Paco Vera Hormigo, Javier Campano, Antonio Cambodas, Josef Rei, Carmen Domíngez Pérez, Antonio Arafao Castro, José Aguilar Montesinos, Juan Rejas López, Mar Claudio Barreneched, Jaime Caloto Fernández, José María, Pedro Quian, Fernando del Cerro, Javier García Pizarro, Carlos Galvin, Eben Sadie, Dominik A. Huber, Félix José Martínez, Mar Sardá de Abreu, José Recio Martín, Florentino Oliva, Julia Gonzáles Serrano, Restaurante Florida, Ángela Martín, Patxi Pastor Salcedo, César Gutiérrez, Antonio González Gómez, Katerina Glazkova, Andrew McCarthy, Aloña Berri, Maite Díez, Ernesto Txueka, Manuel Ruzo, Carlos Ramírez, Cecilio Oliva, Rosa Ferreira, Leonor Molina Sanchez, Gerard Batllevell, Josep Anton Batllevell, Concepció Simó, Leonor Sánchez, Josep Ferrando, Gemma Peyrí, Quima Pellisé, Paco Batllevell, Bego Soldevila, Iria Marqués, Neus Miró, Maria Victoria Masip, Roger Felip (Mas Trucafort Restaurant, Falset), Juli Mestre, Fausto, Tito Robledo, Vangie Venzon, Carmen Gómez Domínguez, Victor Ganoza García, Angeles Gómez Sánchez, the Valez Family, Gemma Marco (Buil&Giné Winery), Toni Bru (El Celler de l'Aspic), Matías Fernández (Quinoa Restaurant), Julià Folch, Mireia Folch, Rafael Pino, Félix Arcones, Juan Lázaro, José Amri Leunda, Andres Etxeberria, Alberto Fuente, Herminda Buezas Oubiña, Jaime 'El gallego de la "Oreja de oro"', Aitor Aguirre, Jesús Guerediagu, Rachel Ritchie (Priorat Regional Tourist Office for Catalan translations), Gabriella Ranelli de Aguirre (Tenedor Tours San Sebastián for Basque language translations), Sociedad Euskal Billera (San Sebastián), Txepetxa (San Sebastián), Pedro Nieto (Guijuelo), Casa Ciriaco (Madrid), El Bordón Embutidos (Viana, Navarra), Casa Bigote (Sanlúcar de Barrameda), Elkano Restaurante (Getaria), Zuberoa Restaurante (San Sebastián), Restaurante Botin (Madrid), Bar Borda Berri (San Sebastián), Mercado de Asbastos de Santiago (Santiago de Compostela), Tuna Universitaria (Madrid), Virgen de Casar (Monte de Casar), Bar Restaurante Las Petronilas (Mirandar del Castañar), O Tio Benito (Ribadumia), Bodega la Muralla, Romerijo (Puerto de Santa María), Sánchez Romate (Jerez de Frontera), Núñez de Prado (Baena), El Navarrico (San Adrian), Castro Martin (Ribadumia), Mas Ardevol (Falset), Elena Valldepérez and Frank Bueno (Costa Daurada Tourist Board). Images of Scala Dei by permission of Catalan Autonomous Government, Department of Culture and Media. And lastly a very special thank you to Enrique Ruiz and the Spanish Tourism Board.

IN AUSTRALIA

The staff of MoVida and MoVida Next Door for allowing me the time to get out of the kitchen and travel Spain. Mr and Mrs Camorra Senior, Peter Bartholomew, Cornelius McMahon, David Mackintosh, Louisa Biviano, Tomás Robles, Scott Wasley (The Spanish Acquisition), Monica Brun (Embassy of Spain, Sydney), Tiffany Treloar, Veronica Ridge, Max Allen, Wendy Connor, Prue Acton, Robyn Cornish, George Cornish, Emma Poole, Christopher Hayes, Adrian Kortus, Diane Roddy, Stephanie Alexander, Tim White and Amanda Schulze (Books for Cooks), Kristin Otto and Javier Degen (The Spanish Pantry).

The authors would also like to thank their partners for allowing them time away from home, away from their young families. The authors deeply appreciate their extra efforts in working and caring for kids on their own.

GLOSARIO
GLOSSARY

Following is a list of words used in this book that may need translation, a few tips on some items of equipment and a few simple instructions. This is a very subjective list and I couldn't resist throwing in a few asides.

Adobo – A Spanish paprika–based marinade for meats. Once used for preserving foods, now a recipe to add flavor.

Agridulce – Sour and sweet. Refers to the juxtaposition of sweet ingredients and something sour in a dish, like sweet carrots and dried fruit with vinegar. Also describes a type of Spanish paprika that has counterpointing notes and is most commonly found in the national sausage — chorizo.

Ahumado – Smoked.

Ajo – *See garlic.*

Almendras – *See almonds.*

Almonds – The annual nut crop is harvested in autumn. Almonds contain lots of flavorful oil that can become rancid with age. Buy whole almonds from specialized nut retailers, whole food shops or Middle Eastern food stores with a high turnover of stock.

Alubias – A type of dried bean.

Anchoas – Anchovies. Spanish anchovies are the best in the world, and as such the Spanish appreciate them on their own as a *tapa* in a bar. Indeed, some bars serve only beer, wine... and anchovies!

Anise liqueur (*licor de anís*) – A clear, colorless, aniseed-flavored liqueur. It is consumed in Spain as a pick-me-up on a cold morning, as a little shot throughout the day, or mixed with brandy to make the aperitif *sol y sombre* (sun and shade). Its strong licorice-like flavor makes it popular in the kitchen in sweet dishes.

Arroz – *See rice.*

Artichokes – Look for tight, heavy artichokes with plump outer leaves. To prepare them, cut off the top of the head using a sharp knife — the first third to a half, depending on what stage of the season it was harvested. Younger artichokes need less trimming than older artichokes. Trim the stem leaving about 1 inch, or a bit less if the stem is shrivelled. Remove the outer, coarser leaves until you find the paler internal leaves. Using your sharp knife, trim away the skin of the stem and around the base and discard. Cut the head into quarters lengthways or as described in the recipe. (Scrape out the hairy choke if it has developed.)

Asador – Roaster. Also refers to a roast house. Generally, roasting in Spain is performed in a *horno de legna,* or wood-fired oven.

Bacalao – *See salt cod.*

Bellota – Spanish for acorn. Fed to pigs that are processed into *jamón Ibérico de bellota.*

Boquerón – An anchovy cured in a vinegar marinade, often served in bars as a *tapa*. Also slang for an Andalusian hick or hillbilly.

Brandy – Common breakfast drink. Sometimes used in cooking.

Bread – Bread is eaten with every main meal in Spain — it is used to sop up the juices left on the plate. The quality of bread varies greatly from south to north, with hard, crusty "industrial"-style bread being popular in the south, and moister, denser and more rustic bread more popular in the northwest. As Spanish cooks waste nothing, the bread used to cook with is generally stale. In this book, we generally recommend that you use two-day-old *pasta dura*, available in Italian bakeries and other good street bakeries.

Butter – All butter used in this book should be unsalted and already at room temperature.

Café con leche – Coffee with milk. Spanish coffee is noticeably darker and over-roasted compared to the coffee consumed elsewhere in Europe. *Café con leche* has a certain appeal of its own and is perfect for dunking cookies and pastries into.

Calabaza – Spanish for pumpkin (winter squash).

Caldo – A hot stock, often left over from another dish. It is incredibly refreshing and invigorating — and in Spain, strangely, is often served in bars.

Camareros – Waiters. They are generally middle-aged males, sometimes sour, often charming, always dressed in white shirt and waistcoat. A bastion of Spanish dining.

Caseta – Temporary fun house often set up in a *feria*.

Cazuela – Ceramic cooking vessel. These are inexpensive, rustic, excellent for slow cooking and available from cookery shops. They need to be "proved" or "cured" before they are used for cooking by being soaked overnight in water, drained, then slowly brought to a high heat over a flame and allowed to cool. After a long hiatus from cooking, re-season your *cazuela*. Never rapidly change the temperature of a *cazuela* by placing a hot *cazuela* in a cold environment or vice versa.

Chipirones – Baby squid. In Spain, they are often line-caught by old men.

Chocos – The name for cuttlefish in the south of Spain. Elsewhere they are known as *sepia*. They are often cooked low and slow (in a pressure cooker, for example) or hot and fast on a *la plancha* (*see facing page*).

Chorizo – Spain's national sausage, made from pork, seasoned with salt and flavored with *agridulce* paprika, garlic and pepper. Fresh chorizo is used for cooking, where it imparts salt and seasonings into a dish, like a floating, meaty bouquet garni. Cured chorizo is cut off into slices and consumed with beer or wine. Good chorizo is hard to find outside Spain, but if you happen to find a good butcher who makes a good chorizo, it will be well worth the effort.

Cocido – Slow-cooked stew of chickpeas, chicken, *jamón*, beef, sausage and vegetables, served as three separate courses. My favorite food! Can also mean "boiled."

Codorniz – Quail. Available from specialty butchers and poultry shops, but also consider buying them from Vietnamese butchers as they generally have good stock. Choose plump little birds with a healthy pink tinge to the skin. All commercial quail is farmed quail and has much less flavor than wild quail.

Cojonudos – Complimentary slang made famous by the current King of Spain. Translates roughly as "balls."

Comida – Food or lunch.

Cornstarch – We use Spanish cornflour, made from corn and bearing the name "Maizena."

Cortador – A professional (almost exclusively male), dedicated to the art of cutting *jamón*.

D.O. – *Denominación de Origen*. Similar to the French *Appellation d'origine contrôlée*. A D.O. can refer to food just as much as wine. It's a way of recognizing that certain foods and wines come from a certain region and are grown and prepared in a certain manner. It's a way of protecting food and wine traditions, among other things.

Dried beans – Dried beans need to be picked over for stones and discolored beans prior to soaking. Rinse and soak them in plenty of cold water for several hours or overnight, then cook as instructed in the recipe.

Dried cherries – Not traditional in Spanish cooking, but a wonderful ingredient.

Eggs – The eggs used in our recipes are extra-large and should be at room temperature before cooking.

Embutidos – Charcuterie or small goods. Highly prized and deeply loved in Spain. *Embutidos* refers to the sausages, preserved meats and pâtés that reflect regional ingredients and preserving conditions. There are a few Spanish-style sausages that bear the same name of sausages made in Spain, but they are pale imitations of the original.

Escabeche – Vinegar-and-wine-based marinade once used to preserve food, but now popular for its flavor.

Espárragos – Asparagus. A vegetable highly regarded in Spain.

Estofado – A slow-cooked meat stew.

Feria – Originally an agricultural show, now a large collection of showground attractions and yet another excuse to eat, drink and celebrate.

Fideos – Macaroni-like pasta, used in broths and soups and to make paella-like dishes.

Fino – Spanish dry sherry. Drink chilled with tapas.

Garbanzos – Chickpeas. Traditionally considered "poor man's meat," and widely used in both home cooking and restaurant meals. Buy large chickpeas from a shop with a good turnover. We shop for chickpeas where Middle Eastern people buy their legumes. When preparing chickpeas, discard any discolored chickpeas or stones. Rinse, soak in warm tap water, and when the water is cool, cover and place in the fridge overnight. Drain prior to cooking as directed in the recipe. Note that chickpeas harden when refrigerated and are best served warm.

Garlic – Use fresh garlic only.

Guindillas – Mild Basque pickled peppers, popular in *pintxos*.

Helado – Ice cream.

Hígado – Liver.

Hojaldres – Puff pastry. Some really good commercial puff pastry is now available from fine food shops.

Huevos – *See eggs*.

Jamón – Spanish ham (pronounced ha-MON). Substitute *jamón* Serrano or thick-cut prosciutto.

Kikos – A snack of roasted corn kernels, popular at soccer matches and bullfights. Sold in some Spanish food stores.

La plancha – Flat grill. A great block of hot steel used to cook food quickly with intense heat. *La plancha* adds its own flavor of hot steel and caramelized cooking juices.

Leche – Milk.

Lomo – Pork loin, both fresh and cured.

Malsouqua pastry – also known as Tunisian brik pastry. Available from Middle Eastern delicatessens — sometimes they sell it as filo pastry, and sometimes they don't have it on display. Tricky, yes . . . but that's part of the fun.

Manchego – Aged sheep's milk cheese from the region of La Mancha in Spain.

Manzanilla – Fino sherry from Sanlúcar de Barrameda. Ask for it by name in good wine shops.

Matanza – Slaughter. Generally refers to the annual killing of the family pig. A time of much celebration for the family, but not so much for the pig.

Media ración – A *ración* is a serving from a shared plate. A *media ración* means a smaller portion of this. A recipe described as "6 medias raciones" means that if you served this at the table, six people could take a small serving, roughly equivalent to an appetizer-size portion.

Meneadas – Lardons, or strips of fat, used to keep meat moist during cooking.

Menestra – A homely dish of mixed, seasonal slow-cooked vegetables, very popular in the north. Runs counter to the misconception that the Spanish don't eat vegetables.

Morcilla – Blood sausage. A rich sausage made from blood, rice and onions found across Spain, and available in other countries from a handful of good butchers. At a stretch, black sausage can be used as a substitute — add a pinch of cinnamon to it as this is a background spice used in *morcilla*.

Olive oil – Olives are harvested in autumn, pressed and the oil sold after settling. I use fresh local olive oil, as well as Spanish varietals such as sharp and grassy Arbequina and sweet and mild Hojiblanca.

Orujo – A 100% proof grappa from the northwest of Spain. In other parts of Spain, it is known as *aguardiente*.

Paellera – A large, flat metal pan in which the famous rice dish paella is cooked. Paella pans are available in cooking supply shops, Spanish food stores and online.

Pan – *See bread.*

Panko – Not a Spanish product, but a type of breadcrumb made in Japan. Always light and crunchy, panko breadcrumbs are available from Japanese food stores and fine food stores.

Paprika – Known as *pimentón* in Spanish. In this book, only Spanish paprika is used — you'll find it in delis, specialty food stores and online, and now even some supermarket shelves. Arguably, the best Spanish paprika is from the La Vera region in the north of Extremadura.

Parrilla – A grill, whether a flat grill or a gas grill.

Pedro Ximénez – The name of a Spanish grape variety. The grapes can be made into a white wine, but generally they are partially dried on the vine and made into a wonderful dark, sweet sherry named after the grape variety, and also known by its initials PX.

Perdiz – Partridge. Very popular in Spain, where it is far more common in restaurants than chicken. It is much harder to come by elsewhere.

Perol – A pot with high sides and a rounded base. You can just use a similar domestic saucepan if you don't happen to have one.

Picadillo – Means "chopped."

Pimentón – *See paprika.*

Pimientos – Peppers. They are used extensively in Spanish cooking and often form the base of a *sofrito*.

Pimientos piquillo – Mild red peppers. Roasted and packed in jars, they are now available in good food stores and some supermarkets. The *piquillos* bearing the "Made in Spain" mark tend to be better than the South American brands.

Pincho – Snack . . . as in *pincho de tortilla*. Can also refer to skewers of meat, as in *pinchos morunos*.

Piñones – Pine nuts. Used extensively in the south of Spain. Again, use only the freshest nuts — follow the Middle Eastern people to their nut shops.

Pintxo – A recent Basque tradition of bar snack food, often involving food on a toothpick, or fish and mayonnaise on bread. The snacks are often prepared long in advance and left out on the bar in the open and under warm lights.

Poussins – Small chickens; traditionally, castrated male birds.

Queso – Cheese.

Ración – A *ración* is a serving from a shared plate. A recipe in this book described as "6 raciones" serves six people as a main-size portion, if served with one or more accompanying dishes.

Refrito – Refried. Also a technique of adding another layer of flavor by dressing a dish just prior to serving with hot oil infused with ingredients such as garlic, parsley, chile or perhaps Spanish paprika.

Rennet – An enzyme made from calf stomachs and used to set milk into curd in cheese-making. Once available as junket tablets in supermarkets, it is now hard to come by, but is available online.

Rice – Rice is eaten around Spain and is grown in the east of the country. Much of it is a medium-grain rice from a Japanese variety. A popular and foolproof variety for making rice dishes is *bomba*—it absorbs three times its weight in liquid, thus drawing in the flavor of the cooking liquid. A lot of Spanish rice is grown near the town of Calasparra, in the inland region of Murcia. Look for *bomba* or Calasparra rice in good food stores and delicatessens.

Rioja – Perhaps Spain's most popular red wine. It is grown in the La Rioja Autonomous Community in the north of Spain, and is often produced from *tempranillo, granacha, graciano* or *mazuelo* grapes.

Saffron – A spice from the flower of a crocus. A few delicate threads add a rich yellowish-orange hue to food and a pleasant taste. Buy only as much as you need from a busy retailer of spices. Also available from online spice shops.

Salmorejo – A traditional Andalusian bread and water soup. *Salmorejo* generally now refers to a soup made with bread and tomatoes, but can also refer to other soups and purées made with bread. (In the Canary Islands, a *salmorejo* can also be a marinade.)

Salt cod – Before refrigeration was invented, this was the fish enjoyed in the interior of Spain, featured in a huge repertoire of dishes. Salt cod can be bought from city markets, Mediterranean delis and some good fishmongers. It always requires desalinating before using. To do this, brush away all the large salt crystals and place the cod in a large bowl of clean, cold water. Soak in the refrigerator for 48 hours, changing the water four times at regular intervals during this period. Remove the cod from the water and discard the water, then use as the recipe directs.

Sardinas – Sardines. Fresh sardines are available in the city markets. They sometimes need to be cleaned. To do this, open the stomach using a sharp knife, place a finger inside and remove the guts. Rinse clean before cooking. Sardines do not need to be scaled.

Secaderos – Drying rooms, often used for curing *jamón* and drying peppers for paprika. Can also refer to cool rooms for drying lesser-grade *jamones*.

Sherry – Sherry lifts and brightens the food it is used in, while adding a hint of yeast and flavors of barrel age. I highly recommend buying Spanish fino sherry to cook the recipes where it is listed.

Sherry vinegar – Vinegar made from sherry. It has deeper, more developed notes than other vinegars and adds both a sharpness and roundness to dishes. Available from good food stores, delicatessens and some supermarkets.

Sofrito – The base of slow-cooked vegetables — often onion, garlic, bell pepper and tomato — which imparts so much flavor to so many Spanish dishes. A *sofrito* is cooked low and slow for 30 to 60 minutes and often needs to look like jam before the next ingredients are added. There are as many *sofrito* recipes as there are Spaniards.

Tapas – Small bar snacks at the center of a national culinary phenomenon. Tapas comes from the Spanish verb "to cover" and refers to the covering of bread that bartenders in Spain once placed over drinks to keep out dust and flies. Now it refers to hundreds of different bar snacks. A tapa is one piece of food, a bit like a canapé. So when you see "24 tapas" in a recipe, you know that it makes 24 little snacks.

Tempranillo – A variety of red grape, native to Spain, that produces an aromatic wine that is ruby-red in color. It is now also grown much further afield.

Tomatoes – Quite a few recipes in this book call for tomatoes to be peeled and/or seeded. To peel and seed tomatoes, score a cross in the base of each tomato, place in a heatproof bowl and cover with boiling water. Leave for 30 seconds, then transfer to cold water and peel the skin away from the cross. Cut the tomatoes in half and scoop out the seeds.

Tortilla – An omelette cooked on both sides. A common tortilla, filled with potato and onion, is *tortilla española* — the savior of vegetarian tourists. A tortilla can have other fillings such as salt cod, asparagus or even spinach.

Txacoli – A white wine made in the Basque country. Served chilled and often poured from a height, it is a young, fresh and sharp, slightly tart wine that is often served with grilled seafood.

Vegetables – All the recipes in this book, unless otherwise stated, call for all vegetables to be medium-sized, washed and peeled.

Vegetarianism – Still in its conceptual phase in Spain.

Vinegar – Unless stated otherwise, we recommend that you use very high-quality vinegar for the recipes in this book — such as a good-quality chardonnay vinegar for *escabeche*.

Vino tinto – Red wine. Also refers to home-made red wine that, like its makers, has variable characteristics.

INDEX